Jean Racine Revisited

Twayne's World Authors Series

French Literature

David O'Connell, Editor

Georgia State University

Jean Racine.

Gravé par I.Daullé Gr. du Roy 1762.

JEAN RACINE.

Jean Racine Revisited

Ronald W. Tobin

University of California, Santa Barbara

Twayne Publishers
New York

Twayne's World Authors Series No. 878

Jean Racine Revisited
Ronald W. Tobin

Twayne Publishers
1633 Broadway
New York, NY 10019

Library of Congress Cataloging-in-Publication Data

Tobin, Ronald W., 1936 –
    Jean Racine revisited / Ronald W. Tobin.
    p.   cm. — (Twayne's world authors series ; TWAS 878. French literature)
    Includes bibliographical references and index.
    ISBN 0-8057-4605-6 (alk. paper)
    1. Racine, Jean, 1639 – 1699—Criticism and interpretation.   I. Title.   II. Series: Twayne's world author series ; TWAS 878.   III. Series: Twayne's world authors series. French literature.
    PQ1905 .T63   1999
    842'.4—dc21   98-37561
                                                                          CIP

This paper meets the requirements of ANSI/NISO Z3948-1992 (Permanence of Paper).

10 9 8 7 6 5 4 3 2 1

Printed in the United States of America

For the Jadoff Sisters, Mary and Anne

Contents

Preface

> Oh, my gentle Racine, it is in your masterpieces that I recognize the heart of
> a woman! I have formed my own according to your noble poetry! If the lyre
> of my soul does not always weep in response to your divine music, it is
> because my admiration for you vaults my whole being into ecstasy.
> —Rachel, Torino 16 October 1857 (1851?)[1]

Like Rachel, I am a fervent admirer of the master of French tragedy.
When offered the possibility of writing a book on Racine, I warmed to
the opportunity to present an accessible portrait of the dramatist
through an original synthesis of Racine scholarship since the appearance
of Claude Abraham's Twayne volume, *Jean Racine*, in 1977. The review I
undertook of research on Racine over the past 20 years was a comple-
ment to a task I completed (for 1957–1977) for the Racine chapter of
the *Supplement* to the *Critical Bibliography of French Literature: Seventeenth
Century*, ed. H. Gaston Hall (Syracuse, NY: Syracuse University Press,
1983). For the present volume, I have added new material of my own
that has withstood the rigorous test of the classroom. Hundreds of students, both graduate and undergraduate, have refined my approach to
Racine through their questions and silences, their passion and indifference: typically, teaching Racine seems to evoke Racinian reactions. A
substantial difference between that audience and the Twayne public is
that the former read Racine in the original French, whereas the latter
most likely know the dramatist only through translation.

Translation concerns any scholar who seeks to present an author
whose works were originally drafted in a foreign language. Racine's
plays constitute, however, a very special case, for they are generally considered untranslatable into English. On the surface, this is paradoxical
because the translator of Racine does not confront the problem of finding suitable words for a complex or highly technical vocabulary. Nor
does one have to seek equivalents for a dense, rich, and folkloric vocabulary of some 20,000 lexical items, close to popular sources, like Shakespeare's. Racine's vocabulary, containing slightly more than 3,000 individual words, is the language of the aristocracy: clearer, more concise,
rarely exotic. Since French classicism dictated a pruning of the luxuriant
linguistic tree that the Renaissance had cultivated, the secret of Racine's

art does not lie in lexical invention, but in innovative recombination. Given that there are probably only 300 original lines in all of French classical tragedy, the rhetorical strategy for any dramatist was to use *dispositio,* the creative placement of familiar words and images. The simplicity of Racine's text is, consequently, one of the obstacles to his translation. As the American poet Robert Lowell, himself a translator of *Phèdre,* concludes, "No translator has had the gifts or the luck to bring Racine into our culture."[2]

Commenting on Lowell's effort, Christopher Ricks adduces a specifically English cultural reason for the difficulty: "One aspect of the matter, both cause and consequence of what has been Racine's untranslatability for us, is the English tradition of being negatively willing not to reject Racine but positively eager not to overrate him."[3] More recently, another scholar has put his finger on the nature of the obstacle: "There is something about the speed, pace, sound, and grammatical disposition of the words in Racine's hexameters that won't go into English. Translators of Racine into other languages find it difficult as well."[4] In the light of such views, it would have been foolhardy to propose translations of high literary merit in this volume. They are intended only to give a literal version of the French, as are my translations of quotations from scholars writing in French.

I had to translate many passages from Racine because my approach is essentially a textual one, and I wanted the reader to appreciate, even in translation, some of the wonders that Racine accomplishes with the French language. I also sought to integrate different perspectives and aspects into each chapter, while reminding the reader of a number of constants in Racinian and classical dramaturgy. That Racine succeeded in enjoying an unprecedented career in the theater—and through the theater—boggles the mind when one recalls the conditions he encountered at the outset. The miracle of Racine is that he began his artistic career at the point in the history of western culture when the theater was under its heaviest attack. When one adds to this all the quarrels over his individual plays in the contentious seventeenth century, one has a vision of theater as battlefield. That Racine survived and triumphed can only be understood by a close look at his life and times.

Chronology

1638 13 September. Jean Racine, father of the poet, marries Jeanne Sconin, daughter of Pierre Sconin.

1639 22 December. Jean Racine is baptized in the church of Saint Vaast in the town of La Ferté-Milon. The sponsors are his maternal grandparents, Pierre Sconin and Marie Desmoulins.

1641 24 January. Baptism of Racine's sister, Marie.

1642 29 January. Burial of their mother.

1643 7 February. Upon the death and burial of Jean Racine, the poet's father, his son is confided to the care of paternal grandparents and his daughter to Pierre Sconin.

1649 22 September. Burial of Jean Racine, the grandfather of the poet.

   From 1649 to 1653 the young Racine is educated at the school attached to the monastery at Port-Royal.

1653 1 October. Racine enrolls at the Collège de Beauvais.

1655 1 October. He returns to Port-Royal des Champs and perfects his knowledge of Greek and Latin authors.

1656 30 March. The school at Port-Royal is closed, but Racine succeeds in staying in the area, in the château of Vaumurier belonging to the Duc de Luynes.

1658 October. Racine is sent to Paris to study Logic at the Collège d'Harcourt.

1659 Racine moves in with Nicolas Vitart in the Hôtel de Luynes and remains until mid-1661. He meets La Fontaine, a distant relative, and composes both religious and secular verse.

   7 November. The Treaty of the Pyrenees is concluded ending the war between France and Spain. Racine praises Prime Minister Jules Mazarin in an ode that has not been preserved.

1660   Racine completes "La Nymphe de la Seine à la Reine" and a play, *Amasie,* of which we have no trace.

1661   June. Racine begins a new play about Ovid but evidently never completes it.

        October. Racine leaves for Uzès where his uncle, Antonin Sconin, is Vicar General.

1662   25 July. Sometime between the date of his last letter from Uzès and that of his first letter from Paris (23 July 1663), Racine returns to the capital.

1663   29 May. To celebrate the convalescence from measles of Louis XIV, who is Racine's elder by only a year, Racine composes the ode "Sur la convalescence du Roi."

1664   20 June. Premiere of *La Thébaïde* by Molière's troupe.

        30 October. Publication of *La Thébaïde* by Barbin.

        November. Publication of another ode, "La Renommée aux Muses."

1665   30 October. Racine receives 600 *livres,* the first of many "gratifications" from the king.

        4 December. Creation of *Alexandre le Grand* at the Theater of the Palais-Royal.

        14 December. *Alexandre* presented by the Hôtel de Bourgogne.

1666   January. Publication of the "Lettre à l'auteur des 'Hérésies imaginaires.' "

1667   17 November. Premiere of *Andromaque,* a resounding success.

1668   *Les Plaideurs* performed. The precise date of the premiere is unknown.

1669   January. Publication of *Les Plaideurs.*

        13 December. First representation of *Britannicus,* a failure.

1670   21 November. Creation of *Bérénice.*

        28 November. Premiere of Corneille's *Tite et Bérénice*

1672   5 January. Premiere of *Bajazet.*

        5 December. Racine elected to the Académie Française.

1673   12 January. Racine delivers his acceptance speech to the Académie.

13 January. *Mithridate* opens.

1674   18 August. *Iphigénie* staged in the Orangerie at Versailles; the public premiere at the Hôtel de Bourgogne will take place four or five months later.

1677   1 January. Premiere of *Phèdre*. The *Phèdre* of Pradon will follow two days later.

31 May. Marriage of Racine and Catherine de Romanet.

30 September. Racine and Boileau named royal historiographers. Much of Racine's time henceforth will be devoted to this task.

1678   11 November. Baptism of Racine's first son, Jean-Baptiste. Five daughters will be born in 1680, 1682, 1684, 1686, and 1688, and then his last child—and biographer—Louis, in 1692.

1679   21 November. Catherine Monvoisin (called La Voisin) accuses Racine of having poisoned the actress La Du Parc, his mistress. The matter is not pursued for long.

1683   Composition of the *Précis des campagnes de Louis XIV.*

1 October. Death of Pierre Corneille.

1685   2 January. Racine praises Pierre Corneille in his speech acknowledging the nomination of Thomas Corneille to the Académie Française.

6 July. Racine composes *L'Idylle sur la paix,* with music by Lully.

1687   Second edition of the collected works of Racine, more complete than the first dating from 1676.

1689   Premiere of *Esther* at Saint-Cyr.

1690   16 December. Racine is named Gentleman of the King's Chamber, provided that he pay a substantial and potentially ruinous sum to the widow of the previous occupant of the post.

1691   5 January. *Athalie* presented at Saint-Cyr.

1694   The *Cantiques spirituels* probably date from this year.

1695   Racine occupied with writing the *Abrégé de l'histoire de Port-Royal,* from 1695 to 1699.

1696   Racine purchases the office of Secretary-Counselor of the King.

1697   Third edition of Racine's collected works appears in two volumes, with important emendations.

1699   Racine dies of cancer of the liver. First buried near his master, M. Hamon, at Port-Royal, he now lies in the Church of Saint-Etienne du Mont in Paris.

Chapter One
Biography

For a man who came from nothing, he easily adopted the manners of the court.
—Ezéchiel Spanheim[1]

The life of Jean Racine has attracted more attention than one might expect, even given his reputation as France's leading tragic author, the "French Shakespeare," as it were.[2] The reasons for this unusual interest are basically threefold: he was the first French author able to live principally from income attracted to his pen; in the soul-searching that followed the debacle of France's defeat at the hands of Prussia in 1870, the nation looked to icons whose study would furnish moral models for the reconstruction of France, and Racine, like Molière, was singled out for analysis and inspiration; and the twentieth-century biographies of Racine, the first by a descendant, Alfred Masson-Forestier, in 1910 and the second by the major Racine scholar Raymond Picard in 1956, depicted the playwright as a self-centered, ruthless *arriviste*, thereby giving the lie to the romantic, exemplary image Racine enjoyed after 1870. As a kind of prolongation of the third aspect—the cultural clash between what an older generation learned about Racine and what modern research has unearthed—Racine has also been the subject of a sometimes sensational quarrel between partisans of "objective," historically based scholarship, like Picard, and those who prefer to use interdisciplinary approaches, like Roland Barthes. This dispute, whose embers still glow, has only served to refocus attention on Racine, the man as well as the works.

The first detail we have about Jean Racine is that he was baptized on 22 December 1639 in the small village of La Ferté-Milon, situated about 60 miles from Paris in the Valois region of France. His family was bourgeois, of the modest means and status associated with the family trade: the maintenance of salt granaries. Racine's early years were spent almost entirely with relatives, owing to the premature deaths of both his parents. His mother died giving birth to his sister, Marie, 13 months after he was born; his father remarried in 1643, but died three months later. Since the new wife refused to take responsibility for the children of

1

the first spouse, Marie was given to the care of the maternal grandfather, Sconin, while Jean was taken in by his paternal grandparents,
Racine. If he had not been orphaned so early in his life, Racine might
well have continued in the family trade and never reached the artistic or
social heights that he eventually attained.

When his grandmother, Marie des Moulins, became a widow, she
brought Racine, then age nine, with her to the convent of Port-Royal
des Champs near Paris, where she obtained permission to enroll him
without fee at a school founded by a group of devout scholars and teachers. Racine, therefore, had the good luck and the precious opportunity—rare for an orphan of modest social origins—to study the classics
of Latin and Greek literature with distinguished masters. They taught
him to compose French and Latin prose and poetry and also to analyze
the great texts of ancient Greece. Racine did this so well that he knew
Greek better than almost any nonprofessional scholar of his day. Ironically, Racine's readings of the classics at Port-Royal included that very
genre, theater, whose practice was to embroil him with the Jansenists
for his entire career. The focus of the school at Port-Royal des Champs
was on an education steeped in the austere Augustinian view of earthly
existence known as *Jansenism,* a theological persuasion eventually condemned by the Catholic Church as heretical. Since the monarchy suspected the Jansenists of being both theologically and politically subversive, Racine's lifelong relationship with his former friends and teachers
remained ambivalent inasmuch as the ambitious artist sought admit-
tance into the secular realm of court society while not breaking entirely
with the Jansenist camp.[3]

Racine spent the years 1649–1653 at Port-Royal. Thanks to an
arrangement between his Jansenist masters and the College of Beauvais,
he transferred to that institution, remaining there for almost two years
before returning to Port-Royal on 1 October 1655 to perfect his studies
in rhetoric with the most famous orator of the time, Antoine Le Maître.
Although the school at Port-Royal was closed by authorities in 1656,
Racine was allowed to stay on with the resident physician, Hamon.
When Racine was 18 years old, the Jansenists sent him to study law at
the College of Harcourt in Paris. Even though La Ferté-Milon was not
far from the capital and Port-Royal des Champs was even closer, Racine
had probably never laid eyes on Paris before this time. Once there, he
became relatively emancipated from the Jansenists and looked to relatives like Jean de La Fontaine as models. He began to write some fash-
ionable light verse, some essays, and one or two tragedies that were

never presented and of which we have no trace: *Amasie* in 1660 and, according to his son Louis Racine (whose testimony is often suspect), *Théagène et Chariclée* in 1661. In 1660 he published an ode on the occasion of the marriage of King Louis XIV and Marie-Thérèse, "La Nymphe de la Seine, à La Reine" (The Nymph of the River Seine, dedicated to the Queen), which first brought him to notice.

Racine had both the disposition and the talent to thrive in the Parisian cultural climate of the late 1650s and early 1660s, where conforming and pleasing—and, in Racine's case, pleasing with his pen—were indispensable assets. One of the first displays of Racine's intentions was his composition of a sonnet in praise of Cardinal Jules Mazarin, Prime Minister of France, for successfully concluding the Treaty of the Pyrenees with Spain (1659). This tribute enraged the Jansenists, who had been persecuted by Mazarin, but it revealed Racine's strategy of social conquest through literature.

There were three ways for a writer to survive in Racine's day: attract a royal pension, obtain an ecclesiastical benefice, or compose for the theater. While the first was out of the question for the neophyte Racine (although he eventually received many gratuities in the course of his career), he did attempt in 1661, through his mother's family, to arrange for a benefice, specifically from the diocese of Uzès in Languedoc. Although his financial goal was not reached at that time, he did acquire an ecclesiastical income in 1667—but it came from Anjou, not Uzès.

The two years in Uzès allowed Racine to grow intellectually and socially. At the invitation of his uncle, the Reverend Father Antoine Sconin, Racine undertook a voyage to the south, where Sconin was the Vicar General, and, more important, the financial director of the diocese. Sconin was looking forward to having at his side a young man who could eventually assume his ecclesiastical position or, if not attracted to the priestly life, raise a family and inherit the large house Sconin had managed to build in Uzès. Racine agreed to become a "postulant," to study the Bible and Saint Thomas Aquinas, while taking advantage of the proximity to Nîmes and Avignon for short trips. Racine did not seem to have a genuine priestly vocation, but at this time a true calling was not required to obtain the financial benefits attached to the office.

When it became clear that the Bishop of Uzès, Monsignor Grignan, would require much more of a commitment to the clerical life than the increasingly nostalgic Racine was willing to give, the latter returned to Paris. During his stay he had continued his voracious reading. He had also learned much firsthand about the Mediterranean world he had previously encountered only in his readings, about the administration of justice that would eventually be put to good use in his comedy, *Les Plaideurs* (The litigants), and about keeping an eye on one's finances, a lesson he never forgot.

Upon his return to Paris at the beginning of the summer of 1663, Racine sought advice on how to pursue royal favor from the influential critic Jean Chapelain, secretary to the late Mazarin's successor as Prime Minister, Jean-Baptiste Colbert. Racine wrote two odes—"La Convalescence du Roi" (On the convalescence of the King) and "La Renommée des Muses" (The fame of the muses), which earned him the protection of the future Duke of Saint-Aignan and the right to be present at the ceremony of the king's awakening from sleep ("le lever du roi"), one of the innumerable rites that characterized the reign of Louis XIV. Having undoubtedly met Molière on one of these occasions, Racine decided to offer him a play, *La Thébaïde* (The story of Thebes, which Racine had probably begun in Uzès), even if a career in the theater meant further estrangement from the Jansenists.

Molière took a chance on the young dramatist and produced the play. A reaction from the Jansenists was not long in coming. In the same month that witnessed the premiere of Racine's second play, *Alexandre le Grand* (Alexander the Great) in 1665, one of his former teachers, Pierre Nicole, published a letter accusing novelists or playwrights of having no more redeeming virtues than a "public poisoner." This was but one of 18 letters that Nicole wrote on behalf of Port-Royal over the period 1664–1666 in defense of the Jansenists' position condemning the theater. Although Nicole made no direct reference to Racine, and the letter was probably meant for Desmarets de Saint-Sorlin (who was both a novelist and a playwright), Racine believed that he was the object of Nicole's wrath and responded accordingly with a stinging and dazzling open letter, "Lettre à l'auteur des 'Hérésies imaginaires' " (Letter to the author of the "imaginary heresies").

There existed three principal theaters in the Paris of 1660: Les Comédiens du Roi, better known as the troupe of the Hôtel de Bourgogne, on the rue Mauconseil; the troupe of the Marais that had been playing on the rue Vieille-du-Temple since 1634; and Molière's company, back from a tour of the provinces, which had been sharing the Petit-Bourbon theater with an Italian ensemble of *commedia dell'arte* actors, until the former moved into the theater of the Palais-Royal in 1660. With the signing of the peace treaty between France and Spain on 7 November 1659, festivities of every kind—especially theatrical—abounded and were even multiplied when Louis XIV married Marie-Thérèse of Spain on 9 June 1660. After seven years of hiatus, Pierre Corneille resumed his theatrical productivity with *Oedipe* of 1659, and Molière wrote his first comedy-ballet, *Les Fâcheux* (The bores) in response to a request by Finance Minister Nicolas Foucquet to compose a play for a lavish reception he planned for Louis XIV. The moment was clearly ripe for ambitious young men with a talent for the theater.

With *La Thébaïde ou les frères ennemis* (The story of Thebes or the enemy brothers) presented by Molière's troupe, Racine's theatrical career began in 1664. The play ran for 17 nights, which was a notable achievement for a novice playwright, especially when we recall that a run of 30 consecutive performances was considered an unqualified success. The typical French theater of the time had about 500 seats. Racine earned 348 francs for the play's initial run and about 100 more when Barbin agreed to publish the text in the normal first-edition run of 1,200 copies. Racine wisely dedicated the play to the Duke of Saint-Aignan, who had been influential in gaining him access at court. Fortunately for Racine, Saint-Aignan was a supporter of the Colbert clan, whose pacifist views generally won favor with the king over the more aggressive policies promoted by Chancellor Michel Le Tellier and his son François-Michel, the Marquis de Louvois.

At this time a dramatist had to win over three publics to make his mark in the theater—the court, the general public, and the scholars/critics. Racine doggedly pursued all three, even though his clashes with the third group (who were mostly friends of his rival, Pierre Corneille), as revealed in his prefaces, were often sharp. Eventually, he accomplished two remarkable feats: he succeeded both in the theater and thanks to the theater, for his art proved to be not only ideally suited for dramatic expression but also a vehicle for the social aspirations of this insecure and quietly driven man.

We must recall that if writing for the theater could bring revenue, it could also reap ridicule. From the earliest days of Christianity, when the Romans began mocking the Christian sect in dramatic spectacles, Christianity has often cast a wary eye on theatrical productions, even if there is no more impressive spectacle than the Mass itself. This long-standing prejudice against the theater was very much alive in the seventeenth century, which witnessed both the rise of theater as its most popular genre and, at the same time, widespread scorn for the practitioners of that art. No one felt this relegation to second-class moral and social citizenship more than the hypersensitive Racine.

In his desire to succeed, Racine often seems to have selected his play topics with an eye to a prevailing trend or a contemporary interest. Molière's suggestion to compose a play on the Theban brothers may have been caused by the announcement in December 1663 of a forthcoming tragedy at the Hôtel de Bourgogne, *La Thébaïde,* by the Abbé Boyer. Wishing to demonstrate his troupe's superiority in head-to-head competition, Molière may have asked Racine to develop a *Thébaïde* for him. Even though the Boyer play turned out to be one of the most crushing failures in seventeenth-century dramatic history, the idea of taking advantage of current events and tastes remained with Racine. This notion may have inspired his choice of subject for his second tragedy. At that time, Colbert had a notion that France could rival Flanders in the making of tapestries, and he asked the artist Charles Le Brun to take charge of the project. Le Brun proposed that the weavers do a series of tapestries vaunting the triumphs of Alexander the Great. Since any reference to the heroic young Macedonian ruler would be taken by Louis XIV as a point of comparison with himself, a play about Alexander that suggested this comparison had enormous potential for bringing its author directly under the approving gaze of the king.

Since Molière's troupe earned some money for Racine with their production of *La Thébaïde,* he decided to give Molière his Alexander play, even if he harbored some doubts about the ability of Molière's comic-oriented troupe to perform tragedy. On 4 December 1665, Molière's company offered the first performance of *Alexandre le Grand* at its theater in the Palais-Royal. The play was so well received that Racine secretly negotiated with the Hôtel de Bourgogne—a rival troupe more skilled in tragedy—to present the "second premiere" of *Alexandre* on 15 December. There was even a soirée organized by the Countess of Armagnac for the king and court, featuring a performance of *Alexandre* by the Hôtel de Bourgogne, on 14 December, which means that Molière's competitors probably were in rehearsal just two to three days after the Palais-Royal premiere. The break with Molière was both inevitable and irrevocable—Racine even seduced Molière's leading actress, Mademoiselle Du Parc, into joining him personally and professionally—and from that point onward all of Racine's secular tragedies found their first voice with the actors of the Hôtel de Bourgogne.

Occupied at least partially with the quarrel with Nicole over the "imaginary heresies," Racine let two years go by before he presented his next tragedy on 17 November 1667 in the queen's quarters and in the presence of the king. Soon after, *Andromaque* (Andromache) had its public premiere and was a rousing success With a structure reminiscent of the pastoral genre, in which lovers pursue each other in circular chains (A loves B, who loves C, who loves A), Racine infused his drama with a strong love plot that the audience found appealing and familiar. What was not familiar, indeed what was strikingly new was the way in which Racine redefined the nature of "love." No longer a gallant linking of noble souls, it became an attempt at communicating the incompleteness of one's existence to a being who, in principle, could offer fulfillment.

The public's taste coincided with—or perhaps was led by—that of Louis XIV's sister-in-law Henrietta of England, to whom Racine dedicated the printed version of the play. Henrietta must have been especially sensitive to the situation of *Andromaque* in which the title character is threatened with the death of her son because she had lost her own three-year-old child within a month after *Andromaque*'s premiere. Although success at court did not guarantee enthusiastic reception in town, as we shall see, *Andromaque* conquered both constituencies and earned a lasting fame rivaling that of Corneille's *Le Cid,* the most renowned theatrical production in French cultural history.

Encouraged by the satirist Nicolas Boileau, whom he had met in the fall of 1663, and perhaps by Jean de La Fontaine, another master of the comic register, Racine composed his only comedy, *Les Plaideurs,* in 1668. While he had no particular reason to write a satire of the legal system, he did manage, with *Les Plaideurs,* to demonstrate that he was a man of several talents. First, he displayed his knowledge of Greek dramatic literature by basing his comedy on *Wasps,* by Aristophanes. Furthermore, he was able to answer the challenge of a new genre—and answer it well, if the court's reaction was any measure. Finally, *Les Plaideurs* offered Racine the opportunity to yield once more to the temptation to best the acknowledged leader in a theatrical genre: he had imitated Corneille in *Alexandre,* and now it was Molière's turn to defend himself. Since it took the public approval of Louis XIV to transform *Les Plaideurs*' initial lukewarm reception into a success, Racine might well have understood that his soundest strategy would be to declare victory and precipitously leave the field of battle, never to return to comedy.

Tragedy was, to be sure, another matter, and Pierre Corneille another rival. Racine undertook his next play, *Britannicus,* clearly in the expectation of beating Corneille at his own specialty of tragedy with a Roman setting. He read the preeminent source for Roman history, Tacitus's *Annals,* as well as plays on the general subject, such as Cyrano de Bergerac's *La Mort d'Agrippine* (The death of Agrippina) of 1654, in an effort to paint a suspenseful portrait of the struggle for power between the teenage emperor Néron, his mother, Agrippine, and his half-brother, Britannicus. Racine's effort was not, however, crowned with success. With Corneille having rented an entire box for himself at the Hôtel de Bourgogne as just one element of a meticulously conceived mobilization of forces against the young upstart, *Britannicus,* which premiered on 13 December 1669, was the worst failure of Racine's career, even if, once again, it found favor at court.

Racine sought to take revenge in a violent, anti-Corneille preface that accompanied the publication of the play in 1670. Most others in his situation would have been content with noticing that Corneille had taken the trouble to attend the play and participate in the cabal himself, a sign that the older dramatist was concerned about the compelling conception of fallen nobility that Racine had conveyed in both *Andromaque* and *Britannicus.* Concerning the latter play, Racine's ultimate triumph was longterm, for *Britannicus* is undoubtedly the favorite Racinian tragedy for late-twentieth-century directors and audiences.

Bérénice, which premiered on 21 November 1670, constitutes the pivotal point in Racine's dramatic career. The play reintroduces the subject of its predecessor by recounting the accession to the Roman throne of Titus, who was raised in the court of Nero; Racine was challenging Corneille again. This time the competition was direct; perhaps thanks to a wish expressed by Henrietta of England, who died before the plays' premieres, both Racine and Corneille worked on the same subject.[4] When Racine's *Bérénice* outdistanced his rival's *Tite et Bérénice* at the box office, it became evident, despite the sniping of Corneille's contemporaries like the Seigneur de Saint-Évremond, that a new generation with a different vision had arrived "on the scene." *Bérénice* has the added importance of being the play for which Racine found a formula that he repeated, without serious alteration, in the rest of his secular tragedies: a love interest, a relatively uncomplicated plot, striking rhetorical passages, and a highly poetic use of time.

Ever experimenting within the limits he—and the tragic genre itself—prescribed, Racine followed the simplicity of *Bérénice* and its three main characters with a violent, relatively crowded production, *Bajazet,* in January 1672. While the themes of unrequited passion, striving for acceptance, and the unrelenting pressure of time are recognizably Racinian, the locale is not. *Bajazet* is Racine's only play to take place in a contemporary setting (Constantinople), sufficiently far removed in distance and in mores from seventeenth-century France to create a mythical exoticism as alluring for the spectator as that of ancient Greece or Rome. Racine took advantage of the curiosity that the France of the 1670s had about things Oriental and especially Turkish—as Molière had in *Le Bourgeois gentilhomme* (The would-be gentleman, 1670)—and presented a harem tragedy that was calculated to appeal to a Christian audience that harbored prejudices that Islamic nations were unenlightened refuges of diabolical oppression.

The exact date of the first public performance of Racine's next tragedy, *Mithridate,* has never been determined, but it may have been as early as mid-December 1672.[5] *Mithridate* weds *Bérénice* to *Bajazet* in that the subject is Roman—the title character is a longtime enemy of Rome—whereas the setting is in Asia Minor, the "Orient" for most citizens of France at the time. The clash of Mithridate's two sons for the love of his fiancée is the manifestation of the primordial tragic situation that Racine first conceived for *La Thébaïde:* the warring brothers. Louis XIV, a warrior-king himself, shared the public's taste for the play and undoubtedly appreciated the declamation by the actors. Indeed, Racine took pains to train La Champmeslé, who played the role of the fiancée, Monime, in a diction best suited to emotional expressiveness. The result was speech that approached song; was Racine already foreseeing that his next rival would not be a person, but a genre—the opera?

Iphigénie, created for the celebration of the second conquest of the Franche-Comté region, premiered in the Orangerie of Versailles on 18 August 1674. With its spectacular scenes of the Greek army waiting to depart for the Trojan War, its legendary characters (Ulysse, Agamemnon, Achille, Clytemnestre), and its allusions to mythological entities, *Iphigénie* contains elements that would also be at home in an opera. Racine's thrust is not lyrical, but psychological, a fact borne out by his insinuation in the Preface to the play that he is the only worthy successor to the ancients, the truest disciple of the master craftsman of Greek tragedy, Euripides. The calm tone of this preface tells us a great deal about Racine's stature and self-esteem at this time. Despite a competing play on the same general subject (*Iphigénie* by Le Clerc and Coras) produced by Racine's enemies, Racine's version was a resounding success and confirmed him as the unrivaled genius of French theater.

If Racine had never written a line after *Phèdre,* his reputation as a dramatist would still have been assured because this tragedy is the highest expression of his art. Looking back on the days when its success was still in doubt, Racine must have found it sadly ironic that *Phèdre,* which was the last play to be performed at the Théâtre Guénégaud and had the honor of being chosen to inaugurate the Comédie Française (the fusion of the Guénégaud and Bourgogne troupes) on 25 August 1680, should have encountered such serious threats to its early existence. His enemies asked a rival dramatist, Jacques Pradon, to compose a competing *Phèdre,* which gave Racine's play stiff competition for some months. But eventually the public gave the definitive nod to Racine. While one can never explain satisfactorily why public taste in the seventeenth century preferred one work or one author over another, the journalist and critic Donneau de Visé pointed out in the weekly newspaper he founded in 1672, the *Mercure de France,* that Racine's treatment of the same basic subject is more interesting because it is more audacious: while Phèdre is newly engaged in Pradon's play, she is already married in Racine's.

On 11 September 1677, Racine and Boileau were officially named historiographers of the king, an appointment bitterly criticized by certain nobles who could not tolerate the promotion of social inferiors to high positions at court. The division of labor between the two appointees was evidently this: Boileau took charge of the history of the reign from the beginning to 1671, and Racine from 1672 onward. Two principles governed the work: one does not denigrate the enemies of the king lest his conquests seem inglorious, and one always indicates that the strengths of Louis XIV lie in foresight and preparation.

Before abandoning the theater (forever, he must have thought) at the age of 38, Racine reflected on his career, its triumphs, its conflicts, and, evidently from his Preface to *Phèdre,* on the distance that had come to separate him from his former friends among the Jansenists. His moral apology for the theater in his Preface must have been conceived, at least in part, with the Jansenists in mind:

> It were much to be desired that our works should be found as serious and as full of instruction as the pages of those poets [of antiquity]. It might bring about a reconciliation between the tragic art and a number of persons, noted for their piety and learning, who have denounced it of late, but might well look upon it with less disfavor if authors cared as much to instruct as to entertain their audience, and carried out thereby the true purpose of tragedy.

Surely a conventional statement of this sort, versions of which can be found throughout the history of drama, need not be taken as proof of a conversion (or reversion) to an Augustinian view of Christianity. Racine may well have been seeking a reconciliation, and he was in a position to eat his cake and have it, too. By renouncing the theater, he could claim that he was following the advice of moral thinkers like Nicole who, in the quarrel over the "imaginary heresies," perorated against the immoral distraction and bad example of theatrical illusion. Racine was also leaving the socially disadvantageous situation attached to all those who practiced the suspect craft of drama for the rarefied atmosphere of the court of Louis XIV. Thanks to his new occupation as historiographer of the king, Racine could effect a rapprochement with the Jansenists by quitting the theater—and at no cost.

Two other considerations may have been influential in what has come to be known as "Racine's silence" after *Phèdre*. In a brilliant essay, Marc Fumaroli sees the history of French tragedy between Corneille's *Médée* of 1634–1635 and Racine's *Phèdre* of some 40 years later as a period of prudent compromise between the pagan origins of tragedy and the Christian society of seventeenth-century France.[6] In this interpretation, *Phèdre* is Racine's representation of the tragic genre caught between hypocrisy (hiding the display of criminal passion that is its essence) and silence. Phèdre's suicide reveals that Racine chose the latter.

A final possible reason has to do with the difficulty Racine experienced in conceiving his play according to the tenets of classical art, whose fundamental principle was unity. Besides the formal considerations of the "three unities" of time, place, and action, and the notion of the "unity of illusion" (the spectacle should never be broken by leaving the stage empty within an act), the concept was expected to be reflected in art, because art, it was felt, was indicative of the national consciousness. Unity thus extended to all aspects of French life; did France not claim to have one king, one law, and one religion? The nation was indeed slowly, but surely, being "unified" (a euphemism for the suppression of difference) under the relentless centralization policies of successive ministers Richelieu, Mazarin, and Colbert. But cracks were showing at the seams, and a cultural crisis was taking hold of France.

[In *Phèdre*, Racinian anthropology proposes fragmentation, not unity, as an elementary human structure.] The uncontested master of French theater in 1677 may have abandoned his career because he was no longer able to support the philosophical and aesthetic principles that upheld classical art, mostly those having to do with unity and order. [Since his vision of the import of the play sprang from the subversive principle of fragmentation, Racine could no longer subscribe to the classical ideal.]

On 30 May 1677—that is, within several months of the appearance of his crowning achievement, *Phèdre*—Racine married Catherine de

Romanet of the Vitart family. It was said that she never read a single one of his plays. They had five daughters and two sons, one of whom, Louis, later became the (not always accurate) source for much of the biographical information on his father for generations to come.

After 1677 the court turned increasingly conservative and the courtier Racine followed suit. As historiographer, he chronicled the king's adventures, especially his war campaigns, and worked on putting them into suitable prose. These official duties culminated in the *Eloge historique du Roi sur ses conquêtes* (The historical panegyric of the king for his conquests) of 1682, which was typical of the collaborative effort involved in royal historiography. The Marquis de Chamlay, a military aide, collated material that he and his assistant, François de La Prée, had collected. Louis XIV and La Prée gave selected events the proper emphasis; Racine—and to a lesser extent Boileau—distilled and refined this material. In 1684, Racine's historiographical works were the basis for his election to the Petite Académie, which became the Académie des Inscriptions, charged with composing texts in praise of the king to be inscribed on medals and monuments. Even if he and Boileau never completed a history of Louis XIV's reign, they did accomplish what was expected of them: lending style to the writing of history. If more of his historical writings had reached us—most of them were destroyed in an accidental fire—we might have been able to judge whether Racine had succeeded in elevating the transmission of facts to the level of literature.

After *Phèdre,* Racine worked hard to establish his status and his fortune. If, in 1679, Racine was accused by Catherine Monvoisin, called La Voisin, of having poisoned his mistress and star actress, the Marquise du Parc, no formal charges were pressed and no consequences ensued. In 1672 he had been elected to the Académie Française and came to exert almost dictatorial powers over it;[7] in 1674 he had acquired the noble title of Treasurer of France, but soon quested after the higher distinctions of Ordinary Gentleman of the King (1690), and Secretary of the King (1696). The latter post cost him dearly (about 60,000 francs), and constituted a financial burden for the rest of his life.

Racine returned to the theater to write two religious plays, *Esther* (1689) and *Athalie* (1691), for the convent girls at the institution Mme de Maintenon had founded in 1686, Saint-Cyr. The complex itself, which housed 250 poor girls from noble families, was of recent vintage; Hardouin-Mansart had completed the buildings only in 1687. Mme de Brinon, the Superior of Saint-Cyr, believed that her young charges should have some theatrical experience as part of their training in diction, memory, and bodily grace. Knowing that secular plays, with their passionate themes, were unsuitable for the kind of education that was offered at Saint-Cyr, she composed some of her own, which were decidedly awful. Since, as Racine points out in the Preface to *Esther,* drama's goal is to instruct while amusing, Mme de Maintenon sought a way to have the girls, ages 8 to 21, practice morally uplifting plays that reflected a sure theatrical sense. She wrote to Racine asking that he undertake, at his leisure, a kind of moral or historical piece, without a love plot, for Saint-Cyr.

After some hesitation, Racine agreed. But how could he have refused a request from the king's morganatic wife (they had married secretly in 1684)? Engaging Jean-Baptiste Moreau (1656–1733), the music teacher at Saint-Cyr, to compose the music for the choral interludes (as he would for *Athalie* as well), Racine undertook the commission. Opening with a prologue spoken by the allegorical figure of Piety, *Esther* had its premiere at Saint-Cyr on 26 January 1689. According to Mme de Sévigné, Louis XIV found it "admirable."[8]

Mme de Maintenon worried about the publicity that the play had attracted thanks to the king's enthusiastic appreciation, for it upset the calm existence of the convent. *Esther* was ultimately put aside and had to wait until 8 May 1721 for its public premiere at the Comédie Française. But Louis XIV was insatiable in his thirst for another religious play by Racine and gave the order soon after the last of *Esther*'s convent performances. Thus, *Athalie* was conceived.

The royal command caused problems for Racine. He seems to have had little initial taste for composing another religious play for Saint-Cyr, and he asked to be excused because he had too much work to finish as royal historiographer. He also may have wondered if he could locate another biblical episode suitable to the constraints under which he had to work. Finally, he was not sure that he wanted to produce another "irregular" drama: with its three acts, chorus, and transcendent message, *Esther* broke sharply with Racine's previous practice in tragedy. These considerations, plus attacks from religious purists scandalized by the presentation of theatrical performances in a convent, delayed the completion of what became a much fuller play than originally conceived.

Athalie had its debut before the king on 5 January 1691. It offered a suspenseful plot with political stakes, good and wicked counselors, five full acts, and a central character who, if villainous, still remains admirable in her epic struggle against a superior adversary. All these elements would make *Athalie* a typical Racinian drama, were it not that fate is replaced in this instance—more significantly than in *Esther*—by divine providence.

Racine may have written other works for the theater, but they were not preserved. For example, according to his disciple La Grange-Chancel, Racine had undertaken a tragedy on the Alcestis theme, a subject reflected in the Preface to *Iphigénie* and in the allusions to Hercules in *Alexandre* and *Phèdre*. But at some point during the last two years of his life, Racine threw it in the fire. His other literary activities during his last years included re-editing, in 1687 and finally in 1697, the complete works he had first published in 1676. He also participated in a collective enterprise of translation, the *Hymnes traduits du Bréviaire romain* (Hymns translated from the Roman breviary, 1688), and then composed what should be considered the third panel of Racine's triptych of musical and poetic devotion, along with *Esther* and *Athalie:* the *Cantiques spirituels* (Religious canticles) of 1694. Collaborating with Moreau again, Racine generally followed the model of the Canticle of Canticles to produce a work of religious orthodoxy (with some Jansenist coloration) that is a remarkable triumph of both piety and poetry.

Racine's last work was probably the *Abrégé de l'histoire de Port-Royal* (Short history of Port-Royal, 1695–1699). In what passes for an historical document, Racine inserts digressive, apologetic comments designed to disculpate Port-Royal without, however, offending Louis XIV. The *Abrégé* is at once an act of faith and an act of contrition by the prodigal son seeking to return to the Jansenist hearth.

In a codicil to a will he had drawn up in 1685, Racine expressed his wish to be buried at Port-Royal at the feet of M. Hamon, thereby permitting the courtier, at the last, an act of independence. He died of cancer of the liver on 21 April 1699. When Louis XIV had Port-Royal razed in 1710, Racine's body was transferred to the site it occupies today: a tomb in the Parisian church of Saint-Etienne du Mont, just across the nave from the final resting place of the great Jansenist apologist, Blaise Pascal.

Chapter Two

Tragedy

The historian thinks of tragedy as a literary genre; the dramatist and his public as a repertory; the philosopher as an essence or a category. Different perceptions, different definitions, different expectations. If one consults the dictionary for orientation, one finds that the *Oxford English Dictionary* gives the etymology of *tragedy* as being from the Greek words for "goat song." (A brief inscription on the famous Parian marbles offers a clue to the enigmatic etymology: the winner of the annual drama competition in Athens received a goat as a prize.) The *OED* continues to list definitions that are more helpful for a general understanding: "1. A play or other literary work of a serious or sorrowful character with a fatal or disastrous conclusion; . . . 2. That branch of dramatic art which treats of sorrowful or terrible events in a serious and dignified style." In other words, tragedy, like all literary genres, is both a form and a vision.

While concepts of tragedy differ according to period and culture, we can state, broadly speaking, that the tragic genre flourishes in an age of transition—and, therefore, of crisis—between a time of belief and a time of agnosticism, between an epoch illustrating humanity's search for the absolute and an age in which it becomes inextricably engaged in history. Since the period of French history extending from the middle of the sixteenth century through the beginning of the eighteenth century contains both the last vestiges of the theocentric Middle Ages and the first traces of the rationalist Enlightenment, it qualifies as a tragic age.

Owing to its searching and questioning nature, a tragic age is one when uncertainty and anxiety are reflected in serious drama, as well as in philosophical and moral thinking. One of the obvious features of the tragedies of Pierre Corneille, for example, is his penchant for putting maxims into the mouths of his characters. In this way, tragedy can become a vehicle for moral wisdom. Even when that is not the point— as in Racine—authors claim an ethical mission for their art, thereby protecting themselves from the accusation of trafficking in immoral spectacles. Whatever the motivation, tragedy always represents the struggle with daunting forces, either exterior (the gods of Greek tragedy), or interior (the passions that besiege humans). For certain authors, the struggle is trial enough; Corneille prefers to submit his heroes to a life-threatening test (or tests), the better to demonstrate their superiority. Hurdles exist in Corneille's theater in order to be overcome.

Racine, on the contrary, intent on portraying human limitation and failure in the pursuit of whatever we prize most, erects obstacles that prove to be insurmountable. Unlike, on the one hand, the characters of much Greek tragedy and French Renaissance drama who exemplify pure passivity in fate's hands; and unlike, on the other hand, Corneille's larger-than-life creations whose actions are generally effective in resolving problems, disputes, and dilemmas, Racine's characters take the middle road: they act, but their actions are in vain. It is, however, the noble quality of the struggle that gives Racine's figures their humanity, a humanity with which we can identify. A French critic once summarized it succinctly when he entitled his essay, "Notre Mère Phèdre" (Our mother, Phèdre),[1] for we are all, like Phèdre, conscious to some degree of our failings.

Classical tragedy, then, is not a revolutionary strategy for changing the world. Rather, out of an instinct that reverses the priorities of our democratic society conditioned by nineteenth-century Romanticism, it teaches that the collectivity's interests are superior to those of the individual. This implicit philosophical statement goes far to explain the rise of tragedy in patriarchal and monarchical societies.

In France there were experiments with composing tragedy in the style of the ancient Romans and Greeks starting in the middle of the sixteenth century. If one sought a model to imitate, it was most often the tragedies of the philosopher and dramatist Seneca, the tutor of the Emperor Nero. Not that everyone thought his plays were particularly well written. In truth, he benefited from two factors: his works were in Latin, which, unlike Greek, was of easy access to the Renaissance reader, and his philosophy, Stoicism, constituted the most frequent recourse of Renaissance thinkers when they attempted to offer an explanation for the world's evils and how to suffer them. Many playwrights—such as Robert Garnier, the best of the French Renaissance tragedians—looked to Senecan tragedy as a means of portraying unbridled passion or of representing the fracturing of the world order that happens when passion is allowed to dominate reason. In such circumstances the Phaedra myth, the Greco-Roman version of the biblical story of Potiphar's wife, becomes a favorite subject, as in the line of Phaedra tragedies stretching from Garnier to Racine and beyond.[2]

There are two broad, generic developments that converge in the classical tragedy of Corneille and his contemporaries and that attain their point of perfection in the work of Racine. The first Renaissance drama following the model of ancient Roman and Greek tragedy is generally thought to be *Cléopâtre captive* (Cleopatra in chains) by Etienne Jodelle in 1553. Since Jodelle was a member of the group of poets known as the Pléiade, he was drawn to tragedy not for its theatrical possibilities, but for its poetic challenge. Essaying a variety of meters, he tells the story of Cléopâtre as captive after the death of her lover Marc Antoine. For the first four acts she and her attendants bemoan her fate and discuss her dilemma: should she live and be transported from Egypt to Rome in disgrace, or should she end her life? Between the end of the fourth act and the beginning of the fifth, she commits suicide, allowing her attendants to fill the final act with complaints on the death of their mistress. *Cléopâtre captive* is paradigmatic of Renaissance tragedy in its basic poetic quality, its focus on the past, its central expression being one of lament, and the powerlessness of the principal figure to change his or her situation. As we noted previously, the Renaissance tragic hero or heroine is a patient: a passive, and suffering individual. The interest of such a play lies undoubtedly in its language and in that language's ability to express passion and pain.

To criticize Renaissance tragedy for not having any action would be to mistake its goals—while making an accurate statement. Action, movement, and indeed onstage violence were brought into the mix of tragedy mainly by the dominant theatrical author of the first 30 years of the seventeenth century, Alexandre Hardy. Reputed to have scripted between 300 and 500 plays (of which, mercifully, only about 30 have come down to us), Hardy specialized in the hybrid genre that attracted more audiences—and authors—than any other in the 1580–1650 span: the tragicomedy. Even in his tragedies Hardy infused much of the free-wheeling action that characterizes the tragicomedy, while closing on an appropriately sad note. His tragedy *Scédase,* first published in 1624, recounts the rape and strangulation of the title figure's daughters in his absence, and ends on the father's frustrated cries for justice. While Hardy's language in no way constitutes linguistic progress toward the clarity and concision of classical French, he evidently conceived of his work as meant for theatrical presentation, and, as such, his oeuvre contributes considerably to the evolution of tragedy as a properly theatrical enterprise.

When the generation of 1630 came "on the scene," figuratively and literally, it featured names like Jean Mairet, whose *Sophonisbe* of 1633 or 1634 is widely credited with being the first French "regular" tragedy (in that it followed "rules"); Jean de Rotrou, author of *Hercule mourant* (The dying Hercules) of 1636; and the young Pierre Corneille, whose first tragedy was *Médée* of 1634–1635. They succeed in infusing a sense of movement—interior movement and conflict often flowing from a deep dilemma—into a highly poetic construct, so that the language serves to translate the subtle internal workings of the characters. Verbal action is the very fabric of classical tragedy.

In the period just before Racine began to write for the stage, there developed two parallel tendencies within the tragic genre. The first, known as "gallant" tragedy, featured a love plot that sought to surprise and move the spectators. The other, more classical and sober, displayed the intrigues behind the sweep of political history. In 1657 Thomas Corneille, Pierre's younger brother, produced *Timocrate,* a remarkable fusion of the gallant and the political; it was the most commercially successful tragedy of the century. Racine followed this model and perfected it such that, if his audiences did weep during some of his plays, Racine never sought a facile exploitation of the emotion of his dramas. Forever tilting the scales in favor of love over politics, he humanized his characters, relative to Corneille's, by stressing their drive for satisfaction of their passion, even at the expense of their power.

While Racine clearly had his own, modern ideas about the genre to which he was to devote almost all of his career, he also claimed to be— and undoubtedly was—a perceptive reader of ancient tragedy. He learned a great deal from Seneca, even if he did not care to acknowledge his debt. But he never missed an opportunity to vaunt his familiarity with the Greeks, and especially Aristotle, whose Poetics he commented on in a still extant text, the *Annotations sur la* Poétique *d'Aristote.* There can be no doubt that Racine was an admirer of Aristotelian theory. What is also doubtless is that he and the other practitioners of French classical tragedy modified Aristotle's view in significant ways to suit their own vision, and it would be useful to review the divergences.

The principal differences between Aristotelian and French classical tragedy are threefold, as Jean Rohou reminds us.[3] First, Greek tragedy has a profound religious dimension. But in the rationalist and Catholic culture of seventeenth-century France, human responsibility precluded a role for blind fate or the capricious intervention of the gods; even in Racine's version of the Oedipus myth, *La Thébaïde,* the emphasis is on the lethal tricks human beings play on each other and not on humanity as the arena for some divine comedy. Outside of the occasional biblical tragedy, few transcendental forces operate in classical tragedy. Rather, the focus is on the political struggle against enemies, tyrants, and usurpers, or against the powerful internal forces that alienate the individual.

Second, the moral goal of Aristotle is changed: no longer will it be a question of experiencing the passions without being overtaken by them, as the Stagirite had proposed, but to purge or calm them through the dramatic experience. Whether this is a laudable and attainable objective is the issue at the heart of the longstanding quarrel between partisans of the theater, like Racine, and conservative moralists, like Nicole.

Third, the nature of the protagonist is radically altered. The hero(ine) no longer needs to commit a wrongful act; it is the nature of his character (e.g., Néron's sadism) or of the situation in which she finds herself (e.g., Bérénice) that creates the tragic dimension. This third factor contributes substantially to differentiating between Corneille and Racine, for the former was interested in the "subject" of the play—the plot, vehicle of the ideas—whereas the latter believed that character was determinate. Insisting, rightly, on Racine as a dramatist interested first and foremost in pleasing an audience, Raymond Picard concludes that "Racine is not a theoretician. . . . He never considered the rules as obligatory conventions . . . but as flexible elements of a technique that he had developed for himself and which had allowed him to do marvelous things."[4] Indeed, far from constraining the imagination of the poet, the famous "rules" of French tragedy—whether their source be Aristotle, Horace, Italian Renaissance scholars, or contemporary French critics—exist to concentrate the emotional impact of the spectacle.

Tragedy, whether Aristotelian or Racinian, involves rules because breaking a rule, even if, like Oedipus, one is unaware of it at the time, is always a source of misfortune. Regulations held a special place in early modern Europe. At court, rules existed for the conduct of human affairs, and reflected the need for repressing individual instincts in highly competitive societies, lest the welfare of the collectivity suffer. Self-control became identified with civilization, and as the sociologist Norbert Elias argues, court-aristocratics took self-constraint to be an advantage they held over all others.[5] Consequently, one finds rules abounding for etiquette, protocol, painting, even food preparation, and, especially with the founding of the Académie Française in 1635, for literature. Complementing these social and artistic movements was the new scientific world view—the New Science, as it was called—that gave rise to a search for patterns that would reveal the rules of the physical universe. Fortified by technological innovations such as the telescope, the microscope, and an accurate timekeeper, scientists and philosophers sought out the secrets of God's well-regulated universe.

French tragedy intensifies the notion of regulation by insisting on certain formal conditions for the tragic genre:

1. Verisimilitude (*vraisemblance*)
2. Decorum (*bienséances*)
3. Noble characters (comedy is inhabited by the middle class)
4. Language suitable to nobility and proper to the lofty tragic genre, including rhyming couplets composed (almost exclusively) of the alexandrine meter of 12 feet per line
5. Division of the drama into five acts, and into scenes within those acts
6. Unities of time, place, and action (the "three unities")
7. Unity of tone
8. Unity of scene or stage
9. Rhetorical structures
10. Two broad topics: passion and politics

If the majority of the 10 components are formal in nature, it is, first, because French dramatists of the 1630s were conscious of creating a new genre whose constituent elements would distinguish it from its predecessors. A second factor lies in the belief, widely shared by artists and philosophers of early modern France, that composition was central to the aesthetic undertaking, even more so than style: "Beauty consists only in order . . . that is, in arrangement and proportion," said the great orator Jacques-Bénigne Bossuet in 1677.

First among the "rules" is verisimilitude: the very "foundation of all plays," according to the Abbé d'Aubignac, whose *La Pratique du théâtre* (The practical art of theater, 1657) was the most influential treatise on dramatic composition published in the seventeenth century. The story need not be factual, but it must be accepted by the audience as worthy of belief, as being part of their realm of experience, lived or potential. The significance of this criterion derives from the change in the public's taste around 1630 from the unrealistic and the fantastic, as represented in the most popular genre of the first 40 years of the century, the tragicomedy, to more realistic, often historically based plots. Ironically, the master of historical tragedy, Pierre Corneille, was occasionally criticized for drawing his plots from unbelievable episodes, even if they were taken from the annals of history. Corneille preferred actual events in all their improbability to any kind of pattern.[6] (This is but one aspect of the larger problem that Corneille had with rules in general; one could even say that his heroes are a successive series of representations of the dramatist himself in that both author and characters seek to become "rules unto themselves.")

"Decorum" or "propriety" is a moral measure: nothing presented on stage should shock the sensibilities of the public. As the seventeenth century progressed, the concept of decorum became refined to the point where violence, an integral part of most tragedies, was banished from the stage and took place in the wings or, more likely, was the object of a formal recounting on stage. Sometimes the two techniques are combined, as when Phèdre takes poison offstage and then enters to describe its effects. Could propriety come into conflict with the requirements of verisimilitude? Of course. A realistic portrayal of those bloodthirsty marauders of antiquity, Homer's Greeks, would have to include repeated acts of carnage. But Racine's Pyrrhus and Oreste of *Andromaque* conduct themselves more in line with French expectations of civility than would any true inhabitant of Epirus. The lesson is that in seventeenth-century French classical drama the culture, the prejudice, and even the ignorance of the audience weighed more heavily on a dramatic poet than historical accuracy.

One of the secrets of artistic success in the classical age of France lies in the intimate relationship between poet and public. Knowing the expectations—and the taboos—of the audience allowed dramatists like Racine to bridge the gap between reality and fiction such that the spectator felt comfortable in the world of illusion. If a play on an historical topic involving kings and queens were presented at Versailles, there would be no great difference between the ideal decor of the play and the physical surroundings. Moreover, the dress of actors on stage often resembled that of spectators, establishing another degree of familiarity. Just as in the novel of the period, what ultimately retained interest was not primarily the exterior elements, however much they added to the spectacle, but the "distinctly conscious aesthetic" that focused the audience's (or the reader's) attention on an expression of feeling that was deemed "plausible."[7]

Though not as elevated as the epic in the hierarchy of genres inherent in the classical mind, tragedy is nonetheless the vehicle for the expression of noble sentiments in a language that distinguishes life from art, for stage language is an enviable, stylized, even idealized discourse rarely attained in the course of daily existence. In the proudly ethnocentric and class-conscious France of the 1600s, the only people deemed capable of experiencing refined emotions and expressing them in a meticulous language suited to internal analysis were members of the aristocracy: nobility of blood gives rise to nobility of feeling, of discourse,[8] and even of action. This cultural conviction explains why the base acts of Racinian tragedy (betrayal, calumny, and murder) are accomplished by social inferiors, even if they are done at the behest of royalty. In this respect it is revealing to note that if Pierre Corneille's most celebrated characters are members of the nobility, Racine's are theoretically even more powerful because they belong to the royal family. Yet, their elevated status is of little help and no solace in their struggle to break out of the constraints of tragedy.

It may appear that the "three unities" constitute "constraints of tragedy" until one notices that in the hands of French classical dramatists, they become marvelous tools for assuring the power and the coherence of a theatrical illusion; that is, they are integral parts of verisimilitude. (It sins against verisimilitude to believe that dramatists, who lived on box office receipts, royalties, and gifts from an appreciative monarch, would ever have agreed to observe rules of any kind that were more of a hindrance than a help in realizing their goal of pleasing audiences.)

If classical tragedy were to be a distinct step forward in the march toward a more realistic dramatic form relative to tragicomedy, then one should ideally create a play that lasts as long as the action portrayed. Since this would indeed be an impractical constraint, playwrights allowed themselves the grace of presenting an action that takes place "within one day": the unity of time (*unité de temps*) is also called the unity of day (*unité de jour*), and the day in question is often only 12 hours in length in the tight concentration of Racinian dramaturgy.

The major theoretical defense of the unities in the seventeenth century comes from the pen of Boileau in whose *Art poétique* of 1674 we read: "In one place, in one day, one action fulfilled, / Is sure to the end to keep the theater filled."[9] According to Aristotle, the "imitation of an action" (mimesis) was the heart of a tragedy, therefore the unity of action is the pivotal factor among the unities. But this "unity" must be correctly understood as a pleasing unification of elements. For Aristotle, the best tragedy is as complex as the human existence it purports to imitate. Except for Racine's unique experiment with the structure of *Bérénice*—which is celebrated for its *simplicity,* its paucity of incidents—

classical playwrights sought to unify the several lines of a plot, the minor ones complementing the principal one and forming part of its resolution.

Aristotle did discuss the unities of action and time, but he did not specifically refer to the unity of place. That thread was woven into aesthetic doctrine by Italian Renaissance commentators on his ideas. Moreover, the trend over the course of the seventeenth century toward a more concise action within stricter temporal limits came to include an expectation that the drama would realistically—in conformity with verisimilitude—occur in "one place." This "place" was rather broadly interpreted by Corneille's generation as, for example, one city and its environs: the Rome of *Cinna* or the Seville of *Le Cid*. If the unity of place was never perfectly observed by Racine's time, its practice was more sharply focused, and this had to do as much with developments of staging as with dramatic conception.

In *Le Cid* of 1637 Corneille employed a multiple decor that had been the norm since the Middle Ages; it was composed of several compartments representing different places. By 1640, however, we have the first tragedy to be situated in a single locus and, therefore, to respect the unity of place: Corneille's *Horace* was set "in a room in Horace's house." Within 25 years the single set was considered not only the standard but the only true possibility. Was this more "believable" than a multiple set? Perhaps not, but it forced both dramatist and spectator to focus on the essential: the single event (usually a decision) that would occur in the course of a short period of time and that would radically alter the lives of those assembled in the tragic space.[10]

This space was usually apparent to the spectator upon entering the theater because having a curtain was costly, inconvenient, and occasionally dangerous (if it fell on the heads of the audience while being lowered). As an item of theatrical luxury, the curtain attracted attention by its very presence for a performance and was most often reserved for spectacles that were sure to earn large and well-paying audiences. Since the curtain was problematic—among other things, it was very heavy—it was used almost without exception to open and close the play and not to cloak the stage during intermissions. In fact, the difficulties in manipulating it explain an otherwise curious practice, that of hiring sailors for occasional work in the theater; their experience with tugging on pulleys to raise sails was most welcome when a curtain had to be hoisted. The problematic curtain was yet another reason why playwrights and directors of dramatic troupes came to prefer the uncomplicated simplicity of the single set versus the simultaneous (i.e., multiple) decor and its potential for requiring several curtains.

For reasons of verisimilitude, propriety, and contemporary technology, not all events could be presented on stage. It was often the case that physical activities impacting on the psychological situation were relegated to the wings and often took place between the end of one act and the beginning of the next. Each of the five acts formed a continuous temporal sequence, which was assured by another "unity," that of scene or stage, that is, the author links one scene to the next within an act by rarely leaving the stage empty (*la liaison des scènes*). Racine was especially effective at putting this "unity" into practice at the service of a more coherent illusion.[11]

The final unity that we should mention is that of tone, akin to what T. S. Eliot called "unity of sentiment": no succession of grave and comic scenes, as in Shakespeare, is permitted; the tone must be serious from beginning to end, although "serious" can include black humor and sarcasm that can provoke nervous laughter (see Néron toying with Junie and Britannicus in act 2 of *Britannicus*). The unity of tone was ever threatened by a particular practice common to the seventeenth and eighteenth centuries, that of allowing high-paying spectators to be seated on the stage itself. It required all the authority of a Voltaire to bring this often distracting convention to a halt. The audience on stage often subscribed to the idea that it was as worthy of notice, indeed as much of a spectacle, as the play itself. At the outset of *Les Fâcheux* (The bores), Molière describes the uproar that attends to the entrance on stage of the colossal self-centered bore, Eraste. Abuse was always possible.

The better to ensure unity of tone, playwrights had recourse to rhetoric. The basis for instruction at school in the seventeenth century, rhetoric was the art of persuasion and the science of analysis. Traditional rhetoric was divided into three types of discourse: judicial (to attack or defend), deliberative (to persuade or dissuade), and demonstrative (to praise, blame, or instruct). Since all of these goals are sought in the course of every tragedy (and high comedy as well), rhetoric is the fundamental means for portraying the passions in classical theater. Furthermore, Racine's use of rhetoric distinguishes itself by its ability to exert a forceful, emotional impact, while coming as close to natural diction as possible within the realm of poetry. One of the best examples in Racine's theater is the powerful simplicity of Titus's line from *Bérénice*, "For, my Princess, we have finally to part" (1061)—which is a summary of the entire point of the play. Racine's rhetoric is at once so powerful and supple that generations of Europeans have given credence to the proposition that if in England the theater is filled with *spectators* (English tragedy being action-filled and visual), in France there are, rather, *audiences,* those accustomed to listening to rhetorical flourishes. Such a point of view, diminishing as it does both Shakespeare's incantatory language and Racine's keen sense of drama, can no longer be tolerated.

Like all the other components, rhetoric is a means to the end of creating a compelling drama based on a mythological, historical, or biblical story involving power and passion. The first important constituent of the play will be the choice of subject based on the author's readings; the broader and deeper the readings, the better the chance that the subject will be well chosen. The critical factor then is the author's general cultural background; it is no small wonder that Racine took every opportunity to vaunt his knowledge of Greek and the privileged access it gave him to sources unavailable to almost all others.

Kings, queens, emperors, and princes will be depicted in struggles that, by the very status of the protagonists, involve the affirmation or the alteration of the political situation at the highest level. Racine was especially gifted in presenting the personal and passionate conflicts behind the great episodes of history (e.g., the development of the Roman Empire), mythology (e.g., the Theseus Cycle), or the Bible (the survival of the Jews). We must be careful to understand the term *passion* as the seventeenth century did. The philosopher René Descartes, for example, listed 40 passions in his *Traîté des passions* of 1649, and stated that six of them were fundamental: love, hate, desire, joy, sadness, and admiration. Corneille thought so highly of admiration that he added it as a third tragic emotion to Aristotle's pity and fear, but Racine specialized in those passions that, according to the etymology of *passion* (from the Greek *pasko*), cause suffering, principal among them, love.

Racine refers to almost all of the above elements in the prefaces to his plays. Although Racine was not one to reveal in public the secrets of his art and though prefaces are notoriously self-serving documents, especially in the case of Racine, they do reveal his preoccupations. The topics he treats most frequently are the unity of action, the imitation of the ancients as seen in the choice of subject, the role of passion, some questions of form, the nature of the tragic, the characterization of the tragic hero, verisimilitude and decorum, and the effect of the dramatic spectacle on the spectator. In fact, since the last item is the goal toward which all the others tend, we can conclude that the recent revaluation of Racine as a master technician of theater does him justice.[12]

In his longest preface, to *Bérénice,* Racine sums up his attitude as a man of the theater with his public always in mind:

> [Some people] believed that a tragedy which had so little action could not comply with the rules of the theater. I had someone ask them if they were complaining that the play bored them. I was told that all were in agreement that, not only were they not bored, but that they were moved at several points and that they would return to see it with pleasure. What more could they possibly want? I urge them to have a sufficiently good opinion of themselves not to conclude that a play which touches them and which gives them pleasure can be absolutely against the rules. The principal rule is to please and to move. All the others exist only to achieve this one.

In *La Critique de l'Ecole des femmes* (The critique of the school for wives), Molière had his spokesman, Dorante, express virtually the same idea: "I would like to know if the greatest rule of all the rules is not to please." Racine knew that to please in the tragic vein, he had to move his audience. He did so by an expert integration of tragic vision and formal elements, including the famous rules that can now be seen as helping create a believable illusion and channel the emotional attention of the spectator in such a way that the desired impact is attained.

Chapter Three
La Thébaïde

La Thébaïde ou les frères ennemis (The story of Thebes or the enemy brothers) was first presented on 20 June 1664 at the Theater of the Palais-Royal by Molière's troupe. The text was published the same year and was the object of serious revision by Racine for the collective editions of 1676, 1687, and 1697. The Preface dates from 1676.

French classical theater, tragic and comic, had several possible audiences, but the most important was the monarch. Louis XIV himself, and all his subjects, were interested in the political implications of art. This interest was heightened when one announced a play that dealt with a famous king and the political aftermath of his demise. Unlike the heroic ending of Corneille's *Oedipe*,[1] in which the institutional integrity of the monarchy is assured, Racine presents a situation in which passion destroys any possibility of a peaceful succession to the throne. In fact, Racine seems to discard both Corneille and his solution by not mentioning the current master of the French tragic stage in his Preface, where, nonetheless, he speaks of most of the other writers tempted by the myth of Oedipus, like Jean de Rotrou, Euripides, and Seneca. For Racine, Oedipus is dead, but *La Thébaïde* may be the exhibition of Racine's own oedipal struggle with that towering father figure, Pierre Corneille.

The action centers around the conflict that arises when Etéocle, the current king of Thebes in the Greek state of Boetia, is reluctant to yield his place to his brother, Polynice, in accordance with a throne-sharing agreement that Oedipus had decreed before his death. Both their mother, Jocaste, and their sister, Antigone, are anguished over the seemingly inevitable clash between the brothers. In an effort to avoid bloodshed—a decisive battle threatens Thebes—Jocaste persuades Etéocle to agree to see his brother in Thebes. An oracle predicts that peace will be reestablished only when "the last of royal blood" dies. Ménécée, one of the sons of Oedipe's brother Créon, believes that he, as the "last born" (i.e., youngest) must sacrifice himself. He does, and the awaited reunion of the brothers can take place. When they meet, however, their mutual hatred flares up and, while trying to separate them, Créon's other son and beloved of Antigone, Hémon, is killed. The brothers are then free to slay each other, which is followed by the suicides of Jocaste and Antigone. Créon, who secretly lusted after the throne and worked against the fraternal reconciliation, takes his own life when Antigone prefers death to becoming his queen.

From a political point of view, the play poses a fascinating question, particularly for the monarchical regimes of early modern Europe: can royal power be shared? Even if he has given his word to do so, can an absolute monarch be less "absolute" and yield some of his authority? The women in the play believe in a solution. Jocaste dreams of a friendly competition between her sons for the favor of their subjects. Créon, as Etéocle's counselor, argues in favor of one permanent king, rather than the instability and probable violence of alternating monarchs. This might have been a possible answer, except that Racine deliberately complicates the issue by making Créon into a French Machiavelli, striving for personal gain at the expense of the prince. Créon proposes theoretically—and is willing to implement practically—the idea of king as tyrant.

When he has Polynice refuse to let the people choose, Racine, in effect, opens up two options: popular choice, or the appeal to imperial law and divine right. Both have their merits, but, clearly, there can be no solution to a situation in which the normal criteria are useless: because the twins are identical, neither has precedence (in age, for example) over the other, nor has one been anointed by the preceding monarch as successor. The only recourse would be to eliminate one of the brothers. Yet, they end life as they began it: together, in conflict. Only the plotter Créon would remain to rule, if his romantic ambitions were not dashed by Antigone. One can only conclude, with Christian Biet, that "Racine describes the failure of this political universe, that is in fact structured by passions more powerful than any politics."[2] In keeping with other manifestations of fragmentation within his first play, Racine creates a national crisis in order to demonstrate the fragility and the discontinuity of the political realm.

The politics of La Thébaïde are hopeless because of the congenital conflict between the brothers. In Paradise Lost 6.259, Milton speaks of the cosmic "Intestine War," as a remembering of the symbiotic body of the garden, in postlapsarian terms. Racine's first performed tragedy is a recollection of the wholeness that once existed, tragically torn asunder by brothers who started warring in their mother's womb—as if she had eaten them, in-corporated them, and in so doing recalled the myth of those earlier "enemy brothers," Atreus and Thyestes. If Oedipus's original sin (incest) is sexual in nature, the result is a malady that infects

everyone. Racine makes pointed reference to it in his Preface: "The catastrophe of my play may be a bit too bloody; indeed, there is almost no
one who does not die at the end; but, to be sure, this is *La Thébaïde,* that
is, the most tragic subject of antiquity . . . [composed of] the story of
Oedipus and his unfortunate family." The framework for the play will,
therefore, be the closest of bonds—familial relations—and Racine will
use family, heredity, and blood as, in the words of Georges May, a
"fourth unity"[3] to tie his tragic characters together.

Racine's Catholic spectators would have immediately understood the
concept of an original sin, even if it were couched in pagan, mythological terms. The irreparable act of Oedipus, the Fall from the Garden of
Eden, or even, as early geographical thinking had it, the division of the
primeval waters by a god into a heaven above and an earth below—all
these are representations of separation. That Racine chose this theme for
the first of his extant tragedies gives weight to the interpretation that
irrevocable sin occupies a distinctive place in his theology and that its
consequence for his drama is a vision of a fragmented universe that some
see as an early indication of the aesthetics of modernity.[4] Indeed, the first
line of the play, and, therefore, of Racine's entire dramatic corpus,
sounds the note of separation and disunion, as Jocaste says to Olympe:
"Have they left, Olympe?"

If this play exists under the sign of Oedipus, so to speak, then what is
his role in *La Thébaïde?* Although Oedipus is already dead before the
opening of the play, his presence haunts it and he is the first in a long
line of major characters in Racine's theater who are never seen, but who
exert enormous influence. (Sometimes, as we will see in *Britannicus* and
Phèdre, these "invisible presences" will be places rather than persons.)
When Oedipus unknowingly made love to his own mother, Jocasta, he
committed a taboo act because the mingling of the same blood is forbidden. This element of the Oedipus myth was known to all of Racine's
spectators. Significantly, however, Racine marks his personal creativity
with respect to the most famous of all myths by not having a single reference to the curse of Oedipus in the course of the play. While he
undoubtedly wanted to profit from the success that the theme had
recently enjoyed in the hands of Corneille, whose *Oedipe* premiered in
1659, we have to assume that Racine wished to leave the beaten path of
the portrayal of Oedipus and Jocasta and focus on the effects of their act
on the "unfortunate family." And so, he has the fruit of their union,
Polynice and Etéocle, begin their fratricidal struggle even before their
birth. If their blood is contaminated by their heredity, it is also identical

because they are twins. (As if to make the point more clearly for our benefit, Racine added four lines in a 1697 edition that spell out that the brothers are identical twins.[5])

Given this configuration, what should be avoided at all cost is a "reunion" of the brothers, bringing the cursed blood into closer spatial contact. But that is exactly the tactic that Jocaste attempts to bring into play, until she finally succeeds in act 4, with predictable, explosive results. The brothers see each other, each sees himself in the other, each detests the mirror image that he discovers. Blood has produced a vision, a re-vision or re-cognition that culminates in a series of deaths and in a view of hell by Créon—the "last" of the royal family—that recalls similar scenes in French baroque poetry of the early seventeenth century: "Lightning is about to strike, the earth is split open, / All at once I feel a thousand different torments, / And I will go and seek my peace in hell" (1514–16).[6] No wonder that, from the very first verses, we are invited to attend a "scene" or a "seeing" of an event.[7]

It is also true that in these same verses Jocaste presents the initial lesson in Racine's theater on the importance of the unity of time, when she sighs, "We have, therefore, come to this hateful day / Which made me quake in miserable anticipation" (19–20). "This hateful day" will be the climax of a long and troubled history, anticipated in dread; the past will "therefore"—a single word rich in reference to previous, sad events— culminate in the present on this day. The political context reinforces the unity of time because the throne becomes the prize at stake, usually during the course of the play, and a decision as to its possession has to be made. Whatever else may happen, everyone on stage agrees that the political situation must be resolved, at least temporarily, within "this day." Politics, therefore, confers a sense of immediacy to the action and fixes the spectators' attention on events as they happen.

But "this day" is also the last of a series; it ends the past by infusing it into the present. Since the past in question in La Thébaïde involves the best known of ancient myths, we are also witness in this tragedy to the inaugural lesson that Racine will give on the impact that Greek and Roman literature will have on his theater. Indeed, much academic ink has flowed on the subtle yet telling way Racine incorporates other writers—modern, but especially ancient—into his work. In La Thébaïde perhaps the least appreciated of these influences is the Roman stoic Seneca (c. 4 B.C.—A.D. 65), who was Nero's tutor, the author of philosophical treatises (e.g., On Clemency), and probable composer of a number of Latin tragedies that were extensively read, commented on, and imitated all over Europe during the Renaissance and the seventeenth century. Among all the ancients, Senecan tragedy displays the greatest preoccupation with passion and its effects, and would consequently have attracted Racine's attention.

Racine does refer to Seneca in his Preface: "As for *La Thébaïde* which one finds among the works of Seneca, . . . I hold . . . that it is not a tragedy by Seneca but is the work of an orator who did not know what tragedy was." This statement is noteworthy because it constitutes the first example of the manner in which Racine consciously avoided mentioning his debt to Seneca. Why? Because Seneca's lot as a respected force in French serious drama had been on the wane for a decade or two and, more important, because Racine, who knew Greek better than anyone in France except for the most erudite scholars and translators, always preferred to elevate Greek sources over the more accessible Latin ones whenever possible, giving himself a decided advantage in any quarrel over literary models. For example, however apparently poor his opinion of the *Phoenician Women,* Seneca's version of the subject matter of *La Thébaïde,* he evidently employed parts of it for his own play. One has only to compare scene 3, which comprises 80 percent of act 4, with the corresponding moment in the *Phoenician Women* to see that it closely follows both the spirit and the letter of the Senecan text.

We should also keep in mind the fact that the remark on Seneca is in a Preface Racine composed for the 1676 edition of his collected works, and it must be interpreted in the light of Racine's status and mentality, not as a neophyte, but as the acknowledged master of French tragedy, some short time before the premiere of *Phèdre.* Having made a career based, by his own calculated admissions, on Greek sources, Racine was not about to expose his sensitive flank to any possible criticisms about the nature of his intertextual borrowings.[8]

One of the innovations that Racine brought to *La Thébaïde* has little to do with earlier versions of the story and concerns the relationship between mother and daughter. The depth of the relationship between Jocaste and Antigone is expressed in Antigone's "stances" of act 5, scene 1. The French dramatic verse form of "stances"—a stanza of verses in which the lines are of varying poetic meters—was used in the first half of the seventeenth century when authors wished to break the traditional alexandrine line to signal to the spectators that they were witnessing a moment of intense lyricism. In the case of Antigone, caught as she is between two loyalties, she gives expression to her personal dilemma in terms that surely recalled to the spectators Rodrigue's celebrated "stances" in Corneille's *Le Cid.* What distinguishes the two "stances" is the nature of the decision each character makes when faced with the choice between self and society; Rodrigue chooses father and family, while Antigone opts for her passion and Hémon. Antigone's verses also possess a function beyond the lyric, since they serve to introduce two new facts: the suicide of Jocaste and the reprise of the battle between the two brothers. By making his lyric moment further the plot line, the fledgling playwright was already showing signs of a literary instinct for creating a large impact with minimum means.

Another attempt by Racine to be original may be seen in the way he dealt with the role of confidants. Before Racine, French classical tragedy had traditionally followed the convenient practice of Greek tragedy of having certain secondary characters, called "confidants," serve as messengers, reporting offstage action, or as sympathetic ears for the sighs and secrets of their masters and mistresses. At times, they might even participate somewhat in the action, but their main purpose was purely functional. As such they ran the risk of violating the precept of verisimilitude, for the spectator could often determine that confidants were not an essential part of the action.

In *La Thébaïde* Racine already displays a talent for experimentation that is a constant of his whole theatrical career. Contrary to writers of a previous generation like Pierre Corneille and Jean de Rotrou, who generally had a relatively generous list of *dramatis personae,* Racine preferred to be economical. His play has six characters, only two of whom have confidants. There is only one truly minor character, a soldier who speaks six lines in act 2, scene 4, to announce that the truce has been broken. Rotrou, in his *Antigone,* has about twice the number of characters. Racine's sense of conciseness drives a play where there exists less need for secondary figures because the confrontation of the major characters is central.

Consequently, Racine's play has only two confidants, who serve two different masters and have varying functions in the play. Since Jocaste has nothing to hide, she and her confidant, Olympe, interact frequently, whereas Créon disguises his ambition until he uncovers it to his confidant, Attale, in act 3, scene 5. Attale is, therefore, more of the traditional, functional confidant than Olympe. In fact, in a desire to give Olympe unaccustomed status by integrating her into the action, Racine has her emotionally involved throughout; it is she who is given the task of describing the touching death of Antigone in act 5, scene 5. As Valérie Worth-Stylianou points out, Racine forced the issue of the confidant in his next play, *Alexandre le Grand,* in which there are no real confidants and in which, as a consequence, Racine sacrifices the clarity of his play to his experiment of creating a classical tragedy without one class of utilitarian characters.[9] It is an experiment he never repeated.

Despite Racine's reworkings of the text over the years, *La Thébaïde* has not moved the forces of posterity to award it a place in the seventeenth-century canon. Most readers familiar with Racine's major plays conclude that *La Thébaïde* is not the equal of other Racinian tragedies; this may well be because of the insufficient attention that Racine gives to questions of space and setting. In the first scene we are told that a battle is about to take place that one can view from the ramparts of the palace. In other words, instead of making us comfortable with the locale in front of us, a palace in Thebes, we are projected to an abstract "else-where," to an event we will not be privileged to see ourselves. The rest of the play is spent in anticipation of the combat between Etéocle and Polynice, which has to take place offstage given the strictures against presenting violence in front of the spectators. This means that, once again, we will be second-hand viewers, asked to content ourselves with what the characters describe from their perch on top of the palace walls, looking down onto the plain below. Since it is during the fifth act that the brothers have their offstage duel, the entire final section of the play can be no more than a series of reports on the action. According to Richard Parish, "the audience finishes up by feeling that if it was also on the ramparts it might be having a better time."[10]

Since this play is the first we have of Racine, it is probably wise to conclude on a brief listing of its strengths and weaknesses. While *La Thébaïde* expresses a tragic vision of the fragmentation of human relations, with Créon as a preliminary sketch of a tragic character haunted by insecurity, the structure is far from seamless, and the characters tend to be either white or black. In the mature plays, by contrast, innocence becomes a problematic issue.[11]

The play's language is rather stilted and formal, slowing down the action, and creating an impersonal atmosphere ill-suited to a tragedy involving intense family hatred. Ultimately, the major flaw is that the spectator's interest and sympathy transfer from one character to another. First we are attracted to Jocaste, next to Antigone; near the end, Créon rises as the central figure. All this despite the title implying that our focus will be on the brothers in this first play as in most others: Néron and Britannicus (*Britannicus*), Bajazet and Amurat (*Bajazet*), Xipharès and Pharnace (*Mithridate*), and Hippolyte and his half-brothers, Phèdre's children (*Phèdre*).

The traits typical of Racinian tragedy to be perceived in this first published effort are, as Bernard Weinberg has identified them, (1) a choice is made, among all possible moments of a story, of an episode near the end so that the events portrayed on stage will be concentrated in a short period of time that leads to the denouement. (2) The spectator's imagination is excited by the report of actions that take place off-stage and must be recounted—whence, the importance of the narrative report (*récit*). Also, the spectator learns about another more significant action: the interior conflicts and dilemmas that have a direct connection to the exterior action. (3) Consequently, the emotional effect on the spectator will depend less on exterior forces than on the development and movement of the passions of the hero or heroine. (4) As a result, the author strives to produce subtle and varied characterizations, a revelation of emotions that is intimate and extensive, and a dialogue that is created not to move along the plot, but to follow closely the operations of the heart and the mind.[12]

An analysis of the play's structure leads to these conclusions: (1) the rhythm is evident—it consists in alternating moments of hope and despair, or accord and discord. (2) There is strict linking of one scene to the next within each act. (3) This is accomplished through the linear structure of each act, except the last; that is, a character who is present in the first scene will remain on stage throughout the succeeding scenes, thereby assuring continuity. (4) The third act is a microcosm of the play's rhythm of hope/despair. It is the "central" act in that sense. (5) Antigone is the unifying character. She is concerned by the conflict between Etéocle and Polynice; she participates in the love plot with Hémon; and she is the object of Créon's passion. She is a member of the accursed family, and she causes Créon's fall. Yet she is not the major character in the spectators' eyes; the emotional focus is undermined by the structure.

La Thébaïde is an incomplete introduction to Racinian tragedy, but it does show the way by insisting on family discord as a central concept. Mythology apparently plays a role, but in truth the gods do not exist: they are the exteriorization of the personal problems of the characters who live in a world of profound instability.

Chapter Four
Alexandre le Grand

Alexandre le Grand (Alexander the Great), early on titled *Porus,* is situated on the banks of the Indus River, in the camp of a local king, Taxile. His sister Cléofile has been captured then released by Alexandre. She urges her brother to leave the alliance with Porus and join forces with the irresistible conqueror, whom she now loves. Porus will not hear of submitting to Alexandre, and Axiane, who loves him, hopes to persuade Taxile to be supportive. When Alexandre's ambassador Ephestion arrives with an offer of peace to the kings and of marriage to Cléofile, Taxile is ready to accept, but Porus refuses.

Since Alexandre and Porus need each other for reasons of military competition and fame as much as Etéocle and Polynice did in *La Thébaïde* for reasons of visceral, fraternal hatred, the battle between their armies takes place while Taxile remains neutral and protects Axiane, whose love he seeks, in his tent. In the description of the battle and its consequences, Racine is less interested in local color than in what he evidently believes would be of greater interest to his audience—the ebb and flow of the action, namely:

1. the report that Porus has been defeated and fled;
2. Cléofile informing Taxile that Porus is not dead;
3. Porus announcing that he has slain Taxile; and
4. Alexandre showing generosity toward Porus.

When Alexandre returns triumphantly, Axiane believes Porus dead and tells Taxile that she will be his, if he exacts revenge on Alexandre. When the news arrives that Porus is still alive, Taxile departs to attack him, but is slain by him instead.

Cléofile urges Alexandre to have Porus, now captured, put to death, but Alexandre finds Porus such a worthy adversary that he pardons him and permits him to retain his lands as king. This unexpected generosity sweeps aside the resistance and resentment of Porus and of Axiane, who now perceive Alexandre as a magnanimous being. They will marry, and Cléofile will undoubtedly accept Alexandre's offer once she has had time to grieve for her dead brother.

The First Preface to the printed text of *Alexandre le Grand* is from 1666, and the Second Preface, which details the historical sources, dates from 1672. Typically, Racine follows his sources only as far as he wants to take them. For example, no mention is made in the ancient sources of Cleophis (the name's spelling in Justin's *Universal History,* while Quintus Curtius gives Cleophes) being the sister of Taxile. Racine takes this liberty in order to develop several interesting scenes between brother and sister.

What goes unmentioned in the prefaces, for obvious reasons, is the history of the "two premieres" of the play. As we have already seen in a previous chapter Molière's company presented the premiere performance of *Alexandre le Grand* on 4 December 1665 at their theater in the Palais-Royal, and it was a notable event. In fact, Mme de Sévigné considered it the equal of *Andromaque* and much better than *Bajazet* (letter of 16 March 1672). Posterity has not been as enthusiastic, and Racine admits that his creation is flawed when he writes in the First Preface: "I never claimed that I was offering the public a perfect work of art [in *Alexandre*]." He also attacks his critics in a manner that became a trademark of Racinian prefaces: his play must have some merit, he argues, because individuals without taste disapproved of it and pretended to find justification for their views in ancient sources, which they were unable to read in the original, like the *Poetics* of Aristotle.

Nonetheless, from all the evidence, the play was such a hot property in 1665 that Racine broke with Molière over it. According to Morel and Viala, the success of the play was due to its "ideological impact."[1] Racine's previous dramatic and poetic efforts did little to distinguish him from his rivals in the eyes of the court, although he had already managed to obtain a royal pension of 600 *livres. Alexandre le Grand,* with its dedication to Louis XIV—grandson of Henri le Grand and future Louis le Grand himself—was undoubtedly conceived by Racine as his ticket to royal favor. Racine would be far from the first to compare Louis XIV and Alexander the Great—in fact, the Macedonian conqueror was all the rage as subject matter in the 1660s—but a stage presentation, at two different theaters at once for a whole week, was bound to attract more notice, for example, than a painting by Le Brun on the same figure, *The Family of Darius at the Feet of Alexandre.* (Interestingly, 10 years later, Le Brun and Louis XIV decided to place an enlarged copy of this masterpiece in the ceiling of the Salon de Mars in Versailles. The painting's message is apparently identical to Racine's: the logical end to war in a modern, Catholic country is not conquest, but the conqueror's magnanimity.[2])

Racine had to be ingenious to make Louis XIV, who had not yet been to war, into a seventeenth-century reincarnation of the military genius of antiquity. In his "Epistle to the King," which was published with the First Preface until being dropped after 1672, Racine took initial pains to identify the two: "Not being satisfied with having placed the name of Alexander at the head of my work, I now add that of YOUR MAJESTY, that is, I have now assembled the greatest that present and past centuries have produced." In the "Epistle," as in *Alexandre* and his later *Eloge historique du Roi* (Historical panegyric of the king), Racine assumed the public role of the writer as defender of absolute monarchy, founded on divine right and capable of justifying tyranny by the sacred duty of the monarch to protect law and order. (The French word for *tyrant* is of high lexical frequency in *Alexandre*.)

It becomes clear in the course of the "Epistle" that Racine's strategy is to promote Louis XIV's moral virtues over Alexander's military prowess. This attempt to reconcile two different conceptions of the hero recalls the longstanding debate over the superior form of heroism, that of Achilles, the violent, or of Hector, the model of civic and familial virtue. It may well be that the problem Racine grappled with in his "Epistle to the King" went unresolved and is reflected in the praise/blame nature of the comments on Alexandre that one encounters from the very first lines, as Cléofile warns Taxile:

> What? You will engage in battle a king whose power
> Seems capable of forcing heaven to defend itself,
> Who has defeated all of Asia's kings,
> And who holds Fortune itself under his control?
> Dear brother, open your eyes and recognize Alexandre:
> See thrones in ashes everywhere you look,
> Nations enslaved, and kings in chains,
> And avoid the misfortune that caused it all.
>
> (1–8)

Conquest has brought Alexandre both an exalted image and an intimidating reputation. In the course of the play, the characters take up this same double optic, recognizing Alexandre's supreme status as soldier while making reference to the unfortunate result of his martial accomplishments.

The ambiguity toward the eponymous character permeates the play, but he is not the only enigmatic individual on stage. All of the characters seem difficult to know, and we are often perplexed by their apparently contradictory motivations. What do we really know about Cléofile, Alexandre's love interest? Is she more interested in saving her brother or in expressing her love for Alexandre, despite reservations about his bloody career? If we recall Racine's desire to give new orientation to the role of the traditional confidants, we may see the reason for the impenetrability of the protagonists of *Alexandre*. There were two confidants in *La Thébaïde*, but there are none in *Alexandre*. Two distinct consequences result from this experiment. First, unlike many characters in Racine's corpus who have difficulty expressing themselves—one thinks immediately of Titus in *Bérénice* and of Phèdre—the characters of *Alexandre* experience no such problem; when their strategy dictates the need for an utterance, they speak. They require no coaxing from a confidant. Second and more telling, Racine's confidantless conception can only be implemented if the characters have no pretext for unburdening themselves and making their true feelings, choices, dilemmas known. Under such circumstances, they cannot help but impress us as less than genuine.

This impression is reinforced by the language of the title character, who has recourse to the same gallant formulas that Hémon used in *La Thébaïde*: He "burns with a beautiful fire" of love, he is all "sighs," he is a "prisoner of passion," and so on. The military elements (his "defeat" and "imprisonment" by the "tyrannical" Cléofile) strike us as time-honored banalities. Furthermore, instead of mutually strengthening each other, the themes of love and war are in fact weakened by the inauthenticity of the language. Racine may have attempted to compensate for the inexpressive language and the lack of confidants by what Michael Hawcroft calls "verbal action."[3] He shows that the lyrical and poetic effusions of baroque dramatists like the young Corneille and Rotrou give way in the second half of the seventeenth century to a conception of dramatic speech as action, designed to have a particular impact on the interlocutor. Given that there are no confidants in *Alexandre*, the principal characters will undertake to influence each other directly by their speech acts.

The earliest examples of this phenomenon occur in the first scene of act 1, where Cléofile tries to dissuade Taxile from combating Alexandre, to which he replies that he cannot betray his allies Porus and Axiane. If Cléofile suggests that Alexandre will give her brother special treatment, Taxile is not moved. At this point, Cléofile changes tactics and appeals to Taxile not to fight the man she loves, but Taxile's own love for Axiane commits him to oppose the conqueror. Cléofile then attempts, rather sadistically, to counter that argument by indicating that Axiane loves Taxile's rival, Porus. She pursues the idea by specifying all that Taxile will lose by supporting Porus and the gain that will be his if he opts for Alexandre. When Cléofile leaves and Porus enters, the same debate commences, but with Taxile having adopted the pro-Alexandre position and Porus the contrary.

From this brief examination of the first 122 verses we can appreciate the importance of words as action for the "exposition"—the first moments of the play when the spectator is given the information necessary to understand the broad lines of the plot—and for the creation of the conflict and tension essential to any drama. To comprehend the inner struggles that Racine portrays, we still require that form of personal confession of intentions and strategies that occurs when a main character speaks "confidentially." The aforementioned lack of confidants in *Alexandre* can lead to ambiguity and even confusion, a factor that goes far to explain the conclusion many critics have adopted—perhaps too hastily—that the tragedy is highly "rhetorical" in a negative sense and ultimately is "bad Corneille." In fact, one of the literary sources for *Alexandre* is Corneille's *La Mort de Pompée* (The death of Pompey).

One of Corneille's favorite and most successful devices was the use of the peripeteia, the radical change (or apparent change) of direction in the course of events. The death of Chimène's father at the hands of Rodrigue in *Le Cid* and the seeming defeat of Horace and his brothers in *Horace* are memorable examples. But, as Jacques Scherer has noted, in *Alexandre* Racine draws no particular advantage from the two peripeteia involving Porus.[4] His death is announced as a possibility at the beginning of act 4; then, in scene 4, he is evidently alive, but Axiane, who is the one most interested in his fate, is not present to hear the good news. Two peripeteia take place with virtually no dramatic consequences; Corneille knew how to do better.

From *La Thébaïde* to *Bérénice* Racine was always dueling with Corneille, even if it was often more like shadow boxing with himself, since Corneille usually had others, like Saint-Évremond, execute the counterattack. *Alexandre* does have a Cornelian allure about it, owing in no small part to its denouement, which resembles the heroic endings dear to Corneille and which would have certainly reminded a seventeenth-century audience specifically of Auguste's clemency at the end of Corneille's *Cinna*. This reminiscence of Corneille accounts for Mme de Sévigné's attachment to *Alexandre,* faithful Cornelian that she was.

But what is the message of the denouement? Is this a "tragedy" in more than the Cornelian sense of submitting the hero to a series of death-threatening experiences in the course of the action? Recent critics have found the play tragic because it inspires pity and fear, and it ends, not on an image of military glory, but of human suffering caused by triumph on the field of battle.[5] As we have seen, Cléofile has mixed emotions about Alexandre, and she expresses them to open the play. She is also responsible for the last mental picture we have of Alexandre, and it is telling. Starting with *Alexandre,* Racine attempted to project the imagination of the spectator beyond the final curtain's close by capturing one or more of the main characters in a pose that is not only typical but, in a sense, mythical: the character's reputation throughout time and fable will correspond to his or her ultimate image in the play.

Alexandre, who, according to Plutarch, claimed to be descended from Hercules, will have the same fate as the demigod born of Jupiter and Alcmena, even if Porus sarcastically refuses to elevate Alexandre to Herculean status:

> We know that the Gods are not tyrants;
> And however a slave chooses to name him,
> The son of Jupiter passes here for a man.
> (572–74)

Alexandre, like the Hercules of Seneca's *Hercules furens* (Mad Hercules), may be the benefactor of mankind, but he is also responsible for the carnage that fills the play's central divisions. Cléofile is eloquent on the subject in the first scene of the last act, as she paints a portrait of Alexandre seeking conquest even in hell:

> But now what, Lord? Always one war after another?
> Will you seek subjects beyond the earth itself?
> Do you need, as witnesses for your brilliant deeds,
> Countries foreign to their own inhabitants?
> Whom will you fight in such austere climes? . . .
> [In places where] Nature itself seems to expire.
> (1325–32)

If the lust for personal glory brings death and destruction, then practicing the virtue of clemency can only be a higher degree of heroism, one suitable to a king as representative of God on earth. The Bourbon monarchy took pains in the sixteenth and seventeenth centuries to legitimize itself by claiming descendance from Hercules and his "great-, great- . . . grandson" Alexander,[6] and also from Imperial Rome. Thus, it had to be doubly flattering to Louis XIV, despite Cléofile's qualms, to see himself portrayed as the (morally superior) modern version of Alexander the warrior and of Augustus the clement. The latter quality especially protects the king from the possible reproach of wishing to emulate a sovereign of unlimited power, with all the attendant dangers for the healthy, secure, and rational functioning of the state. In a well-documented article, Timothy Reiss goes so far as to perceive, in the pacific tone of *Alexandre,* Racine's caution against the provocative acts that Louis XIV—uncontested master of his own country—had undertaken against the Holy Roman Empire to demonstrate his idea that France was the rightful heir to imperial power in Europe.[7]

In *Andromaque* Racine continued to depict dynastic events, but with a change of perspective that must have struck the seventeenth-century audience as profoundly realistic.

Chapter Five
Andromaque

The date 17 November 1667 is one of the signal moments in the history of world theater because *Andromaque* premiered on that date and changed the conception of tragedy. As we have seen previously, the reigning monarch of serious French theater at this time was Pierre Corneille, whose plots stressed political clashes and heroic conclusions. In *Andromaque* realism replaces heroism. It already had, to some degree, in *La Thébaïde,* but the public took serious notice this time because the drama was more tightly constructed, the characters more in sympathy with contemporary mores, and the key word, rich in emotional shadings, was not *sang* (blood) as in the first play, but *amour* (love).

Andromaque's realism may be summed up as the presentation of kings and queens subjected to the fate common to all, or as Paul Bénichou puts it so well about Racinian theater in general, Racine presents "the grandeur of a privileged [royal] situation, joined to the unveiled truth of nature."[1] Racine succeeds in offering a spectacle of human suffering transformed into a pleasing experience for theatergoers. Why did spectators enjoy this new form of tragedy? The answer may lie in the fusion of human attitudes that are revealed in *Andromaque*: dignity, pride, passion, suffering, and madness.

The story concerns the aftermath of the most celebrated struggle in mythology, the Trojan War. In the first extensive display of his knowledge of the literature of classical antiquity, Racine borrows from treatments both classical and modern, prominently, Homer's *Iliad*; Euripides's *Trojan Women, Orestes,* and *Andromache*; Heliodorus's *Theagenes and Chariclea*. Perhaps even more important are Seneca's *Trojan Women* and Virgil's *Aeneid* (he quotes a passage from the *Aeneid* at the top of both his first and second Prefaces). Among several possible modern sources, scholars have found traces of Pierre Corneille (*Pertharite*), Jean de Rotrou (*Hercule mourant, Venceslas*), Thomas Corneille (*Persée et Démétrius*), and Racine himself (*Alexandre*). One of the contributing factors to the success of this play—and one of the constants of Racinian creativity—is Racine's ability to develop previous and contemporary material. These are the sources that "influenced" him, that is, the texts that he imitated and used in the light of his own dramatic needs.

From these sources Racine weaves a tale of frustrated desire, deceit, and death concerning the "second generation" of heroes, those whose illustrious parents were the principal figures in the war between the allied Greeks and the citizens of Troy in Asia Minor. We do not encounter Achilles, Agamemnon, or Helen, but their offspring: Pyrrhus, better known in mythology as Neoptolemus,[2] Oreste, and Hermione— plus the title character, who plays two roles superbly, for she is both the widow of Hector and the mother of Astyanax. Neither one of the latter figures is seen in the play, but they are arguably its two most influential characters.

The drama begins with Oreste outlining the project that brings him, as Ambassador of the Greeks, to Buthrotum in the northwest region of Greece known as Epirus. Fearing that Astyanax will exact revenge on them one day, the Greeks have sent Oreste to obtain Astyanax from Pyrrhus, the King of Epirus, who is holding both mother and son captive as prizes of the Greek victory over the Trojans. Oreste's personal agenda for making the trip to Buthrotum lies in his desire to have Hermione, Pyrrhus's fiancée, leave the king and follow him back to Greece. Hermione, who had desperately been clinging to the hope that Pyrrhus would recognize her as his beloved queen, demands that Oreste prove his love by slaying Pyrrhus, who has announced plans to marry the Trojan "slave" Andromaque and reject the Greek princess who has spent years waiting in Epirus. Pyrrhus is assassinated—offstage, to be sure—by the Greeks, and Hermione commits suicide on his body. Oreste has a fit of madness as he envisions the results of the double betrayal in which he became involved—he transformed his political mission into a personal obsession resulting in regicide, and Hermione did not return his love, even after he caused Pyrrhus's death. In a supreme irony, Racine recasted the ending of the Trojan War by promoting the captive Andromaque to conqueror; she survives the demise of the three other principals in the play and takes satisfaction in pursuing punishment against the Greeks for killing the King of Epirus, her new husband.

It is clear from this resume that each of the characters has the same problem: he or she loves someone who does not return that love. This connectedness, for which the Germans coined the term *liebeskette* (chain of love), produces the following formula that Racine had learned from a dramatic genre popular in the seventeenth century, the *pastorale*: A loves B who loves C who loves D. In the romantic world of the *pastorale,* there

would be a complete circle, because D would love A. If Racine did have
a fondness for circular patterns, as we shall see in *Phèdre,* he preferred to
stress the unilateral nature of the relationships in *Andromaque,* where
Oreste pursues an Hermione taken with a Pyrrhus who yearns for an
Andromaque who cares only for Hector: the circle is incomplete, and
the circuit is broken. A great deal of the ironic impact of the play derives
precisely from the apparent linkage of characters who are in reality
totally isolated in their self-centered drive for possession of the object of
their love. Furthermore, although they all attempt to transcend the
obstacle of unrequited love, not one of them offers a sincere word of
sympathy to any other. This all-consuming passion for passion has an
explanation, which Racine takes pains to elucidate.

In fact, he gives us a clue very early on, even before we read the first
line of *Andromaque.* In the list of "Actors" that precedes the text, the
order of the descriptions of the four main characters reveals much about
their fundamental problem:

> ANDROMAQUE, widow of Hector, captive of Pyrrhus
> PYRRHUS, son of Achilles, king of Epirus
> ORESTE, son of Agamemnon
> HERMIONE, daughter of Helen, engaged to Pyrrhus

In any Racine play, as in much traditional drama, the first task of the
reader/critic is to determine the nature of the relationships that the characters maintain with each other. Racine's list of *dramatis personae* shows
that the primary consideration for each of his figures will be their rapport with an illustrious parent; the play begins, appropriately, with
Oreste, who, for Racine, is defined solely by his relationship with his
father. To highlight this factor, Racine skillfully uses a standard rhetorical technique, genealogical periphrasis, that consists in avoiding the
direct naming of an individual in favor of stating his or her descendance.

The first example occurs in act 1, scene 2, where Oreste, who had just
lamented his fate to his friend Pylade, changes his tone to address
Pyrrhus, the reigning monarch in Epirus, in these arrogant terms:

> Before all the Greeks express their wishes through me as spokesman,
> Allow me to acknowledge the excellence of their choice,
> And to show the joy I feel, Lord,
> To see the son of Achilles and the conqueror of Troy.

> (43 – 46)

As if to make sure that Pyrrhus, whom he has called the son of Achilles and not the King of Epirus, understands that the father will always predominate in the eyes of the Greeks and of posterity, Oreste adds: "Yes, we admire his exploits and your blows, / Hector fell before him, and Troy expired thanks to you" (47–48). The comparisons are sure to wound Pyrrhus; his father committed "exploits," but he is capable only of "blows"; his father slew the protector of Troy, which, tired and defenseless, simply lay down and died before Pyrrhus.

Even if Oreste was seeking to vaunt his own elevated ambassadorial status rather than offend Pyrrhus, he does conjure up the image of the celebrated father against whom Pyrrhus will always instinctively measure himself. Oreste does even more in this vein: three times in the course of this same speech he mentions the other hero who haunts Pyrrhus, Hector, whose fame as the "citizen-hero" rivals that of Achilles as the "warrior-hero." As we shall see, Hector's status as the (late) husband of Andromaque preoccupies Pyrrhus most of all.

To return the favor of genealogical periphrasis, Pyrrhus answers Oreste:

> Greece on my behalf is too upset,
> Of loftier concerns I thought her disquieted,
> Lord, and from her appointed Ambassador
> I had expected great and vast proposals.
> Who would believe that the undertaking you describe
> Would justify the intervention of the son of Agamemnon;
> And that an entire nation, triumphant at every turn,
> Would be driven to slay a small child?
>
> (173–80)

Implicit in Pyrrhus's reproach to all the Greeks is a personal one for Oreste; in essence, Pyrrhus is asking Oreste if he, who was too young to participate in a war effort organized by his own father Agamemnon, has found no better heroic tasks to glorify himself than to serve as escort for a child.

Later on in the play, Oreste attempts to persuade Hermione to join him in a misdirected form of flattery involving genealogical periphrasis:

> To illustrate my strength and your fame,
> Let us replace, you Helen, and I Agamemnon.

Let us reenact, in this land, the horrors of Troy,
So that they speak of us as they have of our fathers.
                                                    (1159–62)

Hermione is aware that she has always lived in the shadow of her
mother, whose abduction by Pâris constituted the grounds for the Trojan War. If Helen's is the "face that launched a thousand ships,"
Hermione will not find her own identity in casting her fate with someone whose heroism is untried. Finally conceiving of a "vast and great
project," a task that might earn him heroic status, Oreste fails because
he does not understand Hermione's motives.

These examples of a widespread linguistic phenomenon in *Andromaque* underscore the "generation gap" of which the main characters are
acutely conscious. Oreste gives the first and the fullest explanation of
the reasons for this feeling of inferiority when he indicates in the first
scene that love is the operative factor. If, as Pylade notes, Oreste has
spent the last six months wandering, it may be that he has no taste for
the official mission that requires his presence in Epirus. We soon learn
from Oreste himself that he has turned his public obligation into a private quest whose success depends entirely on that "inhuman" (26) person, Hermione.

Having confessed, much to Pylade's surprise, that he still loves
Hermione, Oreste goes on to recall how Pylade was witness to the birth of
that passion and to its despair "when Meneleaus betrothed his daughter
[Hermione] to Pyrrhus, the avenger of his family" (41–42).[3] Since the day
a returning hero from the Trojan War was preferred to him, Oreste has
been seeking the opportunity to prove himself equal to the Greek heroes.
He traveled to lands civilized and savage, risking—even pursuing—death,
without, however, being able to erase the memory of Hermione. Even
when he thought he hated her, he was still in love with her.

Oreste's confession reveals the central motivating element for the
characters of *Andromaque*: "love" is the pursuit of the affection of the one
person whose approval can change failure to success. Oreste needs to
have the initial rejection scene replayed with a different ending—this
time Oreste would be the chosen fiancé. No longer a wanderer in search
of personal identity, he would have won out over his rivals by being
accepted by the daughter of Helen of Troy; a rite of passage to heroism
would be effected.

Hermione has the same kind of drive for acceptance, by the outstanding young hero of the Greek alliance, someone whose "love" might com-

pensate for a life lived not as Hermione, but as "Helen of Troy's daughter." Pyrrhus has two ideals with whom to compete, Achilles and Hector. Even Andromaque is not foreign to this feeling, for she believes that she must prove herself equal to the lofty image of "the wife worthy of Hector." *Andromaque* is about the playing out of these personal scenarios.

The characters may often appear to be participating in a dialectic between love and hate toward the beloved, but hate is always love disguised, because one cannot afford to hate the only person capable of performing the desired transformation. The evidence for this lies in the various shades of meaning of the verb *haïr* (to hate) in the seventeenth century: it ran the gamut from profound loathing to simple indifference. Two occurrences of "hatred as indifference" are in fact found toward the end of act 1, scene 1, when Pylade states that Andromaque has rewarded Pyrrhus's love with "hate" and then that Pyrrhus is in such emotional disorder that he could wed the one he "hates" (Hermione) and punish the one he loves (Andromaque). In both instances, as throughout, "to be indifferent to" is the satisfying meaning.

Before we follow the manner in which Racine casts indifference as the most cruel of attitudes, let us consider a defense mechanism that permits the characters to withstand the indignities they suffer at the hands of their beloved, for it has significance in the dramaturgical, psychological, and tragic dimensions of the play: the lie. In his innovative creation of a tortured humanity in *Andromaque,* Racine presents characters who lie as often to themselves as they do to others. Oreste says exactly that to Pylade in the very first scene: "I deceived myself" (37). Pylade tells him that Hermione "apparently" disdains the infidelity of Pyrrhus, but in reality she "weeps secretly" at the scorn with which Pyrrhus receives her expressions of love. Out of desperation, Pyrrhus tries to give Andromaque the impression, from time to time, that he still loves Hermione. And, of course, the whole action of the play is given its initial impetus by the arrival of Oreste, who has accepted the weighty task of representing the Greeks so that he might betray that mission by persuading Hermione to leave with him.

The characters think of others in terms of their own passion—which means that they are really thinking of themselves. As a consequence, each interprets the other's motives inaccurately. As Noémi Hepp has demonstrated, the best examples of the power to recreate others according to one's blind wishes occur in the two successive portraits that Hermione paints of Pyrrhus.[4] In act 3, scene 3, having learned of Pyrrhus's decision to marry her, she exclaims to her confidant Cléone:

No, Cléone, Pyrrhus does not contradict himself;
He means everything he does: if he marries me, he loves me . . .
Do you remember who Pyrrhus is? Has anyone listed for you
The sum of his exploits—but then who could possibly count them?
Fearless, victory following his every step,
Charming, faithful: his fame is full.

(845–54)

However, this portrait of the young man as hero is replaced in act 4, scene 5 by a different treatment—the warrior as sadist:

You don't reply? I see it in your treacherous eyes:
You count the moments you waste with me!
Your heart, impatient to see your Trojan woman,
Suffers begrudgingly that another occupy you.
You are speaking to her in your heart,
You are seeking her with your eyes.
I'll not hold you back, leave now.
Go, swear to her the pledge of love you once swore to me,
Go, violate your oath to the gods,
These same gods, just and good, will not forget
That this very oath once bound you to me.

(1375–84)

Neither view of Pyrrhus is entirely accurate. The first is a Pyrrhus of Hermione's own willful creation, perfect in every way. The second is inaccurate in that it attributes to the young king an intention to make Hermione suffer that is far from his mind. As she herself recognizes, she is not present to Pyrrhus's consciousness.

The passage from act 4, scene 5 is, consequently, illustrative of both deception and indifference. Pyrrhus neither loves nor hates Hermione. She simply does not exist as an emotional connection for him; therein lies the tragedy for Hermione, whose whole identity as a separate being depends on a demonstration of Pyrrhus's preference for her. (That the demonstration should preferably be public is but one instance in Racine of his characters' self-perception as actors in a theatrical experience. We shall see more of this in *Britannicus*.)

Hermione's first description of Pyrrhus (act 3, scene 3) confuses perception and conception. It is a patent example of self-blindness. Of all
the seventeenth-century writers, Blaise Pascal best alerts us to the cause
for this instinct for self-deception. In so doing he offers a fine tool for
dissecting the psyche of Racine's characters:

> The nature of self-love and of the human ego is to love only self and to be
> turned only toward self. But what will it [self-love] do? It cannot prevent
> this object that it loves so deeply from being full of imperfections and
> misery: it wishes to be big, and it sees itself small; it wants to be happy,
> and it sees itself miserable; it wants to be perfect, and it sees itself full of
> imperfections; it wants to be the object of love and esteem of all human-
> ity, and it sees that its defects deserve only aversion and scorn. . . . Desir-
> ing to wipe out the truth, and being unable to destroy it in itself, it
> destroys it, to the degree possible, in the perception of others and of
> itself; that is, it puts all its effort into hiding its defects to others and to
> itself. (*Pensée* 743, Sellier edition)

This phenomenon recurs as a common theme in the writings, both religious and profane, of the French seventeenth century. If humanity's penchant for self-deception explains the perorations of a Pierre Nicole
against the theater—the genre that invites one to stray into a world of
illusion that can provoke moral blindness—Madame de La Fayette
treated the same idea, in a secular context, in her novel *La Princesse de
Clèves*, where a husband has to admit to his wife that he would have preferred ignorance to the truth of her feelings for another.

Hermione is hardly alone in willfully practicing a form of verbal
irony, of telling other than the truth. Oreste lies about the true nature of
his mission in Buthrotum, and Pyrrhus gives the Greeks the impression
that he will remain true to his oath to them. Indeed, his self-blindness is
perhaps most noteworthy when he tries to convince his confidant (and
himself) that he has triumphed over Andromaque and decided to
deliver her son to the Greeks. He ends act 2, scene 5 with "Let us do all
I have promised." The spectator already senses that such a statement is
part of a desperate game that Pyrrhus is playing with his word and his
honor, both of which he seems ready to sacrifice for Andromaque's love.
In Racine's next play, *Britannicus,* he offers us a character who is falseness personified, Narcisse, the traitor—as well as one of his characters
who does not need to lie instinctively about himself because of his power
and his lack of conscience, Néron. On the other hand, the emperor has

no qualms about devising traps and lethal snares, thereby obliging his victims, like Junie, to lie.[5]

To avoid confusing the audience, Racine's practice in the matter of falseness and deception is almost always to have a scene of lying preceded by one in which the truth is told. Hermione tells Cléone the truth in act 2, scene 1, and then practices omissions and outright falsehood with Oreste in act 2, scene 2. This dialectic always allows us to penetrate the real values of the characters—which is Racine's goal. The instinctive lie, which is first and foremost an act of self-deception, forms part of that renewal of the tragic genre in *Andromaque* with which we credit Racine.

Self-deception is necessary owing to the need to conceal the reality of one's self-perception. The world of *Andromaque* is populated by those who feel incomplete and therefore inferior. What they seek in the object of their passion is that which they lack; it might be called *status* in the modern sense of the term. They desire to unite with a being whose approval—expressed as reciprocal love—will at once elevate them (to the level of hero, bride of the triumphant king, warrior equal to Achilles and Hector, and wife worthy of Hector of Troy) and make them whole. Since being recognized and accepted by the beloved other is what constitutes love in this play, indifference will be the cruelest of replies (or nonreplies) to the expression of passion, and the characters are not reluctant to point this out. We have already seen Hermione complain to Pyrrhus about his indifferent behavior toward her (act 4, scene 5). Oreste fills act 2, scene 2 with reminders to Hermione that she would hold him in much higher "regard" (she would "see" him and appreciate him) if he were Pyrrhus. He also makes the point about Pyrrhus: "In any event, he is indifferent to you" (549), to which she reacts so emotionally that she loses control for a few seconds before she once again returns to the sentimental ballet it is her role to dance throughout.

But the most dramatically impressive examples of the game-playing that results from the terrible combination of politics and unrequited love are reserved for those scenes—act 1, scene 4 and act 3, scenes 6–7—almost identical in their rhythm and result, between Andromaque and Pyrrhus, that is, between the lowest and the highest beings in the political hierarchy. In the first, Pyrrhus is clearly the supplicant, opening the scene with the gallant turn of phrase: "Were you looking for me, Madame? / Dare I hope for such a charming event?" (258–59). To which she bluntly replies:

> I was going to where you keep my son under guard,
> Since you let me visit, only once a day,
> The only thing of value I have left from Hector and Troy.
>
> (260–62)

Astyanax, Hector, and Troy (whose patriarch Priam, Andromaque's father, was slain by Pyrrhus)—in three lines Andromaque names the three obstacles to any voluntary union between master and slave. She goes on to mock his heroism—"Has any little Trojan escaped your wrath?" (268)—and reminds him of his illustrious forebear. To give asylum to her child, she notes, "would be a task worthy of Achilles's son" (310). He insists that the means to that end is for her to end her resistance and join him. She would then not look upon him with the same disdain, forever thinking of Hector. When she again throws Troy and Hector in his face ("What a husband!" [359]), he loses patience and resorts to threats against her son. At this point, one expects a Pyrrhic victory—he will force her to yield, even if he still has not earned her heart.

But she knows him well and plays the trump card of suicide. His emotional blackmail is, she suspects, based on bluff, for he has everywhere demonstrated that he lives only for her. She guesses correctly that his quest would go unaccomplished should she die. He lets her go to Astyanax, suggesting that their next meeting will decide the salvation of all three of them. That next confrontation (act 3, scene 6) starts with the characters adopting a contrary pose to the one they had assumed at the beginning of act 1, scene 4. Speaking in principle to their confidants, but aware that the other is listening, Pyrrhus and Andromaque move about the stage like adversaries in a duel, until Pyrrhus strikes the first blow: "Let us go and deliver Hector's son to the Greeks" (901). Now it is Andromaque's turn to act the supplicant, even to flatter the king: "You know full well that Andromaque would have never embraced a master's knee—except yours" (915–16).

Seeking to increase his advantage, Pyrrhus rejects Andromaque's pleas and again says, "Let us go, Phoenix" (924). In the sadistic game she is forced to play, Andromaque recalls her only successful move of act 1, scene 4 and fills the second half of the same line with "Let us go, Céphise, and rejoin my husband" (924). Same tactic, same initial result, as the conqueror once more yields to the conquered, but with an ultimate difference. This time, reminding her that he has waited an entire year, he ends on an ultimatum: "perish or reign" (968). He will soon return to lead her to the place where her son already awaits him—the temple, whose conflicting symbolism is not lost on her. There will either be a royal marriage or the sacrifice of an innocent. The choice is hers.

The concept of a having the play turn around a decision is central to Racinian tragedy. When discussing Greek tragedy earlier, we recalled the peripeteia, the moment when the chorus changed direction during its chanting on stage. The French equivalent, *la péripétie,* transforms outside to inside in Racine; it will not be a visible, physical act, but rather an interior movement in an opposite direction that will change matters, dramatically. Racine highlights the pivotal nature of Andromaque's decision, which will, of course, determine Pyrrhus's, through a remarkable structural configuration. While Racine's plot development is never identical from one play to the next—he remains one of the great experimenters in the history of tragedy—there are similarities one can expect. For example, it is often the case in French classical theater, tragic or comic, that a problem or conflict established in the first act will be addressed in the course of acts 1 and 2, only to have the attempt at resolution fail at the end of act 2. Act 3 will, therefore, open on a return to the initial situation, featuring the original problem, now exacerbated. This is true for *Andromaque,* in which Oreste practices reverse psychology to have Pyrrhus keep Andromaque and her son and give up Hermione. But his efforts are unsuccessful, and act 3 starts, as act 1 did, with Oreste bemoaning his fate to Pylade.

Nor is it unusual to have the last act responding to the first. Oreste's entrance symbolizing the end of six months of physical dislocation (act 1) finds an ironic echo at the close, when he will begin a period of mental instability. Nonetheless, the larger structural pattern of *Andromaque* reveals Racine's skill at allowing form to reinforce the lessons of content, as one can judge from the following pattern:

Act 2, scene 5—Pyrrhus and Phoenix agree that too much hatred separates Pyrrhus and Andromaque. Marriage is, therefore, impossible.

Act 3, scene 1—Pylade warns Oreste of the consequences of his plans: Oreste wants to kidnap Hermione, even kill Pyrrhus, in acts of revenge.

Act 3, scene 2—Hermione claims to be listening to the call of duty by marrying Pyrrhus. Oreste apparently has lost.

Act 3, scene 3—Hermione, triumphant, shows her cruel side to Oreste and to Andromaque, who is arriving.

Act 3, scenes 4–5—Andromaque tries to detain Hermione: "Where are you fleeing, Madame?" (858).

Act 3, scenes 6–7—Andromaque pleads with Pyrrhus and is told that the decision is hers whether to marry or to see her son sacrificed to the Greeks.

Act 3, scene 8—Andromaque is torn by images of the past, of Troy, and of Hector.

Act 4, scene 1—Between the end of act 3 and the opening of act 4 Andromaque has consulted Hector at his tomb, and has made the decision, involving an "innocent trick" (1097), to accept Pyrrhus's proposal. She wishes to avoid an approaching Hermione: "Let us leave and flee her violence" (1129).

Act 4, scene 2—Hermione, reduced almost to silence, plots the death of Pyrrhus.

Act 4, scene 3—Hermione in defeat, Oreste in triumph. Hermione orders him to slay Pyrrhus.

Act 4, scene 4—Cléone warns Hermione of the consequences of her desire, but Hermione insists on vengeance.

Act 4, scene 5—Pyrrhus announces to Phoenix and Hermione that love has won out and he will marry Andromaque.

We are immediately struck by the sentimental echoes in the pattern. A more analytical look reveals Racine letting structure speak. If a central decision will change the direction of the plot, this peripeteia is prepared in act 3, scenes 6–8, and then occurs in the intermission between acts 3 and 4. We can expect, therefore, that attitudes and positions adopted before these three scenes will be reversed afterward, and that is so— with a twist. To an easy symmetry, Racine prefers chiasmus, the rhetorical device that places two antithetical groups in the inverse order of a symmetrical one. Instead of act 4, scene 1 responding to act 2, scene 5, which would be the symmetrical scheme, it rather echoes act 3, scenes 4–5; act 4, scene 2 replies to act 3, scene 3, and so on, until act 4, scene 5 proves to be the exact reversal of act 2, scene 5.[6]

This structural conception shows that Andromaque deserves to be the title character because her decision, determining Pyrrhus's, changes everything. Moreover, the three other characters act in contradictory fashion before and after the *péripétie*; if they first conduct themselves in accordance with some hope of personal satisfaction, they are later forced to see the reality of their situation. Moreover, this wrenching is caused by a "slave." Who, Racine suggests, is more enslaved, the physical captive or the obsessed conquerors? Which fetters are more constraining, external or internal?

If she is freer than the others from an emotional point of view, Andromaque is still bound by her situation, which explains the reason for the "innocent trick" (in French, "l'innocent stratagème") that she outlines to Céphise in act 4, scene 1. She will marry Pyrrhus, thus committing him to protect her son, and then she will commit suicide to remain faithful to Hector. This will work, she argues, because she knows Pyrrhus to be "violent but a keeper of his word" (1085). We can only agree that she knows Pyrrhus well, as her successful defense against Pyrrhus's advances, like any blackmail strategy, is calculated on an unerring perception of what the adversary prizes most. Moreover, she is right to call him violent. But is he a "keeper of his word"? Who keeps his or her word in this play? If respecting one's verbal engagements was a point of honor for the Greeks, it is conveniently forgotten by Racine's French-speaking inhabitants of Greece.

Nor is Andromaque above reproach. Long considered by critics of French literature as a kind of mundane saint, she can now be seen to join the other characters of the play in abusing the truth-telling function of language. She practices "mental restriction" to Pyrrhus, all the while aware that he will react "violently" and probably dispose of the cumbersome political baggage that is Astyanax; that is, she will sacrifice her son to her fundamental desire to earn a glorious image in history as the faithful spouse of Hector of Troy. Recalling earlier, strong heroines of French tragedy, like Corneille's Médée, the Trojan queen summons up the courage to make a wrenching decision. Whatever its moral failings, it is an act imposed from the outside. That is the distinguishing element: if Andromaque misrepresents—to herself and Céphise—the logical outcome of her plan, the sin will be venial because it is the best she can do in the circumstances. The others, who renounce their allegiances and alliances for the sake of passion, are under no such (external) constraint. Who, indeed, are the captives here?

Racine has the eponymous captive share other traits with her captors that serve only to reinforce the ironic reversal of the master/slave relationship. Prominent among them is the theme of displacement. Oreste arrives in Epirus after six months of wandering, betrays his sworn mission, and is condemned to stray physically, mentally, and morally after the play's close. Hermione has been living in a foreign land in anticipation of a marriage that will never happen, and still chooses at the end to "renounce Greece, Sparta, and its empire, / My whole family" (1562–63) to be able to remain in Pyrrhus's land. Pyrrhus may be King of Epirus, but he offers to turn his country into a new Troy, break his alliances with the other Greek states, marry the wife of Hector, and raise Hector's son as his own. Andromaque, who has been brought to the scene of the drama against her will, pleads with Pyrrhus to allow her and Astyanax to pass into "exile."

All the characters in this play—and in Racine's corpus as a whole—are in one sense or another "exiles," for they have either left home or, more important, they have abandoned what gives meaning and stability to their existence—country, family, commitments, honor, self-worth. They become representations of a vision dear to both secular and Christian thinkers of the seventeenth century, *homo viator*, the human being as traveler. In their very estrangement from what used to constitute the core of their lives, Oreste, Hermione, and Pyrrhus embody the concept of alienation in its very etymology (Latin: *alienus*) because they become "strangers" to themselves. Racine permits Andromaque, who occupies a morally superior position to the temporal powers that hold her prisoner, to triumph and seek revenge against the Greeks, thereby turning the result of the Trojan War on its head.[7]

She is not totally alone in her mission, for she has her son, whom she is allowed to visit, and Hector, with whom she "consults" and who inspires her "innocent trick." Her strategy is to play Pyrrhus against his Greek allies, who forever pressure him and who, finally, are responsible for his death. The Greeks, led by Achilles, Agamemnon, and Meneleaus, fought the Trojan War to repay the affront they suffered when Pâris kidnapped Helen. This quick summary serves to show how indispensable are the many "invisible characters" (Astyanax, Hector, the various Greeks, and so on) of whom one often speaks in the play, who weigh heavily upon the action, who have an enormous psychological impact, and who are never seen on stage. Racine deploys these "absent presences" with extraordinary effectiveness to extend the horizon of his drama and enrich its internal resonances, all the while keeping the number of visible characters at a strict minimum. Racine's theater is, therefore, vast in its implications for the world beyond the stage and, at the same time, suffocatingly intimate for the *dramatis personae,* who are seen in the light, not of day, but of the "false day," cast by the candles that lit theatrical performances in the seventeenth century.

However intimate may be the world of Racine's characters, it is not a Sartrean *No Exit,* for a number of characters escape the spatial bonds of their play, prominently among them Oreste. If Racine has Hermione end her days in the tragic space of Epirus, he has other plans for Oreste. The literate seventeenth-century spectator would have wondered whether Racine's Oreste has yet committed the act for which he is celebrated in myth, the slaying of his mother Clytemnestra. The preponderant evidence of the play suggests that the young prince is probably at the beginning of his legendary career.[8] He does speak of his "innocence" in act 3, scene 1, and later Cléone reports that the very name of *assassin* terrifies and immobilizes him (1470). Moreover, it is hard to believe that the Greeks would have named a recent matricide as their ambassador. If it seems that the Furies are already persecuting Oreste at the end of *Andromaque,* a careful reading reveals that there is only one torturer, as ever, Hermione:

> Well, daughters of Hell, are your hands ready? . . .
> But no, withdraw, let Hermione take your place:
> She knows better than you how to render me;
> And I bring her my heart to be devoured.
>
> (1637–44)

Since he does not actually kill Pyrrhus, the Furies have no reason to pursue him—yet. The final irony is, of course, that, despite his statement ("I die content and my fate is fulfilled," 1620), his destiny is not "fulfilled" because his legendary folly will not seize him in Epirus. The events of *Andromaque* are but a rehearsal for the murder of Clytemnestra and Aegisthus, which will transpire later, back in Attica. This projection of the audience's imagination into the future, beyond the final events of the drama, constitutes yet another Racinian device for expanding the imaginary space of his theater. He invites us to speculate about what happens to the characters after the play's temporal close in those cases where they bring up the question. This device is strikingly effective in the instances where well-known figures of mythology or history are involved, such as Oreste or, in *Britannicus,* Néron.

But whatever final image is retained by the spectators, the longlasting impact of *Andromaque* comes from the new psychology of love to which they have been introduced and which requires exceptional subtlety in the expression of strong emotion and a frank demystification of politics. *Andromaque* clearly demonstrates that there are two levels of interaction in the lives of royal personages: the public/political and the personal/passionate. Pyrrhus, for example, is caught between the Trojan world and its impact on his private life, and the Greek world and its implications for his public sphere. The surprise for the public of 1667 was that, in the end, all passionate relationships are seen as fundamentally political in their means and expression; power is the recourse for attempting to transmit the depths of one's emotions to the object of one's desire.

Chapter Six

Les Plaideurs

Racine's sole effort at comedy, *Les Plaideurs* (The litigants), probably premiered in November 1668. Racine tells us in his introductory "Au Lecteur" (To the reader) that he wanted to undertake a new version of Aristophanes's *Wasps,* and that it was originally conceived for presentation by the Italian dramatic troupe that had been sharing the theater of the Palais-Royal with Molière since 1661. Their style, in the *commedia dell'arte* fashion, was to improvise in their own language on a basic sketch and occasionally include some scenes in French. When the leading actor of this troupe, Scaramouche (real name Tiberio Fiorelli), left for Italy some time in the second half of 1668, the focus of Racine's project changed and became a satire of the legal profession to be performed at the Hôtel de Bourgogne, which was in dire need of comedies with which to compete with Molière.

Given the antipathy between Racine and Molière since the "double premieres" of *Alexandre le Grand,* and Racine's penchant for challenging rivals at their own specialty, it may well be that he warmed to the idea of upstaging Molière. One of his main characters does bear a last name that is identical to that of the eponym of Molière's *George Dandin.* This bitter comedy, which first appeared in July 1668, is filled with provincial nobles whose names (Sottenville, La Prudoterie) betray their Norman origin—and *Les Plaideurs* is set in Normandy. Given such "coincidences," it seems probable that Racine was implicitly inviting the audience to make a comparison between the two comic efforts. This is an irresistible invitation that we shall take up later.

At first *Les Plaideurs* met with an unfavorable reception. A month later, however, the Hôtel de Bourgogne risked performing it before the king, who was visibly amused, and the fortunes of *Les Plaideurs* improved to such a degree that no other play of Racine was presented more often in his lifetime. It also became the favorite Racine play in the eighteenth and nineteenth centuries. Its final historical distinction may lie in the fact that, as far as we know, it is the only play performed in France in the seventeenth century to have incorporated subject material drawn from Aristophanes.

Racine's personal estimate of the comedy is not easily discerned. In his preliminary remarks (which do not bear the title of preface that he accords all the tragedies, but are called simply "Au Lecteur"), he explains that friends coaxed him into undertaking a project for which he had just a modicum of enthusiasm. Racine's son Louis indicates that these friends also helped his father write the play. A lawyer, M. De Brilhac, taught him the language of the courts, and Boileau came up with the idea of the quarrel between Chicanneau and the Comtesse. Other acquaintances, like Antoine Furetière, the author of *Le Roman Bourgeois* (The bourgeois novel), which unquestionably influenced *Les Plaideurs,* and probably La Fontaine collaborated with Racine over a series of riotous suppers.[1] The result is not, as might be expected, a patchwork: Racine proved throughout his career that he was a master at seamlessly sewing "contributions" from others into his art, whether the contributions were voluntary or not. As the quote, usually attributed to T. S. Eliot, goes: "Immature artists imitate; mature artists steal."

But Racine reveals a certain pride in his "sketch," claiming, in "Au Lecteur," that it succeeded in making people laugh, and he takes pains to defend it against charges of implausibility, invoking the example of Aristophanes. Since comedy is, by its nature, the art of the implausible, one suspects that Racine did not propose this point for serious debate. Rather, the question of *vraisemblance* once again offered him the opportunity for citing an author whose work he had read in the original Greek, and who was linguistically inaccessible to the vast majority of literate persons in France.

From Aristophanes Racine took the plot line tracing a son's effort to keep safely at home a judge (Perrin Dandin—a name taken from a magistrate in François Rabelais's *Tiers Livre*) who has become obsessed with judging to the point of condemning a rooster for not crowing at the right hour. His son (Léandre), wanting nothing more than to lead the romantic life of a man of ease, tricks the father (Chicanneau) of the woman he loves (Isabelle) into signing a marriage contract, which his own father subsequently ratifies. Despite the mania for litigation of Chicanneau and the Comtesse de Pimbesche (whose name means "whining woman"), the claims and countersuits that Dandin is called upon to adjudicate are not theirs. Rather, Léandre brings before him the case of a dog, Citron, who has eaten a capon. (In Aristophanes's trial, one dog opposes another.) When the defendant's children (puppies) are brought into court, the judge cannot restrain his passion for pronouncing judgment and frees the dog in a burst of sympathy for the defendant's "family."

Racine has arranged each of his three acts around surefire comic scenes. In the first act, there is the monologue of Petit Jean, Dandin's bailiff, and the hilarious scene between Chicanneau and the Comtesse, who are initially seen consoling and encouraging each other, but who, inevitably, fall prey to their irrationality and sue each other when the Comtesse misconstrues Chicanneau and believes he wishes to tie her up. In the second act, L'Intimé's confrontation with Chicanneau yields a rich harvest of verbal threats and physical comedy. Perhaps the most amusing scene in the play is act 3, scene 3, in which the trial is held, complete with satires of legal jargon and of the rhetorical flourishes in which lawyers indulge.

The trial is properly "staged," so that there can be no doubt that we are dealing with a form of dramatic illusion. Racine makes this patent when he introduces a character named the "souffleur," the prompter charged with feeding lines to actors—or lawyers—who have memory lapses on stage. Léandre and L'Intimé disguise themselves, as would actors, to be able to gain entrance to Chicanneau's home. The trial has Petit Jean and L'Intimé (badly) portraying lawyers, while Dandin gives full expression to his madness for judging. Louise Horowitz notes, "As a title, *Les Plaideurs* fits both 'outer' and 'inner' plays."[2] The smaller play is allowed to encompass the larger one to such a degree that questions of some import to the characters before the trial, specifically the outcome of the various lawsuits, remain in a state of suspension as the curtain descends.

Within both the "inner" and "outer" plays one perceives patterns that help support what Claire Carlin calls a "generalized movement from chaos to order."[3] There is a principle of control (Dandin's "imprisonment" in his house by his son) and release (Dandin trying to escape from several points in the house: a window, the attic, the cellar, a basement window). Isabelle is also locked away by her parent, but gains release. The Comtesse fears that everyone is trying to "tie her up" (*lier*, in French). Each obsessed parent wants to dominate his space and trap everyone within it, while the young lovers wish to play out their lives in the sunny space of comedy. Another pattern forms between the states of wakefulness and sleep. Petit Jean opens the play hoping to get some sleep in the street because he is exhausted from frustrating Dandin's attempts at escape. Chicanneau and the Comtesse turn up regularly at Dandin's door before dawn. L'Intimé devises his plot to gain entry to Chicanneau's house once he is awake, a situation that finds its parallel in Léandre no longer sleeping, according to L'Intimé, but plotting to defeat the hindering parents (act 2, scene 2). L'Intimé, in his role as a lawyer, finally puts Dandin to sleep.

These patterns focus attention on the physical aspects of *Les Plaideurs* and, as is always the case in the genre that celebrates the body, particularly on the corporeal. If the limitations of the body are only suggested by the many hesitations and reluctancies in *Andromaque* (Oreste intimidated by Hermione, Hermione unwilling to be aggressive with Pyrrhus, Pyrrhus not inclined to exert his power over Andromaque), they are proclaimed everywhere in *Les Plaideurs*. The play begins with Petit Jean dragging a large brief-bag. His graceless entrance sets a comic tone that is considerably enhanced by the many sightings of Dandin as he vertically traverses the several levels of the house. The vertical is his space, while the others are seen dashing horizontally between houses. Racine devised stage movements so frenetic one would think that all of Feydeau's work was inspired by *Les Plaideurs*. Characters never quite gain access to the person who can assure satisfaction before they are off again in the opposite direction. No sooner is Dandin locked back in his home in act 1 than Chicanneau has left his house, crossed to Dandin's, and begun passing back and forth. The Comtesse then enters and crosses to Dandin's house. Both are seeking the judge, but by the scene's end, they have deserted the stage, one calling for a process-server, the other for a sergeant. In the second act the movement starts in the opposite direction, with L'Intimé crossing to Chicanneau's house to deliver Léandre's note to Isabelle, followed by Chicanneau and then Léandre. The spectators' attention is then reverted back to Dandin's house, where he is seen hanging from the rain gutter.

Repeated entrances abound in *Les Plaideurs,* all of them emphasizing ungainly and comic corporeality. Every time Dandin appears, he is attempting once again to break out. The audience's pleasure derives from the suppression, then release of an object, and with repetition pleasure builds in expectation. Dandin's repeated attempts are all the more ridiculous because they demonstrate a reversal in station. One sees a magistrate, not some clownish valet, squeezing through windows and air vents. His pursuit of freedom demonstrates another reversal or irony: the home is not a shelter, but a prison, not a site of order, but of disorder. This is why Petit Jean must seek tranquillity not within, but without, in the street. Yet, despite these reversals, we never fear for the safety of Dandin or the health of Petit Jean; the twists are salient, but without consequence. If either man paid for his imprudent act by breaking his neck or suffering from exposure, we would be in the realm of tragedy, where all causes have effects. *Les Plaideurs* is an exemplary comedy in its many illustrations of the comic principle of fantasy, of nonconsequentiality, right to the denouement that, as we have said, leaves a number of issues unresolved. The fantasy is aided by the setting consisting of two houses on opposite sides of the stage. We are drawn to one, then to the other, and finally to the neutral space between the two where all the parties are united. The audience finds this symmetry, enhanced by the mania of two fathers, to be agreeable. When symmetry is so blatantly artificial, it lessens any sense of consequence, stifles irony, and propels the comic potential.

To read or see *Les Plaideurs* is to experience mixed expectations. Since the author is Racine, we anticipate common themes with his tragedies. But because it is a comedy, we think immediately of Molière's theater. The truth is that *Les Plaideurs* is neither a tragedy disguised in comic clothes, nor an imitation of Molière. It is *sui generis* and the better for it. But the comparisons with Racinian tragedy and Moliéresque comedy are instructive. Concerning tragedy, Maya Slater counts three common themes that tie Racine's tragedies to *Les Plaideurs*: obsession, betrayal, and claustrophobia.[4] Like Oreste blindly pursuing Hermione, the judge and the two litigants in *Les Plaideurs* are passionate in the pursuit of their goals. If the portrayal of their emotional situation makes them appear mechanical, unreasonable, and ridiculous, then they surely belong in the realm of the comic. This is certainly true of Dandin, the Comtesse, and Chicanneau, even if they have their moments of lucidity, as when Dandin agrees to Léandre's proposal that he pocket money owed to valets. He finds Léandre's idea "pertinent" (618). Dandin is allowed at the end to pursue his mania, albeit harmlessly; this is undoubtedly a comment by Racine on the qualifications of judges in a legal system with which the dramatist had his problems.

In terms of betrayal, neither Léandre nor Isabelle expresses any reservations about deceiving a parent. Léandre seeks "some honest forger" (148), just as Racine's tragic characters mislead and lie in the pursuit of the object of their obsession, often attempting to limit the latter's freedom of movement. The prisonlike quality of Racine's tragic atmosphere has its parallel in the virtual imprisonment of Dandin and Isabelle. Chicanneau and the Comtesse are held under a specious pretext by Léandre. Moreover, "in almost every scene of substance, there are references to guarding, bondage and imprisonment."[5]

In addition to themes, formal considerations link Racine's tragic and comic modes. His tragedies begin with an information-rich exposition, followed by the heart of the action, which is turned around by peripeteia and concluded in the catastrophe and denouement. In *Les Plaideurs,* one discovers the comic counterpart: an exposition by Petit Jean, followed by a subplot (Chicanneau and the Comtesse) soon linked to the main line by Léandre's notion of tricking Chicanneau into signing a contract his magistrate father will approve. There may be a catastrophe in the eyes of Chicanneau, but for the others all, of course, ends well.

Racine's tragedies feature a number of famous dramatic narratives, and one might wonder to what use he put them in his only comedy. While they are limited to only eight in *Les Plaideurs,* they reveal an author so sure of his ability to create them for tragedy that he can easily exploit them for comic ends as well. Whereas, for instance, the tragic narrative binds the audience and the characters—who receive important information, are seized by fearful anticipation, or better understand motivation—comic speeches tend to create dissonance between the two. The audience often laughs while the narrator, oblivious to the comic potential of his words, is not amused. According to Nina Ekstein's count, in *Les Plaideurs* all the narratives have to do with one subject: the judicial world.[6] It is in these speeches that one discovers the greatest concentration of legal jargon; highly specialized, exclusive vocabulary has long been a source of comedy. The pretentiousness of lawyers and the legal system in this particular play is further explored by the connection Racine draws between legality and bestiality in the four longest speeches: animals either cause the legal conflicts (e.g., the donkey grazing on Chicanneau's pastures) or are defendants therein (the rooster, and Citron). Thus, Racine effectively satirizes the objects as well as the process of the law.

The process of narrative also finds itself under comic scrutiny in speeches like Chicanneau's lengthy exposition of act 1, scene 7, in which there seems to be "a consistent absence of logical and temporal connections."[7] In perhaps a fit of self-parody, Racine twists the rigorously organized pattern of tragic narratives to obtain comic effect in *Les Plaideurs,* so as to insinuate the message that all forms of order, including the logical progression of argumentative reasoning, yield to the impertinent genie of comedy. As does content. Instead of being an unbroken vehicle of thoughts and feelings, the narratives are often interrupted so that, in effect, the medium is the message: disruption, inconsistency, and discontinuity reign in the comic world of *Les Plaideurs.*

For someone to be a *plaideur,* he or she must know how to plead, that is, to be an eloquent narrator, attentive to the audience or addressee, and sensitive to the situation or context. On occasion tragic narrators break one of these principles—does Phèdre really appreciate Hippolyte's situation in her labyrinth speech of act 2? Comic narrators, like L'Intimé, explode all the rules, inserting themselves where they do not belong, neglecting the desires of the person addressed, and forgetting the whole purpose of a trial.

Racine turned his background in tragedy to his advantage in one more way by casting his play into verse, whereas Molière's two proximate comedies, *George Dandin* and *L'Avare* (The miser) are in prose. The recourse to the alexandrine meter enables him to parody Corneille's *Le Cid* on three different occasions in the text: "His wrinkles engraved all his exploits on his brow" (154), which recalls almost exactly the same verse (35) in *Le Cid;* "Come, my blood, come, my daughter" (368) is very close to "Come, my son, come, my blood" (268) of *Le Cid;* and, Dandin saying to Léandre, "Do what you must, take this brief-bag, take it quickly" (601) would remind the seventeenth-century spectators of "Do what you must, and take my life after such an affront" (221) spoken by Don Diegue. They might even infer from the intertext that Dandin would give his life for his brief-bags. Molière's Harpagon, from *L'Avare,* would also be so tempted in order to save his precious strongbox.

The reference to *L'Avare* is not gratuitous, for it appeared in the fall of 1668, just a few months before *Les Plaideurs,* and offers fruitful points of comparison with Racine's text, as does the aforementioned *George Dandin.* If Léandre and Isabelle show something less than reverence for their parents, the young lovers in *George Dandin,* Clitandre and especially Angélique, mock authority persistently, with Angélique finally winning the concession of continuing her life (of infidelity) as a condition for remaining married to her bumpkin husband, Dandin. The lesson of the play, at least from the point of view of the lovers, is that adultery triumphs.[8] Is it not to *George Dandin* that Racine is referring when he congratulates himself in "Au Lecteur" for not having yielded to the contemporary mode of immorality in comedy?

Or perhaps, when noting the "dirty double-entendre" and the "off-color jokes" that permeate current comic production, he was (also) thinking of *L'Avare.* There is a particular scene (act 5, scene 3) that responds to Racine's criticisms in this vein, as Harpagon and his daughter's suitor, Valère, speak at cross-purposes. The scene is built on two basic codes (avarice and love) that cause confusion because they both flow from desire: for a purloined strongbox or for the miser's daughter, Marianne.

Harpagon:	So tell me: you didn't touch it?[9]
Valère:	I, touch her? Ah, you do her as much wrong as you do me; and it is with the purest of passion that I burn for her.
Harpagon:	He burns for my strongbox!
Valère:	I'd rather die than to have offended in any way: she is too wise and moral to have suffered that . . . All my desire is focused on enjoying the sight of her; and nothing untoward has sullied the passion that her beautiful eyes have inspired in me.
Harpagon:	The beautiful eyes of my strongbox! He speaks of her as a lover would of a mistress.

The nature of the literary models involved may help explain the difference in what each comic author believed to be the limits of decency. If Aristophanes's *Wasps* was Racine's starting point, Plautus's *Aulularia* (The pot) was Molière's, complete with rapes, beatings, and a freer, more licentious atmosphere. Evidently, Racine had a more conservative taste in comedy than Molière, who succeeded in extending the linguistic, aesthetic, and moral boundaries of the genre.

Nonetheless, Racine did include in *Les Plaideurs* several tactics widely used in the comic genre of his period. The fondness for popular idioms, for example, is reflected in the sayings that dot the first scene, such as "He who laughs on Friday, will cry on Sunday," (2) or "They taught us that, when in Rome, do as the Romans do," (6). One finds, in addition, contemporary allusions not only to the legal system but to dress and food, as one should find in that genre of everyday life, comedy. Moreover, despite Racine's insistence that he took the high road compared to Molière, his play could not do without the props that contribute to physical action, as in a farce: letters, brief-bags, chickens' heads and legs, puppies, a stick, and a torch. David Maskell notes, "The list of stage properties is one of the longest of any comedy appearing in the *Mémoire de Mahelot,* and involved extra expense."[10]

Any comparison between the greatest of France's tragic and comic dramatists should ultimately discuss the fashion in which each treats his principal comic characters and their manias. If we limit ourselves to *Les Plaideurs* and *L'Avare,* the difference is telling, for Dandin is easily "contained" at the end and will continue to "hear cases" at home. He and Chicanneau may have been obstacles to the union of their children, but the latter will marry, leaving at least Dandin to pursue his folly privately; that is, the impact of his condition on others will be minimal.

The hurdles for the young lovers in *L'Avare* are formidable because Molière paints a more realistic picture of parental status than Racine. In the French seventeenth century the father was the figure of authority within the family structure, and his decisions were almost always beyond appeal to an exterior agency—except if, as in the case of Chicanneau, he signed a legal document. The father's power is so strong in *L'Avare* that, at the end, while Marianne and Valère will marry, Harpagon will not lose. He will have his strongbox and continue his avaricious ways as master of the house. In other words, society, represented by those who love (and reproduce), has to accommodate the sterile mania of Harpagon. This vision is expanded in Molière's *Le Bourgeois gentilhomme* and *Le Malade imaginaire* (The would-be invalid) to the point where the collectivity has to yield to the monomaniac's desire by establishing the conditions for its satisfaction. The author of *Andromaque* would have none of this.

Yet, *Les Plaideurs* does indeed concern generational conflict. Parental folly threatens the happiness of children: Dandin's obsession is consuming Léandre; Chicanneau will not allow a suitor in the house to distract him from pursuing endless litigation; and the objects of the Comtesse's lawsuits are her own progeny. Does Racine deal, in a tragedy, with the potentially comic situation of an offspring rebelling against parental authority? *Britannicus* awaits.[11]

Chapter Seven

Britannicus

Britannicus premiered on 13 December 1669 and was poorly received. The bad will toward a competitor on the part of rivals (especially Corneille, who sat alone in a box in haughty silence that first night) and the public's disappointed expectations of a more "gallant," that is, love-centered, drama, help explain the failure of what has become perhaps Racine's most popular play in the twentieth century.[1] Its current success has much to do with its themes of politics, sex, and violence. But it is basically a story of three family members: the young Roman emperor Néron, his mother Agrippine, and his half-brother Britannicus.

The play opens on the arrival at dawn of Agrippine, outside the emperor's door. This constitutes but one of her frustrated attempts to see him, for she is concerned about no longer exerting the preponderant influence on him that she always had. The proximate cause of this visit is the abduction by Néron's men of Junie, fiancée of the emperor's half-brother Britannicus. Agrippine finally gets her opportunity to confront Néron in act 4, scene 2, in which she delivers the longest speech in Racinian theater. Meanwhile, she complains to his principal advisor, Burrhus, about her lack of access, and supports her stepson Britannicus's relationship with Junie, even though she understands that Néron is also attracted to the young woman. Britannicus informs his counselor, the treacherous Narcisse, that he wishes to regain his rightful place as direct heir to his father, the late emperor Claudius. Narcisse tells all to Néron, urging him to break away from Agrippine's domination and signal his autonomy by condemning Britannicus, whom his mother has been protecting. In the course of an apparent banquet of fraternal reconciliation that takes place offstage, Néron has Britannicus poisoned, thereby marking his independence from his domineering mother and suppressing a challenger for imperial power. Agrippine accurately predicts that he will soon have her killed, and the play ends on Burrhus's description of Néron in the first stages of that madness for which he will become infamous in history.

If Racine chose a subject for his first two plays, *La Thébaïde* and *Alexandre,* that indicated a desire to follow Pierre Corneille's lead, but at the same time eventually to leave the path the older dramatist had set out for French classical tragedy, *Britannicus* is the point where Racine decided to offer a direct challenge to Corneille's acknowledged mastery of tragedy with a Roman background. As Corneille had frequently done before him, Racine infused a strong political sense into his tragedy, a struggle between mother and son for ultimate power, complicated by the legitimate pretensions to the throne of another son. This recalls the enemy brothers of *La Thébaïde,* but the difference between the first recourse to this structure and the case of *Britannicus* is instructive.

In the Preface to the latter play Racine indicates that "my tragedy is no less the fall of Agrippine than the death of Britannicus."[2] This tragedy has, therefore, the advantage of treating two classic stories at once: the son who slays his mother (as if *Andromaque* were prolonged to include Oreste's murder of Clytemnestre), and the enemy brothers. But, unlike Etéocle and Polynice, Néron and Britannicus are not true brothers. Agrippine was married to Domitius when she gave birth to Néron, while Britannicus (and Octavie) are the fruit of the marriage between the emperor Claudius (Néron's uncle) and Messalina. When Agrippine married Claudius, the young cousins became brothers by family alliance. The marriage of Néron with Octavie then made him and Britannicus brothers-in-law. Finally, Claudius's adoption of Néron made the two brothers under the law. Since Néron was older by three years, Agrippine, after arranging Claudius's death, did not experience great difficulty in having her own son accepted as the only heir to the throne.

As a result, the situation contains all the elements of an inevitable clash because Britannicus was deprived of a supreme power to which he should have acceded by blood, but to which the law no longer permitted him to pretend. As Georges Forestier makes clear, Racine's innovation surely consists not in having a fraternal—and fratricidal—rivalry, but in making two young men rivals before they become brothers.[3] Proof of Racine's intention in this respect may be gleaned from the fact that Néron and Britannicus never consider themselves brothers. It is only when Britannicus is threatened by Néron's jealousy and his own feelings of rebellion that Junie and Burrhus appeal to the "fraternity" between the two.

Racine translates the play's basic sense of rivalry and conflict from the first scene, which is replete with antitheses. Agrippine tells her confidant Albine that Néron, "tired of making others love him, now wants them to fear him" (12); Néron may be "generous" or "ungrateful"

(21–22); if he has "begun" his reign the same way that Augustus "finished" (32) his, one still has to fear that "the future erasing the past, he end the way Augustus began" (33–34); and, Agrippine sees her ceremonial honors "increase" as her influence "decreases" (90). These oppositions refer mostly to the past history of the emperor Augustus who ascended to imperial power through ruthless suppression of his rivals, but became in time an exemplary emperor, as Corneille showed in *Cinna*. Agrippine is concerned that Néron will repeat history in reverse and that, in essence, he will write her out of the narrative of his reign.

The reasons for the numerous and forceful antitheses are, therefore, the adversarial, conflictual atmosphere that Racine wanted to create in general, and the particular instance of the conflict within Néron himself, which will be played out within the 12 hours of the ideal time frame of the tragedy. What Racine wished to represent is, as he puts it in his Preface, the "birth of the monster" (Néron), as well as the fall of Agrippine and the death of Britannicus. But, because the last two developments cannot happen without the first, the focus must be on Néron's moral struggle. In effect, we are witness to *Nero in bivio*—Néron at the crossroads. In the same manner as the ancient world and the Renaissance had already portrayed *Hercules in bivio,* Néron must choose his path.

That the struggle within Néron's soul is the heart of the tragedy is confirmed not only by a reading/seeing of the play itself but by an intriguing point that appears in the Prefaces. Racine undoubtedly suspected that, in offering a drama based on the most consulted historian of Rome, Tacitus, his text would be scrutinized by his critics for its faithfulness to the historical source. The farther he strayed from history, the greater he risked being judged incompetent in the specialty that Corneille had firmly established as his own. We would expect, therefore, that the hypersensitive Racine would not give his detractors much ground for launching an attack on his (ab)use of history.

In the Prefaces he takes pains to defend his portrayals of Néron, Narcisse, Burrhus, Agrippine, Britannicus, and Junie. The weak link in the chain is Junie, and Racine knew it, if we can judge by the length and insistence of his apologia for her. His defense is also tortured and ultimately fraudulent. The case of Junie deserves examination not only for its value within the parameters of the moral world of *Britannicus* but also for its revelation of Racine's attitude toward the often competing imperatives of history and artistic freedom. Racine writes:

It remains for me to speak of Junie. One should not confuse her with an old coquette called Junia Silvana. This one is another Junie whom Tacitus calls Junia Calvina, of Augustus's family, brother of Silanus to whom Claudius had promised Octavia as wife. This Junie was young, beautiful, and, as Seneca says, "the most playful of all girls."

This explanation poses two immediate problems. First, the Junia Calvina who was a relative of Augustus was never implicated in Néron's love life. Second, if we consult the source for the final quote, Seneca's *Apocolokyntosis* (VIII, 2), we find that "Silanus had a sister, the most playful of all girls, whom everyone called Venus." Nowhere, however, does Seneca say that this was Junia Calvina. While the quote is accurate, its application is intentionally misleading. In a drama where Junie will be central to the love plot, Racine has recourse to a historical figure whose contribution could only be to the strong political dimensions.[4] Why this confusion? Why did Racine run the aforementioned risk?

Let us enlarge the creative choices to discover Racine's motive. If there was no one like Junie in the history of Néron's reign, why did he not turn to other women who played key roles in Néron's sentimental life? Racine's knowledge of the historians was such that he must have recognized other possibilities, such as Actea, Poppea, Octavia, and Aria. Rather than being indifferent to Nero's advances—a fundamental aspect of Racine's Junie—Actea was passionately in love with the emperor and even took charge of the details of his funeral. She was, however, a former slave. In the eyes of the seventeenth-century audience, if she were not born noble, she could not be expected to feel or act "nobly." Her affection for Nero and her lack of status, especially compared to Junie, who is described as being descended from Augustus himself, were reasons for eliminating her from possible inclusion as the object of Nero's lust.

The fates of Poppea and Octavia are linked in one important respect: the former replaced the latter in Nero's bed. Beyond that it is difficult to conceive of two women as diametrically opposed. Tacitus tells us that the first day of Octavia's marriage was like a living death, while Poppea, her servant, became Nero's wife only 12 days after his divorce from Octavia. She bore the emperor a child and died at his hands.[5] Clearly, this passionate historical figure could not serve as the basis for the reserved Junie. But Octavia could, if, as is likely, Racine knew the apocryphal Senecan play *Octavia* in which she is portrayed sympathetically. But history recalls her as the rejected wife, not the temptress of the young ruler.

Historical specificity was also the disincentive for Racine concerning Aria. She is known as the woman who, learning that Nero had condemned her husband to death, wished to commit suicide rather than yield to Nero, but who was eventually dissuaded. This story was frequently conflated with that of Aria's mother, who did, in fact, stab herself as an example of heroic revolt against Emperor Claudius. Even though Aria, in Tacitus's *Annals* and in the tragedy of a precursor of Racine (*Arrie et Pétus ou les amours de Néron* [Aria and Paetus, or the loves of Nero], by Gabriel Gilbert, 1660),[6] resembles Junie by her youth, beauty, and faithfulness to the man she loves, her image in the (confused) public consciousness is that of someone who slew herself. In a concession to public sensibility, Racine chose to protect the virtuous Junie at the end of *Britannicus*. He had, therefore, to eliminate Aria as a possible heroine. But she also shares with the three others an insuperable disadvantage, since none of them any longer possess the one quality that Racine believed so indispensable to his female character that he braved the inevitable barbs of his enemies for it—virginity.

Now that we have determined the answer to the question "Why Junie?" let us ask the next logical one—the one that is the catalyst for the action of the play: why did Néron have Junie kidnapped? The two questions are intimately related and find their explanation in act 2, scene 2, just moments after Néron has made his first appearance on stage. As Agrippine has surmised, Néron's act is at once an adolescent's symbolic signal of freedom from the mother and a desire to replace one female presence with another. In this drama of choice, Junie plays a significant role in all the oppositions that Racine traces from the first verses. She is the love interest of both Britannicus and Néron; she is the "other woman"—the competitor for Néron's affections—in Agrippine's eyes; she represents a potentially positive force in Néron's sentimental education, and joins Burrhus in symbolically opposing Narcisse and his evil counsels. In addition to her value as a moral icon, she also, therefore, enjoys a privileged situation in the drama's structure.

But it is first of all her purity that attracts Néron, a fact made evident in the dreamlike verses 385–406. Since an analysis of these lines will reveal the struggle in Néron's soul, they are quoted at length:

> Aroused by a curiosity and desire,
> I saw her arrive here last night,
> Sad, raising to heaven her eyes wet with tears,

That flashed amidst the torches and the spears.
Beautiful, unadorned, in the simple attire
Of a beauty one had just snatched from her bed.
What do you expect? I cannot say whether her disarray,
The shadows, the torches, the shouts and the silence,
And the savage demeanor of her cruel kidnappers
Enhanced the shy sweetness of her eyes.
Whatever it was, taken with such a beautiful sight,
I wanted to speak to her, but my voice would not come.
Paralyzed, filled with amazement
I let her pass by me into her apartment.
I retired to mine. There, all alone,
I tried in vain to turn my thoughts from her image.
Still I thought I saw her, spoke to her.
I loved even the tears that I had made her shed.
A few times, but too late, I begged her forgiveness.
I tried sighs, then threats.
That is how, focused on my new love,
My eyes, without once closing, awaited the dawn.

                                         (385–406)

The operative word is spoken in the first verse: *desire*. Néron will recreate the scene of his first meeting with Junie through the eyes of
desire, which explains his attention particularly to her eyes and, more
broadly, to her physical state. One even wonders whether his memory
has not been deformed by desire to the point where, imagination replacing perception, he has mentally undressed her more than she actually
was a few hours before. In any event, he is (un)clothing her for the scene
that follows, which is heavy with suggestions of sexual violence.

    After listing the composite elements of that scene—the decor, the
sounds, the lighting, the actors (391–94)—he internalizes it, projects it
on his interior screen, and becomes a participant, albeit an ineffectual
one. He retires to his apartment, where he cannot get her out of his
mind. He tries to speak, but is reduced to sighs by this image of virtuous
innocence. He also loves her tears and tries threats. She remains present
in his imagination throughout the night, provoking speechless admiration as well as sadistic impulses. In other words, the sight of Junie—in

this play where the action can usually be reduced to seeing, watching, spying on, and so on[7]—excites both sides of Néron's personality. (For that reason, the scene is full of contrasts: the dark of night and the light of flames, sound and silence, sweetness and brutality.) Neither side wins the contest at this point, and Néron indicates that it is "this virtue, so new to the court, whose perseverance excites my love" (417–18). We might have expected Néron, who spent years of corruption at court (as detailed by Tacitus), to seek to suppress virtue out of some antisocial instinct. Rather, he is awed by the novelty of Junie's purity, and again manifests this "mute impotence"[8] at the end when he silently watches her enter the temple of the vestal virgins.

On the threshold of maturity—he is still a teenager—Néron is faced with an existential choice. Although he pursued a secret life of vice during the first years of his reign, he could not have gone unmarked, in a positive way, by these "three years of virtue" (463).[9] Junie causes him to experience contradictory impulses: for a moment, her image allows him to glimpse the possibility of a world of innocence. This dream exerts such an impact on him that, in a rare development, he becomes powerless, preferring abstraction to reality. As he had predicted, he comes to "idolize Junie" (384).

If *Britannicus* represents Néron's rite of passage as he leaves a state of moral indifference to become the monster of history through the defining act of fratricide, the phantasmatic scene of act 2, scene 2 constitutes the central feature of the ceremony. While Agrippine passes her criminal tendencies on to Néron through what we might call "genetic transmission," Néron perceives in Junie his last chance to effect that escape from the past that is the instinct he shares with all Racinian characters. Néron is fundamentally attracted to Junie because she possesses what he feels he has lost.

To turn toward Junie is also to turn away from Agrippine. Act 2, scene 2 is the pivotal moment of this other development, for, clearly, by having dreams about another woman, Néron is marking his independence from Agrippine. Néron is not looking for another mother in Junie; on the contrary, his desire for purity joins his need for freedom, which, at the end, will dominate and cause him to revolt against all authority figures, including Junie. But his first objects of hatred are his mother and his half-brother. His attitude toward Britannicus shows that his dreams do not always flood him with positive feelings. To cite only one of several instances, he specifically states about his half-brother that "I imagine his pain with great delight" (751).

The second scene of act 2 may be the most laden with meaning of the dream scenes in *Britannicus,* but it is far from unique. Jacques Scherer has detected five "oneiric" scenes elsewhere in the play,[10] to which one should add a sixth (number 2):

1. Verses 99–110, which begin with "That day, that sad day . . . ," describe Agrippine's memory of how she was turned away from the throne by Néron;
2. Verses 484–88, "My troubled love already imagines her [Agrippine]," translate Néron's recurring nightmare of Agrippine scorning him for his ingratitude;
3. Verses 839–55, "I will go, do not doubt it, and show him [Britannicus] to the army," contain Agrippine's threat to Burrhus to make trouble for him and Néron;
4. Verses 999–1014, "How many times . . . ," are Junie's vision of how Néron would reproach her for any kindness to Britannicus;
5. Verses 1587–98, "Ah, if you had only seen . . . ," show Agrippine flushed with pride and satisfaction as she portrays her affectionate son;
6. Verses 1676–86, "I foresee that you will lay your hands even on your mother," compose Agrippine's prediction about her own death and her curse on her matricidal son.

The function of these moments is twofold. First, they delineate the essentials of the plot: (1) Agrippine will lose her political power; (2) Néron is intimidated by his mother; (3) Agrippine will use Britannicus against Néron, if necessary; (4) Junie, caught between the young rivals, fears Néron will act with violence against Britannicus; (5) Néron may temporarily play the role of the prodigal son who has returned to his mother's arms; but (6) he will kill Agrippine, thereby cutting the symbolic umbilical cord. It is all there: the birth of the monster, the death of Britannicus, the fall of Agrippine, and the indispensable figure of Junie.

The second reason for these scenes lies in their insistence on a noticeable feature of this tragedy: its characters have vivid imaginations. They can easily conjure up scenarios in which they are the principal players—in this regard, act 2, scene 2 is paradigmatic of the entire drama. Moreover, they give the impression that they would prefer to be participating in a representation other than necessarily the Racinian tragedy *Britannicus.* If, for the sake of instruction, we cross the theoretical line that separates tragedy from comedy and look for comic elements in *Britannicus,* the results are surprising and rewarding.

Claire Carlin has demonstrated that, if one analyzes the action of *Britannicus* while equipped with the taxonomy furnished by Charles Mauron in *Psycho-critique du genre comique* (A psychocritical approach to the comic genre), one can conclude that Néron represents the authoritarian (father) figure attempting to prevent the union of the young lovers that one finds in traditional comic structures.[11] (We shall encounter another example of this in *Mithridate.*) The scene (act 2, scene 6) in which Néron spies on the two lovers while hiding behind a screen not only elicits a nervous laugh from the spectators but is reminiscent of such scenes in the literature of comedy, most prominently for an Anglo-Saxon public, the famous "Screen Scene" in Richard Brinsley Sheridan's *School for Scandal* (1777).

To see Néron as playing a role is totally congruent with the facts of the history of his reign, during which he often took pleasure in appearing on stage with the "histrions," the performers of his day.[12] The penchant of the characters in *Britannicus* to dream about better days, past or future, invites speculation about their aspiration to play a role in comedies of their own creation. At the outset Agrippine expresses impatience with the slowness of the curtain's rise on a play that she has created and stars in, which might be entitled *The Mother of Caesar* and which had, until recently, enjoyed longstanding success. She rehearses her part several times in the course of the play, notably in the presence of Burrhus and her confidant Albine, because she insists on holding center stage to achieve a performance that is both striking and persuasive. Both Agrippine and the audience learn, nonetheless, that despite all the rehearsals, Néron is not impressed with her extensive plea in act 4, scene 2.

Burrhus might be expected to resist the temptations of the stage because he should set a good example as Néron's tutor. But Racine's choice is instructive: if history names both Burrhus and Seneca as the emperor's guides, Racine preferred to present only Burrhus because the public would expect Seneca to be censorious, whereas Racine needed a complacent and "flexible" figure—a former soldier used to taking orders. Burrhus seems to be hoping, to the last line of the tragedy ("May it please the gods to make this the last of his crimes"), that he will be featured in *The Faithful Counselor,* in which a tutor's wisdom is responsible for the benevolent reign of his young charge. The other (unofficial) counselor, Narcisse, gives us a clue to the role he would like to bring to life:

Fortune calls you a second time,

Narcisse: are you willing to listen?

I will follow to the end her kind orders:

And, to assure my happiness, ruin every wretch in sight.

(756–60)

Happiness for Narcisse would surely consist in the enthusiastic reception of a tragicomedy about *arrivisme* whose title would be *The Perfect Courtier* or perhaps (if seventeenth-century France had only known Shakespeare) *Iago Redivivus.*

Britannicus and Junie, the two lambs lost among the "wolves" (Néron and Agrippine, as Picard aptly describes them),[13] seek to regain the world of shepherds and of the *pastorale* that contributed significantly to the creation of French classical tragedy. The young lovers appear conscious of the fact (she certainly more than he) that fate has relegated them thus far to roles in a tear-inducing romance that could perhaps be transformed into a more pleasing spectacle, if it adopted the same "chain of love" principle that informed *Andromaque.* Thus, Agrippine loves Néron, who loves Junie, who loves and is loved by Britannicus. Not realizing that a broken chain of love is a proper subject of tragedy, the young lovers never cease trusting that the good genie of comedy, someone like Mascarille of Molière's *L'Etourdi* (The blockhead), will take charge and offer them parts in a new play, *The Shepherd's Tale.* However, neither of them has a father whose unexpected arrival will resolve the plot of this comedy as it had for so many others, and they are condemned to the universe of the tragic genre located, in this instance, in Néron's court, that "foreign land both for you and for me" (1526), according to Junie.

Néron does not know in which play he would like to participate. Agrippine, Burrhus, and Narcisse endeavor to control him by inviting him to act in their playlets,[14] while for Britannicus and Junie, he embodies the foil of comic theater who is the obstacle to young love and happiness. But Néron seems to hesitate about the choice of a theatrical genre suited to his talents and suitable to his goals. Sometimes, sensitive to the image that history would retain of his performance on the throne, he appears about to renew his contract as the lead in a comedy that has been running for three years and that is called *The Good Emperor, or the Clemency of Néron.* Burrhus recounts a central scene of the play:

One day, as I recall, the Senate justly
Pressed you to sign the death warrant of a criminal;
You resisted, Lord, in your heart
Their severe condemnation judged too cruel;
And complained of the unhappiness attached to power,
I would like, you said, *never to have learned how to write.*
                                                          (1367–71)

At other times, when Junie particularly occupies him, he considers himself one of those numerous romanesque heroes one finds in seventeenth-
century theater—a Céladon perhaps, to cite the one named by Racine in
his Preface to *Andromaque.*

Yet, rebel with a cause, Néron eventually decides to abandon the
comic genre, the better to participate in a bloody spectacle, once Narcisse alludes to the danger for the person who, having renounced the
profession of dramatist, is forever condemned to substituting others'
lines for his own. He quotes this opinion, as if it were a speech from a
theatrical presentation:

Néron, if they are believed, *was not born to be emperor;*
He says and does only what he is told:
Burrhus leads his heart, Seneca his mind.
His only ambition, his one talent,
Is to excel in chariot races,
To vie for prizes unworthy of his status,
To become a public spectacle in Rome,
To waste his life on the stage,
To declaim speeches he wants everyone to adore,
While soldiers, at appointed moments,
Force spectators to applaud.
                                                          (1468–78)

Néron's definitive role will be crowned in the course of the event that
often closes a comedy: a banquet. Baudelaire once asked, "Have you
ever seen tragic characters eat or drink?"[15] Typical of the practice of
tragic authors, Racine has only two banquet scenes in his tragic corpus

and they occur offstage:[16] one in *Britannicus* and the other in *Esther.* Having invited Britannicus to a festive occasion as a sign of confraternity, Néron parodies the symbolism of repast as communion by poisoning his half-brother. Shunning the collective celebration that ends so many comedies, the emperor opts for tragedy and center stage in a play whose title would surely be *The Madness of Néron.*

More than in any other tragedy by Racine, the characters of *Britannicus* mistake their dramatic genre: each considers him/herself to be the star in a comedy—which I will define here simply as a play with a happy ending—whereas in reality they are all forced to become part of a tragic lesson on the absurdity of belief in happy endings. Agrippine, who would probably complain that we have made too much of Néron's star status, is the only one conscious of the theatricality of this play—or rather, these plays—that she initiated. Realizing that, in tragedy, illusion yields to illumination, Caesar's mother recognizes that the 12 hours she spends on stage will not have a comic ending. Rather, her efforts to give the performance of her life will become integrated into a tragic spectacle entitled *The Death of Agrippine.* In sum, the theatricality of *Britannicus* serves to condemn theatrical representation.

Néron is condemned at the end as well. Although we have seen him viscerally committed to the task of liberating himself from his mother's domination, his choice (of paths and of plays) does nothing to free him from Agrippine but, ironically, only confirms him as inheriting her murderous lineage. Both heredity and history have assured his transformation from Néron the impulsive adolescent to NÉRON, the tyrannical madman of legend. His first act—which will hardly be the "last of his crimes"—makes him responsible for the death of his half-brother; that is, he breaks a fundamental law of nature. Racine insists on the unnatural character of this deed by depriving Néron of the unique human faculty of reason. Thus, the "monster"—defined in the seventeenth century as a non-natural being—is born.

Chapter Eight
Bérénice

To name *Bérénice* is to evoke a series of anecdotes: its premiere at the Hôtel de Bourgogne on 21 November 1670, followed exactly a week later by Corneille's latest production, *Tite et Bérénice;* the competition between the two *Bérénices* supposedly explained by the proposal by Henrietta of England, Louis XIV's sister-in-law, that both authors undertake a play on a subject of her choosing; the Preface to Racine's tragedy being his definitive poetic manifesto, punctuated by the famous line, "the majestic sadness that gives tragedy all its pleasure"; *Bérénice* possessing such exquisite poetry that it is really an elegiac poem rather than a dramatic spectacle; the play representing, as Racine would have us believe in his Preface, the essence of tragic drama: an action that was "extremely simple." All the foregoing examples offer the advantage of familiarity because everyone who knows Racine and his theater will have heard one of these canards at one time or another. Only the last consideration—the structure—is, however, worthy of counting among our occupations in this chapter, for once the drama has been carefully analyzed, we will see that structure is truly a subject worthy of interest.

Racine resumes the plot at the beginning of his Preface: "Titus, who passionately loved Bérénice, and who, so it was said, had even promised to marry her, sent her away from Rome, despite both of their wishes, soon after becoming emperor."[1] If one adds that Antiochus, the King of Comagène, completes the triangle of major characters, and that it is Bérénice, the Queen of Palestine, who finally breaks the impasse by agreeing to leave, the broad outlines are sketched. What is immediately striking is the similarity of this play to *Andromaque* in its linking of characters. In the earlier tragedy, Oreste loved Hermione, who loved Pyrrhus, who loved Andromaque, who was still in love with her dead husband, Hector; in *Bérénice* we have Antiochus, who loves Bérénice, who loves Titus, who is forced to "marry" Rome. Antiochus is another Oreste, Bérénice rivals Andromaque in strength, and one could even suggest that *Bérénice* is a nonviolent *Andromaque* in which all the characters are virtuous. Both tragedies also emphasize a feature found everywhere in Racine: the importance of visual contact, in French, *le regard.* In *Andromaque,* the title figure, despite herself, is fascinated by the erotic vision of the warrior Pyrrhus amidst the flames of destruction and the cries of the dying in Troy (999–1004). In *Bérénice,* Antiochus reminds Bérénice of the moment that inspired the love between her and Titus: "Titus . . . came, saw you, and pleased you" (194). The sight of the other paralyzes, hypnotizes, and is the source of much oneiric activity in Racine's corpus, as we saw in the phantasm of Néron in *Britannicus.*[2]

Instead of stressing the commonality of *Bérénice* with the other plays, one could adopt another point of view from which *Bérénice* could pass for a self-parody of the typical structure of a Racinian tragedy that awaits a decision before it can find its climax and its denouement. In this case, before the curtain rises the catalyzing event has taken place (the death of emperor Vespasian), as has the decision by his son Titus to be true to his imperial duty and not take a foreign queen as his wife. (For Titus, tragic illumination takes place *before* the play begins.) What remains—the action of the play proper—is for Titus to bring himself to announce his decision to Bérénice. The characters seem aimless; in John Campbell's words, "one of them appears to have nothing to do, the second waits for the third and the third does nothing."[3]

Of course, one should not be content with appearances. Despite Samuel Beckett's admiration for Racine (of whose works he was a lifelong reader), Racine's play is not a seventeenth-century version of *Waiting for Godot.* But it does have a simplicity, almost a minimalism, that surely attracted Beckett. Here is a plausible explanation for the configuration of *Bérénice,* the drama of incommunicability:

Titus (finally) speaks: act 4

Consequences and denouement: act 5

First attempt by Titus to transmit the message: act 2

A messenger (Antiochus) is sought to deliver the message and he is intimately tied to the plot because he loves Bérénice: act 1

The messenger performs his duty: act 3

If one begins with the moment around which the entire play revolves, Titus's wrenching statement to the queen about the necessity of their separation (act 4, scene 5), both what precedes and what follows fall into place. Bérénice will not be able to accept the young emperor's decision until the last instant; Titus tries at one point to speak, but cannot;

through a normal human impulse, he seeks an intermediary—a spokes-man—and Racine ties Antiochus intimately to the plot by making him a friend of Titus and a secret admirer of Bérénice; the message is so shocking that the queen is tempted to "kill the messenger," at least ver-bally, and Antiochus's role in the love plot has a direct influence on the denouement. There is not a superfluous moment, not a wasted gesture in this play.

Each of Racine's plays bears witness to his desire to experiment. *Bérénice* is innovative in several ways and reveals the care that Racine lavished on the composition of his works. In this, the shortest of his tragedies (it is usually performed without an intermission), he reaches heights of emotional impact that he rarely attains elsewhere. As if he understood the physical principle that the more compact a space, the greater its explosive potential, Racine situated the action of *Bérénice* "in a closet [i.e., private space] which is between the apartments of Titus and Bérénice." The "closet" (*cabinet* in French) is unique in Racine's theater in its intimacy—all the other settings are relatively public spaces, or, even if they are forbidden to the public, they are at least meant for occu-pation by more than just two people (e.g., the seraglio of *Bajazet*). The closet's symbolism becomes clear as the play progresses, for, if it has been a refuge from the imperial court and a passage belonging to nei-ther Titus nor Bérénice—but rather belonging to both as their special place of assignation—it becomes an intermediary zone, a kind of purga-tory where they are destined to wait and suffer. It is also the locus of the clash of cultures between Orient and Occident, as Harriet Stone explains: "This space which fills the stage but which partitions off West from East is the mediating space through which all the meanings of the play eventually pass, and where they inevitably remain associated in the mind of the spectator who contemplates Bérénice as she leaves Rome for Palestine."[4]

Racine takes pains to specify certain details of the setting in the open-ing speech by Antiochus, including the existence of two doors, each leading to the apartment of one of the lovers. These doors are, in effect, apertures to different and intimidating worlds. Vacillating at the sight of Bérénice's door, Antiochus says, "Let us withdraw, let us leave" (33), but soon after "May we enter?" (51). In act 4, scene 4, Titus is paralyzed in front of Bérénice's door, through which she then bursts; the act ends on Titus being relegated once again to the indefinite space between the two doors. Bérénice also takes the opportunity to ironize on the pomp of the closet as it contrasts with the austerity of the message Titus has pronounced (1320–27). David Maskell draws attention to this tactic: "It is a brilliant invention on Racine's part to emphasize the discrepancy between the emperor's speeches and the decor chosen by him for this private room."[5]

The intermediary nature of space in *Bérénice* has a parallel in the relationships among the characters. Of the seven listed in the *dramatis personae,* five are go-betweens. Given that the tragedy concerns a secret decision that has to be publicly spoken, the majority of characters act as messengers and/or as confidants, with Antiochus primary among them—and Antiochus, the confidant, has his own confidant, Arsace. To avoid the impression of staging a child's game in which everyone hides to escape being caught, Racine conceived of the closet, which, being extremely private, does not offer easy access. The obstacle to finding the recipient of the message only underscores the play's theme of the difficulty of communication.

But even when the two main interlocutors are in each other's presence, the desired connection is not made because of their differing assumptions. Act 2, scene 4 offers a number of examples of the opacity of language owing to the changed nature of the relationship after the death of Vespasian. When Titus exclaims, "May it please the gods that my father were still alive! / How happy I would be!" (600–01), Bérénice interprets this cry as the pained expression of a son at the loss of his father. Not having guessed the moral evolution of Titus, she is totally unaware of the radical transformation that has taken place. Since language always has a context that can change with the circumstances, the characters in *Bérénice* face the unbearable necessity of having to react to fluid situations. The play may be known for its simplicity, but the motivations of the characters are quite complex.

Well before the beginning of Racine's theatrical career, Abbé d'Aubignac proposed, in his influential *Pratique du théâtre,* that "to speak is to act." He was, in essence, defining French classical theater, both comic and tragic, with this statement. From this linguistic point of view, *Bérénice* may be the representative tragedy,[6] for its characters feel that to speak is to exist and that their being is reduced to nothingness because they cannot communicate. That is why everyone is unhappy in this play, whereas it is often the case in Racine that one person's misfortune turns to the advantage of another (e.g., if Oreste is depressed, Hermione must be ecstatic).

As we know from other plays of Racine, to tell is not necessarily to tell the truth. The characters seek to speak in such a way as to have a profound impact on the others, to change the way they think and act. Specialists of "speech-act theory" among linguists call this kind of speaking "performative," and Richard Goodkin noted that "The entire drama of *Bérénice* revolves around a series of unsuccessful oral performatives."[7] They fail because their author cannot say them and has them conveyed instead by a third party, which undermines any effectiveness the words might have had. Their impact is also seriously hindered by the instinctive, but very understandable, self-deception of all three main characters. The past is the scene of Titus's blindness, for, before the play begins, he had entertained the possibility of resolving the two irreconcilable propositions: to become emperor of Rome and to marry a foreign queen. The play's temporal span is, then, the opportunity for the "performance," that is, the (unsuccessful) endeavor to be performative.

Bérénice is probably the best example in Racine's theater of a character's ability to construct a defense of self-serving fictions; she does so in the course of the play in reaction to the increasingly clear evidence that Titus has an unpleasant message to transmit. She passes from one false conclusion to the next: if Titus seems cold at her approach, he must be jealous of Antiochus, and if he is jealous, he must be in love:

> Be assured, my heart, I can still please him;
> I counted myself too soon among the unhappy.
> If Titus is jealous, Titus loves still.
>
> (664–66)

Antiochus, as is his lot, joins the others, but in a less spectacular way: he flatters himself that he can forget the queen, but then quickly inquires about her (act 3, scene 5). If Titus had not practiced an initial self-deception and if Bérénice did not steadfastly refuse to acknowledge plain evidence, there would be no tragedy.[8]

But tragedy there is, and it proceeds from a great irony: the separation of Titus and Bérénice is necessary because Titus possesses a personal sense of honor—the French would say *gloire*—that he owes to none other than Bérénice. How does one understand the "glory" of Titus, that motivating factor behind his distressing decision? How does Racine integrate the Cornelian quality of heroism into his play and still devise a tragic denouement? And how is Bérénice implicated?

History offers a good starting point from which to pursue answers to these questions. It is noteworthy that Néron is mentioned four times in the text of *Bérénice*. Moreover, according to Suetonius, Britannicus and

Titus were brought up together and, once the latter became emperor, he had two statues erected to the memory of Britannicus. Titus is another of Racine's characters *in bivio,* having to choose, in this instance, between the paths laid out by the virtuous brother and the villainous one. But in the first part of his life, Titus chose poorly: it was predicted that his debauchery would make of him another Néron. Racine, however, makes him undergo a moral conversion that Titus explains at length in the play:

> I fell in love with Bérénice. What won't a heart do
> To please the one it loves, and to win over its conqueror!
>   . . . But blood and tears
> Did not seem sufficient to me to deserve her love:
> I sought to make the entire world happy . . .
> I owe her everything, Paulin, and, cruel reward!
> All I owe her will return to haunt her.
> As the recompense for such glory and virtue,
> I will tell her: leave and never see me again.
>   (509–22)

Instead of becoming Néron, Titus became Britannicus—and it was at that time that he sent Bérénice away. Clearly, not to do this would confirm Titus as being as self-centered an emperor as Néron. Nonetheless, to dispatch Bérénice, Titus had to be as cruel as Néron. This is Titus's dilemma: Néron, whom Titus identifies with his past, is paradoxically both an object of horror and a requisite object of imitation for him. Néron was a sort of father to Titus; Titus may curse him, but he is still, to some degree, his son. In choosing to sacrifice his personal happiness, Titus exorcises the hallucinating image of Néron and elects to become a second Britannicus—a Britannicus who, this time, succeeds in overcoming the obstacles in the path of his destiny.[9]

Occasionally, destiny is manifested by a marker as apparently insignificant as rhyme. One could say that the whole problem of the play is encapsulated in Arsace's statement of 59–60, which ends with a rhyme that in itself expresses at once the wish and the frustration of the title character: "Perhaps before nightfall, happy Bérénice / Will exchange the name of queen for empress." In French *Bérénice* rhymes with *impératrice* (empress), and this rhyme appears once again in the first act at verses 175–76—but never afterward, as if that transformation will

henceforth be out of the question. Antiochus is also defined by a word—
témoin (witness)—that, unlike the *empress* of Bérénice, follows him everywhere. Whereas he wants to be a principal figure, he is relegated to
being a confidant-messenger-witness, the third element in a situation
designed for two. At the end, Bérénice tells Antiochus to imitate the
conduct of the other two; he is reduced to being, in effect, a reflection of
the others—a living mirror.

But, at least he will live, and the nonbloody solution to the drama is
both unexpected and original. From the play's early expressions of the
yoke that the Roman sense of glory imposes on its emperors to the
penultimate moments of the tragedy, we have been conditioned to
believe that personal happiness will be sacrificed to national necessity.
Consequently, if Titus is to follow the traditional Roman model of what
one does if one cannot suffer the Roman law, he should commit suicide.
Indeed, this is the expectation that seems present to all minds, characters and audience alike, until Bérénice's final speech. The "foreign queen"
rejects the Roman solution and its inherent sadomasochism:

> You love me, as you proclaim constantly;
> And yet I am leaving, by your own order!
> Does my despair please you so?
> Don't I shed enough tears for you?
> (1345–48)

If the play had ended in death, *Bérénice* would have been the spectacle of
both the cruelty and the noble obligation of Roman glory. But the play
is called, very appropriately, *Bérénice,* because she is the force behind
Titus's drive toward moral perfection, and also the one who conceives of
a non-Roman (non-Cornelian, too) ending. As a foreigner and a woman,
she interprets events differently from the others, and is, therefore, capable of determining a new issue to the dilemma.[10] Her final speech is
unique in Racine, in that it combines *coup de théâtre,* climax, and denouement. Unique as well are the stage directions surrounding it. Immediately before the beginning of the penultimate scene of the play (act 5,
scene 6), Racine indicates· "(*Bérénice lets herself fall into a chair*)" so that she
is in a passive position, serving as the audience for the speech by Titus
(1363–1422), and then, in the last scene, for the one by Antiochus
(1443–68). When the latter finishes, Racine has this stage direction:
"*Bérénice rises*"—she will now pass to the attack, to what J. Dainard

describes as "at once the culminating point of human communication in the play, and the moment of recognition that this communication must henceforth cease forever."[11] That these are "final" scenes, in all senses, is emphasized by the stage directions that constitute the only time Racine specifies the point at which a character will both sit and rise.[12] She rises to the occasion, speaking first to the two men, then to Titus, next to Antiochus, and reserving her final phrase—"For the last time, farewell, Lord"—for Titus.

At first crushed by the import of Titus's declaration that disgrace or self-immolation are the only paths open to him, Bérénice then listens to the "witness" (1427) who makes it clear that the only solutions for him are flight or death, that is, moral or physical suicide. That is the price he is willing to pay for the happiness of his friends. Bérénice replies by calling them "too generous princes," as if they were Cornelian characters attentive only to "glory" and personal sacrifice. (*Bérénice* may be the most Cornelian and the most Racinian play in Racine's dramatic corpus.) The queen proposes another way, one that prefigures the end of Mme de La Fayette's *La Princesse de Clèves*. In the novel, the title figure becomes dangerously ill and almost dies. Once she is physically restored, she views life through different eyes and with new values. She sees that marriage with M. de Nemours would have taught her emotional misery as a daily fact. By renouncing it, she comes to know the unhappiness of separation from him tragically, metaphysically.

So too Bérénice. Realizing that death would be an easy and disappointing issue to beings of such moral rigor, Bérénice proposes that they live an "exemplary" life ("Let the three of us serve as examples to the universe" [1502]), one that transcends the experience of everyday misfortune to attain a level of tragic wisdom. They will experience the tragedy of separation, owing to a vision of life as exile expressed by the "foreign" queen, she who was initially willing to accept expatriation if it meant union with Titus. This is the only tragedy by Racine in which exile is accepted as a solution.[13]

This is also the first play by Racine in which the characters are punished for their virtue. (His next production, *Bajazet,* contained a variant on this.) The clear willingness to accept one's own unhappiness for the sake of others, and the examples of "generosity," as in Titus asking Antiochus to take care of Bérénice, in an act of sacrifice, like Christ on the cross or Hercules on the funeral pyre, lend a religious coloring to the play. Picard may, therefore, be right in characterizing the end as possessing a "secular grace," for the synthesis of purity and passion in *Bérénice* is unequaled in French classical theater.[14]

If, as previously suggested, this play offers the enactment of Titus *in bivio,* we may now redefine the options. The choice is ultimately between the father figure, Néron, and the symbolic mother, Bérénice.[15] Rather than obeying the deadly dictates of Roman imperialism (Titus occasionally compares his life without love to the sterility of a statue), Bérénice points the way to a nobler exit. None of this holds true, if, as some believe, Titus does not love Bérénice. Among critics, Roland Barthes is the best known of those who read the play as an example of "bad faith" on the part of Titus, who has remained with the queen out of habit. Among directors, Roger Planchon presented a *Bérénice* (Lyon 1966, Paris 1970) in which Racine's hero does not yet fully recognize that he has fallen out of love with the heroine. Planchon's interpretation is particularly challenging because he highlights the constraints that weigh on court society (the courts of Titus and Louis XIV) by directing his actors to move mostly in straight lines or in right-angle patterns. The geometrical designs are very effective in conveying a sense of stylization and the death of emotion. To watch this spectacle is to be reminded of Barthes's repeated image of Racine's theater as a prison.[16] Nonetheless, if one looks at the speeches in which Titus is still in doubt and questions himself about which path to follow, the evidence indicates that the struggle within Titus is real: see, for example, Titus's monologue of act 4, scene 4, which contains 24 question marks.[17]

Not everyone will agree on Titus's motivation, but the tragedy is unanimously praised for a number of reasons, foremost among them its poetry. While not yielding to the view of those for whom *Bérénice* is a poem, not a play, we can still stand in awe of Racine's talent for putting into words the most intimate of sentiments. Is there a more romantic definition of love than Titus's (even in my crude English translation)?

> All the strongest attachments of love,
> Soft reproaches, ever-renewing ecstasy,
> An artless desire to please, fear ever new,
> Beauty, glory, virtue, she is all for me.
> For the past five years I have seen her every day,
> And think it is always for the first time.[18]
>
> (541–46)

Has anyone described separation from the beloved as exile more lyrically than Racine's Titus?

Abandoned in the Orient how wretched I became!
I wandered all over Caesarea,
Beloved place where my heart had adored you.
I called and recalled your name in your sad land;
In tears I sought your footprints in the sand.
                                                    (234–38)

If so, perhaps it is Bérénice:

In a month, in a year, how will we suffer
Lord, that so many seas separate me from you?
That the day begins and that it ends,
Without Titus ever able to see Bérénice,
Without, throughout a whole day, my being able to see Titus!
                                                    (1113–17)

No small wonder that *Bérénice*'s poetry forms part of the fabric of French culture, to the point where a popular twentieth-century author, Françoise Sagan, entitled one of her early works *Dans un mois, dans un an* (In a month, in a year) [1957].

Bérénice is also acclaimed in French theatrical history for its poetic use of time: in fact, this tragedy marks a turning point in Racine's theater precisely because of his imaginative deployment of time in all the plays from this point forward. Though ideal time in all Racinian tragedies is characterized by being modified in relation to the intensification of tragic emotion, in *Bérénice* it assumes such proportions that it competes with Rome for the primary role as an "invisible presence." It passes with excruciating slowness, torturing the characters as they await Titus's declaration. Bérénice is especially sensitive: "Phénice, is he not yet here? Too rigorous moments / How slow you appear to my impatient desires!" (953–54). As a consequence, the present is intolerable: "this slowing down of the passing of time gives to moments a cruel power of expansion and their dramatic intensity is derived from their quality of never-ending suffering and the succession of conflicting moods they contain."[19]

The weight of the past is crushing in Racine's work because it contains all the events that will find their culmination in the brief space of the tragic spectacle. Even if it were a promising, happy past, under the protection of a parent, at some point the protector disappears. Titus and Bérénice lived an edenic existence for five years, until the death of Vespasian marked the temporal point at which their lives were changed forever. The future—the period to which *Bérénice* points—will be the time of that form of existence feared by the characters throughout: absence. The past determines the present, which is preoccupied with the future. In such a scheme, the present is the least substantial unit. It needs, therefore, only 12 hours of ideal time to complete its task. Since *Bérénice,* like the rest of Racine's tragedies, represents the verbalization of an interior act, the time of the tragedy always ends at the same point: when the last, single word is spoken—*Alas!* (1506).[20]

The unity of time is but one of the components of classical tragedy, a topic that occupies most of the Preface to *Bérénice*. While the Preface contains the legendary reference to the dramatist's obligation "to please and to move," and the equally famous, aforementioned "majestic sadness" of tragedy, it focuses on verisimilitude and simplicity. That the latter is not, despite what Racine may wish us to believe, a criterion for his work before or after *Bérénice* is attested to by the evidence of his next play, *Bajazet,* which is one of his most complicated. It is also very bloody, and contradicts Racine's thesis in the Preface to *Bérénice* that neither violence nor death is necessary to tragedy.

Behind the apparent lecture that Racine delivers on the most effective elements of tragedy is hidden a pointed criticism of Corneille's practice as a dramatist, since Corneille's plays were open to charges of excessive complication, approximate observance of the unities, and lack of plausibility. The Preface to *Bérénice* is not a manual on the composition of Racinian tragedy (Racine never believed in publicizing the secrets of his art), but a salvo against the more established dramatist who had criticized Racine's historical accuracy in the case of *Britannicus.* The quarrel between the partisans of Corneille and of his young rival over the comparative qualities of *Tite et Bérénice* and *Bérénice* continues to our day in, for example, a lengthy article by Georges Forestier critical of the way that Racine has been allowed, from the beginning, to set the parameters of the debate.[21]

I will let H. C. Lancaster echo my personal position on Racine's tragedy of a couple united by love but separated by history:

> One may prefer more violent subjects, a larger number of characters, themes that are more clearly a matter of life and death, yet the play remains closer than most tragedies to ordinary experience and the penetrating simplicity of the heroine's words will haunt the memories of readers as long as the French language is understood.[22]

Chapter Nine

Bajazet

Bajazet, first performed on 5 January 1672, is Racine's only play with a contemporary setting, and a special one at that: "The scene is in Constantinople, formerly called Byzantium, in the seraglio of the Great Lord." The play's triumphant success summoned praise from all quarters, even, begrudgingly, from Corneille's staunchest admirers, like Mme de Sévigné, who thought it a beautiful play, but surely not better than *Andromaque.* Commentators noted the sumptuous decor and the splendiferous costumes, which must have delighted spectators for a particular reason: these trappings flattered their curiosity about things Oriental.[1] Among other things, this interest was sparked by the invitations that Suleiman Aga, Mutaferraca, ambassador of Mohammed IV, ruler of the Turkish Empire, extended to guests to come to his Paris lodgings and enjoy what became known as the "arabesque liquor," coffee.[2] Gastronomy was indeed a weapon in the tense diplomatic and cultural relations between the courts of Louis XIV and Mohammed IV, and we now know that the writers of seventeenth-century French cookbooks, like La Varenne and his *Le Vrai Cuisinier françoys* (The true French cook) of 1651, were attempting to change the taste of their compatriots. They eliminated the sweet smells and the golden colors that Islam had brought to European cooking of the Middle Ages and the Renaissance, and they favored the acid and salty taste of the Greco-Roman tradition over the sugary savors of eastern cuisine.[3] In so doing, La Varenne, for example, was putting the emphasis on the "French" in *Le Vrai Cuisinier françoys.* It is in this nationalistic context that we should appreciate Racine's genius for choosing, once again, a timely topic.[4] In *Bajazet,* West meets East, an East that must not strain the principle of verisimilitude. To depict the Orient in the light of his contemporaries' limited knowledge and cultural prejudices, Racine presents it as, to coin a phrase, the Evil Empire.

But this repressive regime has its rebels, notably the title character. Bajazet is kept under guard in the seraglio of his absent brother, the Sultan Amurat, who considers him a threat to the throne of Constantinople. Since the Sultan's departure to lay siege to Babylone, his Machiavellian Vizir Acomat has brought Bajazet and the Sultana Roxane together in the hope that they will join forces and revolt against Amurat. Seeing that his life depends on pleasing Roxane, who has complete power in the Sultan's absence, Bajazet does nothing to dissuade her from falling in love with him. But he cannot long hide his love for Atalide, and the Sultana condemns him to death, soon to be followed by her own. Amurat's victory at Babylone assures him the continued support of the army and, therefore, total and ruthless sway over the nation upon his return.

In keeping with the principle that the eponymous figure in Racinian tragedy causes all the others to act and react, Bajazet is the moving force. He is as active as Titus was passive; that is, in the logocentric world of Racine, he dares to say "yes" to love, even if that means "no" to life. In the erotic context of the seraglio, Bajazet tries to shake off the shackles of civilization, of the empire, of duty, of his brother, of Roxane, of all that stands in the way of an existence rich in sensuality. But the character of his fate is transmitted by the nature of the stage setting. The seraglio must have inspired uneasy feelings in the French public, for it conjures up images of dark, repressive, claustrophobic confines best suited to the satisfaction of violent instincts. Moreover, there is an ambiguity about the term that we need to understand. To this point I have used *seraglio* to translate the French *Serrail* for two reasons. First, the word *harem*, which exists in modern French and which I will henceforth employ because of its familiarity, was unknown to Racine. Second, *seraglio*, by its very cacophony, causes the reader to pause and consider the term. This is a useful reaction because *Serrail* means two things in the text of Bajazet: the harem and the palace.[5] When, at the beginning of act 3, Atalide's confidant Zaire says that a slave "At the door of the *Serrail* received the Vizir" (796), Racine is designating a palace. But, verses 875–77 indicate another, more circumscribed place—the harem:

> Recalled to the palace for this sad purpose,
> Full of joy and hope, I ran, I flew.
> The door of the *Serrail* opened to my call.

The drama's physical site, the *Serrail* is obscure even spatially, thereby increasing its enigmatic quality.[6] The word is significant to the point of recurring 13 times in this play (and in none other). Another special term, *noeud* ("knot"), to which we will return, recurs more often in this tragedy than in any other and for good cause: it is again an element that

Racine can use for two purposes. One begins to notice a pattern of deliberate lexical imprecision in several key items. This expands the poetic field of the item; it also strains the spectators' focus, makes them work harder at coming to conclusions about what they are seeing, and in general creates an atmosphere of uncertainty.

The first lines of the drama bathe in this atmosphere. Acomat alerts Osmin to the Sultana's imminent arrival in the harem, where, nonetheless, they can speak.[7] The law of the harem proscribes two acts: to speak and to show oneself/be seen. (The shadowy mutes that attend in this place embody the reigning principles of invisibility and silence.) Since he and Acomat will be seen in the harem and since they are now speaking, Osmin is understandably puzzled:

> And since when, Lord, are we allowed to enter this place
> Which, previously, was forbidden even to a glance?
> Formerly, a prompt death would have followed such audacity.
>   (3–5)

Words, then, can be as least as subversive as acts in this milieu, which explains the frequent request for someone to make a "declaration." Roxane pursues such a statement—of love—from Bajazet throughout. She, whom Amurat has put in charge in his absence, has opened the portals of the harem just as she has opened her heart to love. The entrance of Acomat and Osmin into the taboo area is a sign of the double penetration that has occurred. The world has been allowed into the harem, and the harem, represented by the former slave Roxane, has been opened to the outside where, according to Osmin, the destiny of the Ottoman Empire depends on the success of the Sultan's siege of Babylone; that is, Babylone is as closed to Amurat as the harem is now open to external influences.

Since it has taken Osmin months to return to Constantinople, his recounting is necessarily anticlimactic. The battle of Babylone, on which hangs the continued reign of Acomat, has taken place during Osmin's trip home. Uncertainty over the status of the war has its parallel in another siege: Roxane's attack on Bajazet's heart. Racine has established his parallel worlds—the inside and the outside—so that they constantly reflect each other. Given this reflexivity, all attempts at keeping the two separate—for example, by ordering the harem closed—are sooner or later doomed to failure.

Acomat, however, has no patience for awaiting the result of the battle of Babylone. Fomenting a palace coup in which Bajazet would assume the throne of the absent Sultan, he hopes to hear Bajazet and Roxane "declare themselves" in solidarity with his plan "today" (95). Racine insists on temporal considerations throughout to exacerbate the cruel desperation that besets all his characters, starting with Acomat's expectation that his scheme to be the power broker of the new regime will be fulfilled during the one day of the tragedy. Since he is anxious to see his goal realized, he has a tendency, shared by Roxane and Atalide, to interpret conduct in the light of his desires. It often appears that the light is insufficiently bright. His first description of the meeting between Roxane and Bajazet is typical:

> Bajazet, worthy of her love, saw that his survival
> Depended on pleasing her; and soon he succeeded.
> Everything worked in his favor: . . .
> Sighs, so sweet they had to be suppressed,
> The discomfort of not being able to speak openly,
> Sharing the same audacity, dangers, common fears,
> Linked forever their hearts and their fortunes.
> (155–62)

Like an editor proofing his own text, Acomat is deceived into seeing what he hopes to find rather than what is actually there. In this drama of ambiguity, reading the body is fraught with problems. (A written message would be a much less ambiguous piece of evidence; we shall see what credence Roxane lends to a letter in act 4.) In this instance, we later learn that Bajazet's sighs and discomfort, unlike Roxane's, are signs of reluctance at having to play a deceitful role.

Role-playing is an inherent activity when everyone is occupied with hiding their real intentions, especially from Amurat who is, in a pagan context, what the god of the Hebrews is in *Athalie*: the dominant, but absent, force. According to Acomat, Atalide is pretending to be in love with Bajazet so that no one will suspect the "truth" of the liaison between him and Roxane. Once again, the information that the Vizir is so confidently transmitting to Osmin is inaccurate, for Atalide is involved in a play with two levels. She is acting both as Roxane's understudy, assuming a role that is not hers in a drama intended for public consumption; and she is simultaneously fooling everyone but Bajazet by turning her public spectacle into a private reality: her love for him can be nothing but forbidden fruit as long as Roxane rules.

Within the limits, therefore, of the first scene, we notice the emergence of a theme that Racine will reprise in his next tragedy, *Mithridate*: the search for certainty in a world of moral, intellectual, and, in *Bajazet*, physical obscurity. Susan Tiefenbrun describes the situation to the letter: "the characters caught up in *Bajazet*'s network of conspiracies, undercover surveillance, and unreliable communication systems crave the truth, demanding evidence of fact before the senses."[8] The difficulty is not with the end, but with the means, for the characters rely on intuition, faith in their power to "read" others correctly, and, most frequently, intermediaries who transmit second-hand messages. The initial scene of the play between Acomat and Osmin is symptomatic of all these problems, which are complicated by an ethical climate, unique in Racine's theater, whose rules have been conceived and heartlessly implemented by an immoral despot. Amurat is immoral, in the eyes of the seventeenth-century audience, first by not being Christian and, as a consequence, by being capable of instituting a violent reign. One of the interesting questions implicitly posed by *Bajazet* concerns the nature of morality. If, to be moral, one must conform to the mores—the accustomed order of things—how does one act "morally," in the Ottoman Empire as Racine depicts it, and how will he integrate this ethical imbroglio into his tragic scheme?

The major key to the solution lies in the reversal of values that Racine effects, starting with the ingenious setting of the play in a locus of lust and confinement where communication is based on rumors, gossip, espionage, and the like. To dominate the harem one must be unusually perceptive, able to distinguish truth from illusion and detach oneself from sensual pleasures, the better to "see" reality. As a consequence, Acomat, the visionary Vizir, he who believes himself to be a superior "reader," assumes a central position within the palace that has its parallel in the omniscient status attributed to Acomat, the external, quasi-divine force. If these two, with their marked penchant for trickery and ruthlessness, embody the standards of the collectivity in *Bajazet* (N.B., both survive at the end), then Racine has expressly perverted Christian values to create a milieu in which conduct that flows from western moral concepts—such as the obligation to overthrow unethical regimes—would be punished as treason.

Racine furthers his tragic design with a repeated recourse to the notion of "order." The word itself reappears in *Bajazet* with far greater frequency than in any other of his plays. The reason clearly is that "orders" of all kinds are operative in *Bajazet,* from the commands that are delivered by the Sultan, Roxane, and Acomat (the latter two dare to exercise their own verbal authority, beyond what the Sultan has prescribed), to the customary, "orderly" conduct of the palace and the harem, to the larger question of the moral order that underpins the tragedy. First of all, directives and commands of all kinds are the coin of the realm in a harem where the governing principles are pain and pleasure. There are several references to dictates that Amurat has sent from afar, and the arrival of his messenger Orcan—the second one he has dispatched with orders for Roxane—forces the action to reach its climax.

There is also the matter of the "accustomed order" of things. At the beginning of act 2 Roxane and Bajazet are on stage together for the first time. In a long speech filled with threats and compliments, the Sultana attempts to coerce Bajazet into joining her politically—and otherwise. If her approach seems inappropriate and counterproductive, one must recall that she treats others as she herself has been treated in the harem. Ironically, then, if she is attracted to Bajazet because he symbolizes what she, the former slave, cherishes most—freedom—, she threatens to continue his imprisonment if he does not yield to her advances. She notes that the hour of his deliverance has finally arrived (421–22) and that he should dash through the "Glorious field that I have opened for you" (440). She is rather crudely recalling that his liberty depends on her goodwill, and she wants a suitable sign of assent from him. Her goal, like that of most characters in Racine's work, is to try to elicit speech from her interlocutor. But when Bajazet does decide to speak, it is with the purpose of delaying any initiative. She can barely contain her fury:

> I see my lack of prudence;
> I see that nothing escapes your foresight . . .
> But have you foreseen, if you do not marry me,
> The very sure dangers to which you will be exposed?
> Do you realize what adversity will strike you without me?
> That your goal should be to please me above all?
> Do you realize that I command the gates of the palace;
> That I can open or close them forever;
> That I have total control of your life;
> That you breathe only as long as I love you?

And, without that very love that your refusal offends,
Do you realize, in a word, that you would no longer exist?
                                                    (497–512)

The last line is echoed shortly afterwards in verse 542: "If one word
escaped my lips, your life is forfeit."

This remarkable passage is exemplary in its concentration of themes.
The call to seeing and foreseeing (497, 489, 503) by the one most
addicted to illusion is deeply ironic. The insistence on opening and closing the palace as a translation of the accessibility to her heart (508) would
perhaps be touching were it not meant to be baldly intimidating. The
following metaphor about "breathing" (510) appears to be simply a trite
substitute for "living." Given, however, the method by which one was
often slain in the harem—garroting—, the metaphor becomes demeta-
phorized to disclose a brutal reality. This recharging of traditional and
often euphemistic images with a passionate content is one of Racine's signal contributions to French literature. He is also a master at turning
ambiguity to his best, ironic advantage. When, to cite an instance, characters speaks of a "knot," it can mean either the bond of marriage or the
means of strangulation. Roxane offers both to Bajazet at one time or
another and indulges in frightening sadism when, near the end, she tells
Atalide that she will unite her to Bajazet "by eternal knots" (1625). The
appeal to reason ("Do you realize?" 505, 507, 512), deserves attention
because it recurs throughout Racine's corpus, usually, as here, in the form
of the verb *songer* ("to think"). In *Bajazet,* and especially from the mouth
of as unstable a figure as Roxane, such a call seems curious. In the Age of
Reason do characters really need to remind one another to think? Would
not Roxane herself be better advised to bring logic rather than emotion
to bear on difficult situations? Of course. And in her passionate contradiction Roxane, like Phèdre after her, is profoundly human and tragic.

Finally, let us consider the "one word" (512, 542), which is Racine's
clever manner of seeding the text for future harvest. Roxane knows that
her power extends to the gates of the palace and not beyond. Mistress of
the Inside, she understands that Outside is a perilous zone. She seems,
once again, to be uttering a banality of the kind "all I need say is one
word, and your doom is sealed"—except that she eventually says only
one word which seals everyone's doom: *Sortez* ("Go outside," 1565). The
trite becomes prophetic, and Roxane is true to her (one) word.

It is because she has been insulted and frustrated by Bajazet's total
lack of enthusiasm for her that Roxane commands that "everything

return to its accustomed order" (572). Yet, once the orders and the politicomoral order of the Sultan have been violated, there can be no return. Odette de Mourgues has written brilliantly on the broader question of the moral order in *Bajazet* as it relates to the "accustomed order." She reminds us that in a tragedy there is usually some form of order—political, moral, or religious—that gives the drama a framework necessary for the audience's comfort. The order is the backdrop against which the spectators measure the conduct of the characters, and it varies, therefore, with contemporary ideas on politics, ethics, or religion. The order found in Racinian tragedy reflects, as one would expect, a certain conception of the monarchy and the values of Catholic France. This order is threatened in the course of tragedies like *Andromaque* and *Britannicus,* but is finally reestablished when, for example, Narcisse and Néron are punished. In *Bajazet* there is no moral order with which the public would feel at ease, especially because, as we have seen, the two standard-bearers of the morality of Constantinople are Acomat, who would sell his soul for power, and Amurat, who exercises his authority almost without conscience.[9]

There is, nonetheless, an order, the "accustomed order" instituted by the Sultan, based on slavery and in contradiction to the conception of order entertained by seventeenth-century France. It is cruel, arbitrary, and amoral, as if it were another species of passion or fate, and is incarnated by Amurat at a distance and by Orcan proximately. Since it finally succeeds in destroying all the characters except Acomat, it reconfirms its prevailing status at the end. Virtue (as we see it) is punished, and evil is rewarded. Where else could Racine have situated this kind of tragedy, except in a pagan land capable of every atrocity in the eyes of his contemporaries? On a symbolic level, given the triumph of negative values over positive ones, *Bajazet* takes place in hell.[10]

Hell is above all a place whose "accustomed order" enforces eternal imprisonment. When in act 2, scene 2 Roxane commands the closing of the harem and the return to the former state of things, she is, in effect, casting everyone back into prison, including herself. Throughout the play Roxane seeks legitimacy in marriage; she is only the favorite concubine of Amurat, only the "Acting Sultan." She is not his wife, and given the prejudice against former slaves, would never be allowed to ascend to that lofty position. She is also instinctively drawn to the heroic potential that she, and everyone—including Amurat—find in Bajazet. One sometimes wonders if this universal confidence is well placed. Who, in fact, is Bajazet? Bajazet's actions are more often reported (that is, interpreted) than seen, and, very significantly, he has no confidant and delivers no soliloquy. To what extent does he solicit Roxane's affection in their offstage meetings? Is his performance meant only for Roxane and Acomat? There are no satisfactory answers to these questions. If Antiochus was a mirror of the others in *Bérénice*, at least we knew what his motivation was and what he represented. *Bérénice*'s people have secrets that they find difficult to express, unlike the characters of *Bajazet* who always enjoin each other to "pretend"—to abuse the truth-telling function of speech. Given the enigmatic yet attractive quality of its eponym, *Bajazet* might best be performed with a highly polished pillar at center stage, reflective of all aspirations.

Roxane is, of course, the prime audience for Bajazet's illusion. If, at verse 572, she exits in the loud and resounding manner typical of most stage exits in Racine, she is renouncing her role as spectator and closing the gates on her own chance for escape, both physical and moral. This penchant for self-condemnation attains its dramatic heights when she utters *Sortez*, which is, at once, an act of abandonment of her drive for status and her political relationship with Amurat, the renunciation of her passion for Bajazet, the death sentence for Bajazet and herself, and the end of an almost impenetrable illusion.[11]

Racine makes it abundantly clear that Roxane will accept multiple indignities for the sake of keeping her hopes alive. If she sees through Bajazet's lukewarm rhetoric of act 2, she is willing to suspend disbelief in the next act, in which Acomat, once again, describes a wordless encounter between the Sultana and the prince (869–88) and interprets the gestures according to his personal semiotic code. (His legendary powers of perception lend a credibility to his report that leaves Atalide in despair, until Bajazet disabuses her.[12]) Roxane then appears and is shocked by Bajazet's coolness. The third act retraces, in effect, the rhythm of the first: Roxane is duped, she perceives the possibility of deceit, but she prefers the (temporary) security of belief in Bajazet. Nonetheless, it is evident that Roxane has narrowed her focus: she has subordinated all thoughts of political gain to the one goal of assuring the reciprocal love of Bajazet. This concentration, betraying Roxane's lack of confidence in her ability to obtain her passionate objective, is translated by a spatial evolution. The first two acts take place in Roxane's territory, to which she convenes Acomat and Bajazet and brings Atalide. As of act 3, it is Atalide's space that attracts the others. In fact, she opens each of the last three acts and closes the last with her death.

As Atalide's influence grows, so do Roxane's suspicions until she understands, in act 4, that the play within a play that Bajazet and Atalide were staging depended entirely on her gullibility for its continued success. When Atalide faints upon hearing Roxane read the letter in which Amurat confirms his order to have Bajazet slain, Roxane delivers a lengthy speech (1209–50), in which she reviews all the damning evidence of Bajazet's betrayal and then concludes: "I wish to ignore all." But her wish will not be respected because Zatime enters to show her the personal note Bajazet had written to Atalide. This letter, the only one in Racine's theater whose text we know, is read out loud and "actualises the voice of Bajazet in a way he sought to avoid."[13] Yet even this indisputable proof, that has none of the credibility problems of second-hand reports and rumors, does not extricate Roxane from the depths of her illusion (only a verbal "declaration" by Bajazet will do). Instead of following Acomat to take immediate revenge, she proposes a delay, pretexting a desire to savor Bajazet's embarrassment when the truth is told.

It is in act 5, scene 4 that we have the parallel speech to the one we discussed in act 2, scene 1, but this time it is Bajazet, the harem prisoner, who dares to show himself and speak (1490–1526). He tells of a heart ready to "open," but "closed" to anyone but Atalide, of his life being in Roxane's hands, of "seeing" Roxane's misperception, and so on. His arguments, particularly the one based on his desire not to disabuse Roxane of an illusion that she evidently cherishes, smack of evasiveness and bad faith. It is only when she requires him to witness the death of Atalide that he permits the truth to burst forth. This final, unequivocal statement dispels all doubt and is the direct cause of the most famous one-word condemnation in Racine: *Sortez.*

The whole time since the announcement of the arrival of Orcan in act 3, scene 8, Roxane has been delaying the confrontation between the truth and what she herself refers to as her "blind love" (1071). The intertwined pressures of politics and especially passion grow—"Time presses us" (1117)—and are measured by an exceedingly cruel acceleration of time. If the temporal scheme of *Bérénice* is noteworthy for a painfully slow development that causes each moment to weigh and be weighed, the passage of time in *Bajazet* serves the opposite effect. The characters are aware of the brevity of the temporal framework in which they must operate, and the catalyzing elements are, first, Acomat's drive to overthrow the Sultan, and second, its indispensable component, Roxane's pursuit of Bajazet. The arrival of two messengers from Amurat puts great pressure on the inhabitants of the palace to act precipitously, even if the first envoy was slain by Acomat's orders. The phrase *dans cette journée* ("in the course of this day"), occurring four times in the play, translates the necessity of immediate action. Another result of the pres-

sure of time is the extraordinary number of "orders" that are pronounced throughout, without even counting the ones from Amurat that
are reported by intermediaries. In this atmosphere, it is to be expected
that one will have little time for hesitation, deliberation, or reflection (as
in *songer*). Haste is the order of the day, so to speak, and yet immobility
reigns. Roxane and Bajazet may have met numerous times, offstage and
on, but nothing is resolved until the final scenes, whose rhythm is positively frenetic; that is, for better than four acts, tragedy has dominated
drama, undoubtedly because the wily politician Acomat, who thought
himself capable of leading the "subversive speakers," has been curiously
ineffective in urging courses of action on others. His words have little
impact, and he is often reduced to sputtering series of questions ("What
have I heard? What an enormous surprise? What will you become?"
etc.; 573–75). At the end, his verbal power of persuasion ineffective; he
leaves to offer his services to the highest bidder (act 5, scene 11). His
departure for points unknown causes the note of ambiguity to resonate
at the very moment of the drama's closure.

In accord with the setting for *Bajazet* in the "barbaric" Ottoman
Empire, the denouement is not only the bloodiest but the meanest in all
of Racine's corpus. If we examine it though the prism of time, we discover that, if the future is the imposing force in *Bérénice*, the past-
become-present fulfills that role in *Bajazet*. In the first scene we learn
from Osmin and Acomat, whose meetings frame the play (act 1, scene 1
and act 5, scene 11), that the former has traveled for months from
Babylone before reaching Constantinople, and that a messenger, dispatched before Osmin's departure, has already arrived and been executed. The play proper begins with Osmin making his report to Acomat, and ends on a series of violent deaths—Bajazet, Roxane, and
Atalide—caused by the arrival of Orcan, who is also slain, and who has
come to announce Amurat's victory over Babylone. Since, as everyone
recognizes, the fate of all rests on Amurat's success or failure, and since
Orcan's trip must have taken as long as Osmin's, Amurat must have
won his battle and the loyalty of his army before the action of *Bajazet*
began. The all-encompassing tragedy of *Bajazet* is that everyone, audience and characters alike, was deceived into thinking that the Babylone
situation was still unresolved and that the *die* was not yet cast. The truth
is that the tragedy was nothing more than a gratuitous exercise, a dramatic illusion imposing the necessity to act out their parts on a number
of characters whose destinies were sealed before the curtain rose. If ever
there were a lesson on the futility of human action, it is *Bajazet*.

Chapter Ten

Mithridate

Beginning in 1667 Racine produced a play a year; in 1673 *Mithridate* was born. The historical context of 1672 may provide a clue to Racine's motivation in choosing to treat the subject of the famous warrior: in that year negotiations were begun between France and almost all the rest of Europe to form an alliance against the Dutch in a war whose first blow was struck on 6 April. The war was costly, but inspired much patriotism among the French and much admiration for the young warrior-king, Louis XIV. In all likelihood, Racine was caught up in the nationalistic spirit of the period that could only have been intensified for him by the heady feeling of being nominated and then elected to his country's most prestigious literary institution, the Académie Française, in late 1672. In January 1673 he gave French theatergoers *Mithridate*, whose backdrop is the struggle between an alliance of nations, led by a crafty king, and the Roman Empire.

Mithridate, King of Pontus and enemy of Rome for 40 years, is reported defeated and dead. His young fiancée, Monime, is courted by his older son, Pharnace, but is secretly in love with the other son, Xipharès. The return of the king, whose death was a strategic rumor of his own invention, forces Monime and Xipharès to renounce their relationship. Suspecting Pharnace of having designs on his fiancée, Mithridate has him arrested. Pharnace, however, exposes the sentiments his brother entertains for Monime to Mithridate. Wishing to uncover the truth, Mithridate tricks Monime into admitting her love for Xipharès. Mithridate then plots a terrible vengeance. Before he can execute it, however, Roman invaders, aided by Pharnace, are seen arriving. Believing Xipharès to be dead in battle, Monime is about to commit suicide with poison that Mithridate has sent her when Mithridate's confidant Arbate stops her and announces that Mithridate is dying by his own hand and that Xipharès has put the Roman army to flight. In his last moments, Mithridate gives Monime in marriage to Xipharès whom he recognizes as his true successor as warrior-king.

In Racine's tragedies, plot is the handmaiden of character. *Mithridate* is the tableau of an aging king, his wiliness, his indecision, his frustrations. Racine makes that explicit in his Preface when he describes his wish to elucidate the "habits and the feelings of this prince" and when he declares that everything will be seen in the light of Mithridate's death, "which is the action of my tragedy." By collapsing events that took place 26 years apart—a fact that did not escape the notice of his critics[1]—Racine offers an encapsulated biography of a major historical figure. Biography is often a component of tragedy, as titles like *Julius Caesar* and *Alexandre le Grand* show. But *Mithridate*'s focus remains on the moral portrait. Donneau de Visé said as much in a review of the play that appeared in the newspaper the *Mercure Galant*, in 1673: "and although this prince [Mithridate] was a barbarian [i.e., non-Christian], [Racine] transformed him, through his death, into one of the great princes of the world . . . and this great king dies with so much respect for the gods that he could be cited as an example to our most Christian princes."[2]

Given this concentration on the eponymous character, we might expect Racine to introduce him straightaway. Yet his entrance is delayed for good reasons. First, in accordance with a common seventeenth-century dramaturgical practice, he defers the appearance of the controversial character so that differing points of view on him can be expressed beforehand—thereby exposing the nature of the person under discussion and the attitudes of the discussants as well. In the case of Mithridate, if the spectators are made aware of the motivations of Monime, Pharnace, and Xipharès before the king arrives, they will be in a position to judge the characters' sincerity once he has returned. As we will see, the ability to "read" others is a problem for the inhabitants of *Mithridate*'s world and would one be for the theatrical public, were it not for the prominent scenes in which Racine lets his characters declare their feelings openly.

Another reason for not introducing Mithridate at the outset derives from the deception instigated by the king himself. To gain time and the advantage of surprise, Mithridate has circulated the false rumor of his death. This is the only time Racine opens a play with the report of a death narration. The first act with which we associate Mithridate is, therefore, revealing: he is a master deceiver. This talent is both a strength and a weakness when dealing with others. Indeed, Racine leaves no doubt as to Mithridate's inveterate mistrust of others when he first comes on stage in scenes 2 and 3 of act 2. His initial statements to his sons are accusatory, and then, in a change of tone—and tactics—he adopts the stance of the caring father:

No matter what you may say, Princes,

Reasons of duty do not explain your presence here,

Nor make you leave, for pressing obligations,

You, Pontus, and you, Colchos, for which I made you responsible.

However, your father, who is also your judge, loves you.

(423–27)

We shall see that it is difficult for someone who considers himself a "judge" to be a good "father" too.

The delay in Mithridate's arrival is the first of a series of deferrals made necessary by the lack of accurate information. Indeed, the play's rhythm staggers along owing to the inability of the characters to act decisively, based on a knowledge of the truth. Only in act 4 do all the principal characters come to an appreciation of the true nature of the events. After that, Mithridate's revenge still remains to be elucidated—which means that there will not be complete knowledge for either spectators or characters until well into act 5.

"Complete knowledge" and the "truth" are goals that might be expected in a century that produced René Descartes, the father of modern rationalism, whose *Discours de la méthode* (1637) offered a "path" (one of the philosopher's favorite images) to map out the distinction between truth and falsehood. This pursuit is a veritable preoccupation in *Mithridate* from the very first verse, which is part of a passage that Racine's son Louis later distinguished for its natural, almost prosaic quality.[3] It is Xipharès who speaks:

We did indeed receive, Arbate, an accurate report:

Rome is triumphant, and Mithridate is dead.

Near the Euphrates the Romans attacked my father at night,

Thus surprising his normal wariness.

After a long battle, his army in flight

Left him surrounded by the dead,

And I learned that a soldier placed in Pompey's hands,

Not only his crown but his sword as well.

(1–8)

Despite Xipharès's assurances, the first line is factually erroneous, thus immediately posing the problem of how to determine the criteria of cer-

tainty. The report is false because Mithridate practiced deceit. Undoubtedly the greatest irony of the play is that it is the great tactician of
deception who ultimately becomes a victim of uncertainty: he suspects
that his sons are cuckolding him, and he hears false news that Xipharès
has joined the Romans. Furthermore, it is only when he comes into possession of the full truth that Racine allows Mithridate to expire. One can
argue that Racine frames the action of his play between the false reports
of the father's death (act 1) and the son's death (act 5), followed in each
case by a rectification.

In this drama, where truth and falsehood are staked for gain or loss,
the verb *savoir* ("to know") recurs more often than in any other Racinian
play, reflecting the difficulty of knowing in a world in which rules were
devised by a mendacious despot. In Michael O'Reagan's words: "The
whole action of the play is based on Mithridate's three deceptions: the
false rumor of his death, the testing of his sons when he announces his
plans to invade Italy, and the temptation of Monime."[4] Another key
word in the text of the tragedy is *secret*. Its frequency is such that *Mithridate* vies with *Britannicus* for the most occurrences of the term and its
variants: 21.[5] As in *La Princesse de Clèves*, secrets give rise to interpersonal
strategies of silence and concealment. This has two immediate effects:
the characters experience a terrible urge to speak, and their reticence
sparks curiosity. Silence summons speech, and secrets will be spoken.
The classical writer La Rochefoucauld once noted, "How can we expect
another to keep our secret when we cannot do so ourselves?"[6] Moreover,
once speech is liberated, it cannot be recalled. The most memorable
examples of this occur in the several declarations of love in *Phèdre*, but
those in *Mithridate* are not for that reason to be minimized.

All the major figures in the play seek to say or penetrate the reality of
what has been said. After Mithridate puts his sons to the test, he probes
Monime, like a general searching out the vulnerable points in an adversary's defense. Xipharès, possibly Racine's most admirable—Mme de
Sévigné would have said "Cornelian"—male character, abhors dissimu-
lation and declares that he can no longer reduce his love for Monime to
"silence" (35): he must speak. When Monime alludes to the "secret
treaty" (282) between Rome and Pharnace, the latter speaks of her
"secret sentiments" (287). Xipharès alludes to the existence of the "hidden sentiments" (318) of Monime, and Pharnace confesses to Xipharès:
"You know my secret and I have learned yours" (368). These instances
evoke once again *La Princesse de Clèves* and its dialectic between secret/
hidden/dissimulate and discover/expose/surprise. When Xipharès first is

enjoined by the king in act 2, scene 5 to remain at Monime's side, and then, in the following scene, is advised by Monime to avoid her, Mme de Clèves's predicament comes immediately to mind: caught between the advice of her two most prominent beings, her mother and her husband.

Racine institutes his inquiry into appearance and reality in the first scene, and pursues it right to act 5. This final act, which is designed to resolve all enigmas and obstacles, opens, characteristically, on Monime and Phoedime, who are awaiting an "accurate report" of Xipharès's supposed death. Exceptionally, Racine does not avail himself of a device he used to great effect in every play from *Bérénice* through *Iphigénie*: communication by letter. Even if the recipient dislikes the content, the evidence of a letter is compelling: it can serve to dispel mystery and clarify motivation. Racine could have had Monime write to Xipharès, or the other way around, but it seems as if Racine did not want any illuminating text to intrude into his portrayal of the moral chiaroscuro of *Mithridate*'s world.

This "grayness" is necessary because it is inherent to Racine's conception of his central character. There has been much wrangling about the "conversion" of Mithridate at the end of the play, when the ruthless soldier of fortune displays that remarkable generosity that so impressed Donneau de Visé. For some, it is an inconsistency that points to a weakness in *Mithridate*; for others, it adheres naturally to Racine's allegorical portrayal of the king.

What indication is there that Racine wanted his king to be a model of inconsistency? The response comes from the play's structure, particularly in act 4 when seen in the context of what Racine typically does with his fourth acts. Act 4 is the most important one in Racinian dramaturgy, for there is usually found the moment of decision, or if not, at least the consequences of a decision effected between the end of act 3 and the opening of act 4. Pyrrhus announces his resolution to marry Andromaque; Néron opts for revenge; Roxane discovers the letter from Bajazet to Atalide, and should, in all logic, order the execution of Bajazet; at the crucial deciding point, Mithridate displays indecision. Ironically, the "defining moment" for Mithridate—the character as well as the play—is rendered deficient by ill-defined sentiments. In Racine's view, Mithridate is the very essence of indecision.

The full complexity of the portrait is evident in the salient passages of act 4. The play gravitates about two centers, Mithridate and Monime, and each is in a double bind. She is torn between her duty to the king,

to whom she is betrothed, and her affection for his son Xipharès. Politically, she is against Rome and for Mithridate and Xipharès, who represent the anti-Roman faction. Mithridate is fighting against rivals for
Monime and against her resistance. He is also struggling against the
advancing Romans and their treacherous ally, Pharnace. These dualities
appear in act 4, which opens with Monime expressing her anguish over
her betrayal of her love for Xipharès to Mithridate at the end of act 3.
Her confidant, Phoedime, reassures her so well that she responds with
eight and one-third verses of hope before being interrupted by Xipharès,
who comes to tell her that they have been betrayed. She sends him off
before the king can see them together. Mithridate then returns, demanding that she marry him.

    Mingling threats with attempts to make her feel obligated and guilty,
Mithridate pursues a direct line of verbal attack that she counters easily.
Alone on stage in scene 5, he is struck by the changes he has undergone:
"Who am I? Is this Monime? And am I Mithridate?" (1383). In a monologue remarkable for its ability to translate Mithridate's conflicting sentiments, verses 1379–1421 begin with a statement that the character
himself finds paradoxical ("She leaves—and in a fit of cowardly silence, I
seem to approve her insolent flight!") and end on a question ("How can
I extricate myself from this fatal situation?"). A victim of antagonistic
emotions—torn between his love for Monime, his fatherly affection for
Xipharès, an instinct for revenge, and a need to dominate—Mithridate
lacks a clear plan of action and is reduced to immobility. This is hardly
what anyone, and surely Mithridate himself, would have expected of the
violent conqueror. Henry Phillips notes felicitously, "The most interesting case [in Racine] of a character suddenly faced with a consciousness of
difference from his former self is that of Mithridate."[7] Mithridate's vital
flaws are his need for revenge and his impetuousness. Before act 4 we see
him carefully preparing his acts—or his revenge. But in act 4 Racine
allows us a glimpse of a king in decline, beset by indecision.

    The problem for the old king is that he can dominate in war, espe-
cially through ruse, but in love (as in fatherhood) the same tactics do not
work. As Racine's tragedies show time and again, true love requires true
communication. All "reports" must be "accurate" for love to flourish.
Yet, from the very beginning of the dramatic portrait of this "dispos-
sessed king," as Pascal would say, it is difficult to obtain credible information. This presents a problem for the characters and would be one for
the public, if Racine did not furnish us with other analytical clues. One
of them is geography.

Since *Mithridate* is about a military man who has fought Rome across much of its empire, we might expect geography to be destiny in the play. The geography of *Mithridate* is, in fact, grist for the mill of orthodox Freudians. Racine gives the setting as being in "Nymphea, a seaport on the Cimmerian Bosphorus in the Tauric Chersonesos." The Bosphorus in question is a long, narrow slit connecting the Black Sea with the Sea of Azov; *Cimmerian* means very dark or gloomy; Tauric evokes a bull-like virility; the Chersonesos is a peninsula, a strip of land penetrating the water; and Nymphea are, in an anatomical context, lips. An old-fashioned Freudian might interpret the play as the representation of an oedipal instinct to connect with the mother or as a need to return to the obscure safety of the womb. Conversely, and more in keeping with the historical setting, this might be interpreted as a drive to leave the dark and dank recesses of the maternal culture in search of autonomy. Since *Mithridate* is a tragedy concerning "the King of Pontus and of many other realms," as Racine puts it, the story also involves a symbol of freedom to the peoples subjugated by Rome whose movement has lately been circumscribed and who is no longer capable of breaking out, traversing, and transgressing the Roman law. For Mithridate, lack of mobility means a denial of his essence; it mirrors the ultimate stasis, death.

Racine attempts to infuse some local color into the drama in a couple of allusions to the legendary fierce climate of the region. Pharnace refers to "this wild country" (228), and Monime speaks of this "barbaric country" (1528). For the seventeenth-century public, the moral connotations of *wild* and *barbaric* would have presided over the meteorological or geographical referents. But this same public might well have been aware that the Black Sea region where *Mithridate* takes place (the Crimean peninsula) was known for so long for its inhospitable character that the Greeks named it "Pontus Euxinus, the Welcoming Sea," in an unsuccessful effort to change its nature through euphemism. It was also closed to commerce from the west during most of the seventeenth century.[8]

Mithridate clearly knows Nymphea well because he has ruled over it for 40 years. All the figures in the play realize that there are attendant spaces beyond Nymphea, and there are loci evoked in the cognitive mapping they have done since arriving in the port city, such as the palace, the rampart, the tower, and the altar.[9] Early on, we discover that one of Mithridate's strengths as a military strategist is his ability to break out of geographical boundaries to attack Rome.

In his speech of act 3, the king outlines his plans for fomenting revolt against Rome as he travels through the territories that separate

Nymphea from Italy. In so doing, "Mithridate . . . moves from a realistic appraisal of his situation to no less than a reconstruction of space, from reality to ideal conquest, not only over the Romans but over space itself."[10] Yet Mithridate will be moved out of his territories by the Romans and out of Monime's heart by Xipharès. Despite the diminishing of his territory and the waning of his influence that is the plot of the play, Racine allots him one final conquest of space, when the king sends Monime poison from the battlefield.

As every political leader has quickly learned, it is easier to conduct a foreign campaign than to ensure peace at home. Home for the returning hero is a place occupied, to Mithridate's surprise, by his two sons, each of whom seeks to supplant the father in his own way. This particular father, this "judge," as we have seen, will countenance no impudence, especially since his forte is making war rather than being a parent. For some critics, Mithridate represents the turning point in the evolution of Racine's tragic corpus, because it depicts the Return of the Father who stands as a major figure in Racine's last three profane plays: *Mithridate, Iphigénie,* and *Phèdre.*[11] Be that as it may, what is beyond doubt is that Racine has set father against sons in this tragedy.

William Cloonan sets the parameters of the drama of fathers and sons in *Mithridate*: "Mithridate is torn between a heroic self-image and a yearning for praise which threatens the well-being of individuals and nations. The characters and aspirations of his two sons reflect this dichotomy in their father's personality."[12] To be sure, the sons are not of equal merit in the eyes of the father, as small clues in the text make clear. Mithridate usually refers to Xipharès as "son," but to Pharnace as "prince"; Pharnace earns this political title because he is as attuned to power as his father, but is even more pragmatic in his pursuit of it, perhaps because of the generation gap. Pharnace seeks success for its own rewards, while Mithridate still longs for that fame characteristic of Corneille's heroes. Pharnace's lack of scruples recalls Acomat's in *Bajazet*. At one point he even sounds the note that is essential to the delicate equilibrium that the sultan Amurat has established in *Bajazet*; just as Amurat's ability to keep the army faithful to him depends on winning the siege of Constantinople, so Pharnace suggests (882–86) that Mithridate's defeats may spell the end of his soldiers' loyalty. (In fact, his troops rise in mutiny in act 5.) Pharnace goes so far as to deny Mithridate's essence when he points out (873) that the king has several possible places in which to seek asylum and repose (i.e., immobility), whereas Xipharès reiterates that "war and danger" (i.e., risk and action) are the only recourses for a man of his father's stripe.

Xipharès, like Hippolyte, is yet another son who went in quest of his father, only to "learn" that the latter was dead. Just as Hippolyte did in scene 1 of *Phèdre*, Xipharès will insist on his father's positive qualities. Yet, while Xipharès may confess his love and admiration for his father, he does not much resemble him. One desire unites them: the destruction of Rome; but another separates them: love for Monime. Precisely because he possesses his father's heroic instinct, untainted by Mithridate's unprincipled cunning, Xipharès bristles at Monime's suggestion in act 4 that he flee temporarily. But in rejecting his father's essence (mobility) and his favorite tactic (trickery), he surpasses him ethically and accedes to the throne as the legitimate heir of the recently reconstructed king, who, in bringing together Xipharès and Monime at the end "signals his assimilation into the civilized world."[13] It should be noted that all of Racine's plays deal with succession. The play opens with the possibility of an unfortunate succession and ends on an acceptable passage of royal power. But once again one asks whether the change in Mithridate that permits this happy ending is credible.

Unlike Néron, who was a good emperor before becoming a tyrant, Mithridate, the tyrant, becomes a good emperor through his two "deaths." The turning point is the moment of indecision in act 4. The aggressive, self-confident king becomes rattled by the resistance of his fiancée and is forced to take stock of himself. In so doing, he almost seems to escape the confines of tragedy, just as he has habitually avoided the encircling Romans. He is more like a figure from tragicomedy or even comedy.

First, Mithridate's capacity for metamorphosis and movement recalls the typical hero of tragicomedy, who revels in the multiple possibilities that the genre offers. Mithridate defines himself in verse 563 as "Wandering from sea to sea, less a king than a pirate." Pirates, whose renunciation of allegiances is proverbial and who were known for catching their prey unawares, were frequently mentioned in tragicomedies.

But tragicomedy is only the initial step toward the genre that informs Mithridate's dreams, namely, comedy. The infrastructure of the play is the world of peace and pastoral bliss inhabited by carefree lovers. All the romantic permutations (Monime with Mithridate, Xipharès, or even Pharnace) would, in a comedy, result in a loving couple taking refuge from the inexorability of tragedy. Mithridate in particular expresses himself at times like a comic character. In act 3, scene 5, he sets a trap for Monime and in doing so sounds like Harpagon, the old man with the young fiancée Mariane (from Molière's *L'Avare*) when he is speaking to Valère, who secretly loves Mariane:

I've been thinking about my age, and it occurred to me that people could criticize me for marrying such a young person. This thought made me decide to change my plans; and since I've sent for her and am committed to her by my word, I would have given her to you, if the idea hadn't struck you as distasteful. (act 4, scene 3)

Mithridate makes a similar offer to Monime:

> My eyes are finally open, and I see myself clearly.
> Your beauty will be sadly sacrificed if I offer you,
> With my marriage vow, my age
> And all the misfortune which is my life's baggage. . . .
> I owe you my throne. Rather than regret it,
> I will place you on it even before leaving,
> Provided that you agree that a hand I hold dear,
> A son, worthy object of his father's love,
> In a word Xipharès becoming your husband
> Avenge me against Pharnace and fulfill
>   my commitment to you.
>
>   (1035–62)

Like Harpagon, Mithridate is very adept at pretense. Like Harpagon, he is unsettled by the possibility that someone has designs on his prized possession. As in Molière's theater, love in *Mithridate* illuminates the soul, makes one vulnerable and consequently unsure, indecisive—and human. A sense of isolation and exposure is a constituent element of Racinian tragedy, and characters are most exposed when they love. Comedy, then, rather than undermining the impact of *Mithridate*, adds a humanizing element to the complex portrait of the king in decline.[14]

   Mithridate is reputed to have been Louis XIV's favorite Racinian play. This is probably because Mithridate was not, like Pyrhhus, a "weakling" in love, but rather a conqueror, an international political figure, like Louis XIV leading the allies against the Dutch. This appears to be confirmed by contemporary critics who note that the love tragedy one expected of Racine had a surprisingly strong political dimension. While *Mithridate*'s echo of Louis XIV's military campaign surely attracted the king's attention, one wonders if the portrait of the warrior-king in love, with all its attendant complications, did not also strike a sympathetic chord with a monarch whose own private life buzzed with passionate intrigues.

Perhaps the unexpected complexity of Racine's presentation of the title character helps explain *Mithridate*'s relative lack of popularity on the stage since the seventeenth century. The challenge for this play, as for others in the corpus of classical—especially Racinian tragedy, is the avoidance of monotony, given the repetitious nature of classical anthropology and the problems involved when a genre is built on so few characters. (Pharnace appears in only five scenes.) It is also true that the vocabulary of *Mithridate* is neither rich nor original,[15] despite an exotic locale that would normally occasion an extended number of lexical items designed to establish local color. What we do have in this tragedy is that intense concentration, that "passionate monotony" so typical of writing in the second half of the seventeenth century. Few events, few characters, few words—less is more in French classical literature.

Chapter Eleven
Iphigénie

Eighteen months passed between *Mithridate* and Racine's next tragedy, *Iphigénie,* which premiered at Versailles on 18 August 1674. In 1747 Louis Racine sought a plausible explanation for this break in his father's usual practice of presenting a play at the beginning of the year by publishing a detailed outline of an *Iphigénie en Tauride* (Iphigenia at Tauris) that he found in his father's papers. Racine probably began to pursue the subject of the sacrificial priestess Iphigenia and then rejected it for the one he eventually developed of the (almost) sacrificed Iphigenia. There may have been another idea that he had been nurturing since at least *Bajazet,* and that deflected some of his energy from *Iphigénie.* In E. B. O. Borgerhoff's words, "One comes always finally to *Phèdre,*"[1] and it is not inconceivable that he was already contemplating the outlines of his next Greek play while composing *Iphigénie.*

Whatever the reason for the delay, Racine did succeed in producing the tragedy in the course of 1674, which was a distinctive year in French literary culture for it witnessed the publication of a series of works that are crucial to a knowledge of the seventeenth century. Boileau's *Art poétique* (Ars poetica), a remarkable résumé of thinking (and of some prejudice) about French poetry in its several genres, first appeared in 1674, as did the first four parts of his burlesque poem, *Le Lutrin* (The lectern). The philosopher and theologian Nicolas Malebranche published his major treatise, *La Recherche de la vérité* (The search for truth), in 1674–1675, thereby paving the way for a renaissance of Cartesianism (Malebranche was a disciple, albeit of independent character, of René Descartes). That same year saw the first edition of Louis Moréri's masterful work of erudition, the *Grand Dictionnaire historique* (The great historical dictionary), the Jesuit René Rapin's critical essays, *Réflexions sur la Poétique d'Aristote,*(Reflections on Aristotle's *Poetics*), and La Fontaine's collection of tales, *Nouveaux Contes* (New short stories), whose sale was ultimately forbidden because of their licentious nature. But the highlight of the theatrical season, both at court and in Paris, was Racine's immensely successful *Iphigénie.*

Racine seems to have sensed that he had risen above the competition, that he had in fact become the preeminent man of letters in France, if we can judge by his Preface in which he stakes out his claim as the reincarnation of Euripides in France. Having shaped the definition of French tragedy in the prefaces he wrote for the first collected edition of his works in 1676, Racine then makes *Iphigénie* into a model that fits his criteria for the genre. In what is surely one of the first salvos in the Quarrel of the Ancients and the Moderns, a cultural debate that wracked French literary circles in the last years of the seventeenth century, Racine speaks on behalf of Euripides to attack the Moderns as not sufficiently erudite. In so doing, he sets himself as the model of the tragic dramatist in French.

In his "Euripidean" play—which, in fact, owes much to authors both ancient and modern—he pays close attention to the principles of decorum and credibility:

> Without [Eriphile] I would never have undertaken this tragedy. For how would it appear if I had defiled the stage by the horrible death of a person as virtuous and as lovable as the Iphigenia I had to represent? And again, how would it look for me to resolve the plot of my tragedy through a recourse to a goddess, stage effects, and a metamorphosis that could perhaps be believable in Euripides's day but that would be too absurd and unbelievable in ours?

The first issue posed a thorny problem for Racine, the self-styled "French Euripides," because in his *Iphigenia at Aulis* Euripides had saved Iphigenia from sacrifice through the intervention of a goddess. His ending insults the modern demand for rational solutions. But the strict observance of such a requirement would necessitate Iphigénie's death. Racine saw that, in contrast to the denouements he had devised for most of his other plays that respected the broad lines of the myth or history from which they were borrowed, he had to change this one. He would protect Iphigénie as a concession to the sensibilities of the public who would not have accepted the punishment of vulnerable innocence. This strategy is practiced in Racine's theater especially when the characters are women. Men, such as Britannicus, Bajazet, and Hippolyte, do not fall under this rule because, unlike women and children, they are thought capable of defending themselves. As ever, the dramatist keeps his fingers on the public's pulse, even if it means taking his eye off the literary source.

The second issue addressed in the quote, plausibility, constituted yet another possible trap for Racine. While he was anxious to compete with the opera, which was enjoying great success in France at this time and which drew heavily on mythology, he dared not propose pagan gods as worthy of belief in the reign of His Most Christian Majesty, Louis XIV. Furthermore, unlike the opera, tragedy had a rationalist foundation, it had rules, it involved causality. Even when, as in *Iphigénie* or *Phèdre,* the plot called for a double level of activity, divine and human, involving a problematic relationship between the two, the denouement had to be effected by human means.

Racine had to make sure that the pervasive mythological allusions in the text of his Greek play did not complicate an appreciation of the moral dimension, for a literal reading of *Iphigénie* might conclude that the gods, not the mortals, control events. For Racine, in the modern psychological tragedy that he invented, the focus will always be on human, horizontal relationships rather than on transcendental, vertical ones. When Agamemnon says to Ulysse, "Lord, I recognize the futility of my efforts: / I will leave it to the gods to oppress innocence" (389–90), one might conclude that Agamemnon was here serving as a spokesperson for a Jansenist vision in which humanity has no recourse but to yield to a superior supernatural force. This would be, however, a shortsighted interpretation of *Iphigénie* because the many cries of outrage at divine sadism in the play are counterbalanced by strong statements of human freedom, such as Achille's "Yet, Lord, our fame rests in our own hands" (260).

Whether or not there exist mythological figures in a particular play, some critics have concluded that the Jansenist vision of God had a determining influence on Racine, that, in effect, his formative years with the Jansenists explain his tragic vision. Such an interpretation makes a connection that is difficult to establish with any specificity. That Racine gave unusual emphasis to the role of the passions in his tragic view may well have a Jansenist origin. Nonetheless, Racinian tragedy, like any other literary creation, is at once a medium and a message, a sound and a sense, a signifier and a signified. The "medium" in this instance is that species of serious drama called tragedy with all the artistic conventions and philosophical expectations outlined in an early chapter. Whatever the religious signified of the plays—and Philippe Sellier sees a kind of (non-Jansenist) "religious conversion"[2] reflected in the tragedies beginning with *Iphigénie*—they were theatrical creations destined for a secular public. Perhaps the fairest comment on the question of Jansenism and

Racinian tragedy comes from the pen of Maurice Delcroix: "The Jansenist influence on Racine is beyond a doubt, but it is also beyond definition . . . Beyond a doubt because one cannot conceive that such a relationship, confirmed by history, would not have left its mark on a man."[3]

Like other classical artists Racine sought out Greek and Roman mythology for its poetic value and its ability to create atmosphere and ornamentation designed to deepen aesthetic impact. If *Iphigénie* becomes more than the banal story of a father's predicament, it is due to the extension and enhancement of the play's import though mythology. Some of the exotic ornaments of the play concern its geographical situation, which, as is frequently the case in Racine, is the source of much allusion in the first two acts. The scene is "in Aulide, in the tent of Agamemnon," that is, amidst the tents of the Greek army. Aulide is in Eubea on the Aegean Sea and the point of departure for Troy in Asia Minor. (This is the fourth consecutive tragedy by Racine that faces east in some sense.) Even though the play involves the Trojan War, as had *Andromaque,* it takes place far from Buthrotum in Epirus in northwestern Greece, the scene of the earlier tragedy. *Iphigénie* may be the later play, but its action precedes *Andromaque*'s; indeed, the happy resolution of *Iphigénie* is the condition for the Trojan War, whose aftermath is the context of *Andromaque.*

There is nothing happy about Agamemnon's dilemma as the curtain rises on *Iphigénie.* He may be the commander in chief of the Greeks, but because the Greeks are fractious, his political basis is far from solid. At this pre-Homeric stage, the Greeks have as yet no self-consciousness as constituting a country, but conceive of themselves as belonging to separate states banded together in this instance by a series of sworn alliances. *Iphigénie* dramatizes the story of the fulfillment of a number of destinies—political, national, personal—owing to the spilling of a woman's blood.

Appropriately, Agamemnon is the first presence we encounter on stage because he is the one to make the decision that is at the heart of this tragedy: like Abraham, the king will be asked to sacrifice his child. Racine insists on this point by beginning his Preface thus: "There is nothing more celebrated by poets than the sacrifice of Iphigenia." To sacrifice is, etymologically, to "render sacred." We can expect the play to have a religious dimension that was not apparent in immediately previous offerings, like *Bérénice, Bajazet,* or *Mithridate,* nor even, for that matter, in the earlier Greek plays, *La Thébaïde* and *Andromaque.* We can also anticipate that Racine will put to good use the anthropological concept of sacrifice: one gives so that one will get. The sacrificial act is conceived as part of an exchange in which the return on one's "investment," so to speak, is seen as of greater value than the object offered.[4]

Agamemnon is immobilized in Aulide because no one can lift anchor for Troy until Artemis, who has been angered (by events that Racine never specifies), releases the winds that propel the sailing ships of the Greek navy. The price for this divine appeasement is, according to the seer Calchas, the "sacrifice of Iphigénie." If we first see Agamemnon as choosing to protect his daughter, this constitutes a radical shift. Before the play's beginning, he had tricked her and his wife, Clytemnestre, into undertaking a trip to Aulide, where the sacrifice would take place. Despite the dispatch of the servant Arcas to delay their arrival, Clytemnestre and Iphigénie succeed in gaining Agamemnon's encampment, accompanied by Eriphile, a young woman who had been captured by Achille. The conflicts multiply: Agamemnon against the Greek oracle and Ulysse, one of the leaders of the army; Clytemnestre against Agamemnon once she learns the real reason for being summoned to Aulide; Eriphile, who loves Achille, against Iphigénie, whom she hates; Agamemnon against the aggressive Achille, who is engaged to Iphigénie; and, from the first lines, Agamemnon against himself. The context for all these contentions is the world of Greek mythology, where gods take a capricious pleasure in intervening in human affairs. Indeed, the frame for the play's action is constructed of two speeches by Calchas, interpreter of the gods' will: verses 56–62 and 1743–60. Calchas, one of Racine's "invisible characters," is the opposite of Agamemnon, whom one always sees. Racine sets up this contrast because, on one level, this tragedy concerns the conflict between royal power and religious authority.

Despite political pressure from the Greeks and his personal sense of honor and duty, Agamemnon is about to yield to Clytemnestre's passionate defense of their daughter when Eriphile betrays their plans to Calchas. At this critical moment Calchas is quoted as revealing that the woman sought by the gods is the daughter of a secret liaison between Helen of Troy and Theseus. Her real name is Iphigénie, although she has been called differently since birth. Eriphile, recognizing herself and her fate, commits suicide on the altar prepared for the sacrifice of "Iphigénie." The winds blow, the fleet will leave, Troy is doomed, but Agamemnon's Iphigénie is saved.

This résumé mentions Agamemnon more frequently than Iphigénie. Why, then, is the play not entitled *Agamemnon*? Although the portrayal of women is surely Racine's strength, he does not necessarily prefer women to men as title figures (see *Alexandre, Britannicus, Bajazet,* and *Mithridate*). His principle, we will recall, is to award the title to characters serving as catalysts for the other major characters who define themselves and express their understanding of the crisis through their reactions to the eponymous figures. (But which Iphigénie is the title figure in *Iphigénie?*[5]) Since Iphigénie has apparently been chosen for sacrifice, Agamemnon is impelled into action—and to act in Racine is to effect an inner disposition, to choose, to decide.

The play opens, therefore, on Agamemnon, who has a heart-rending decision to make, saying, "Yes, it is Agamemnon, it is your king who awakens you." In one line we have a number of important pieces of information for the public. "Yes" indicates that we are privy to an action that has already begun, since Agamemnon's word is a re-action, a re-assurance. We are also introduced to two characters, one of whom is a king (who names himself) and the other obviously a subordinate. (Costuming and body language would, of course, make the relationships even more patent.) It is quite early in the day, as the servant is still sleeping. (His awakening "well before dawn," as he notes in verse 4, is the first sign of the connection between humanity and nature. To be precise, the play is set in motion by nature's refusal to cooperate with the Greek heroes: it resists their impulsive and impatient desires.) Finally, the fact that the king is already up and stirring before the servants rise suggests that something momentous is under way. Racine, who was hailed for the economy of his expositions, is nowhere more concise than in the opening lines of *Iphigénie.*

Another significant element of the exposition occupies verse 9: "But everything sleeps: the army, the winds, and Neptune." The sleep from which the lowly Arcas was awakened is only one manifestation of the general atmosphere of immobility that reigns. In the structure of this verse Racine indicates, by placing the "winds" in the middle, that the elements that surround them—the soldiers and the god of the sea—attend upon them. Just moments later we will learn that to cure the all-encompassing stillness, another kind of sleep is demanded: the sleep of death.

Verse 17, spoken by the servant Arcas, who is amazed at Agamemnon's depression, contains the germ of the king's torment: "King, father, happy husband, son of powerful Atreus." Each one of these connections is problematic. Since, for Arcas, to be a king is to be freed of all the cares of daily life that would beset a servant, he accords that occupation the highest place in his hierarchy of reasons for Agamemnon to change his attitude. Next, he touches on Agamemnon's family relationships, starting with his cherished daughter, then his wife Clytemnestre, and his father Atreus. Since our reading of Racine's corpus to this point has made us sensitive to the role that family ties play, we should stop and analyze Arcas's list in the light of Racine's usual practice of presenting, as John Lapp phrases it, a "family in disorder."[6]

When Agamemnon declares in verse 40, referring to Iphigénie, "No, you will not die," we see the resolve of the father to protect his daughter; that is, the self-defining "king" of the first verse ironically shows himself to be more a father than a monarch. Yet, he has been unable to sleep because the sacrifice of Iphigénie has also become a matter of state. (He soon admits that the sacrifice of his daughter holds a curious attraction for him, it "charms" him, and "excites the penchant for pride" in his heart; 80–82). But when he later decides to acquiesce to pressure and have Iphigénie slain, he has to deal with his enraged wife. Arcas lastly recalls a sensitive aspect of Agamemnon's genealogy, for Atreus was responsible for slaying his brother Thyestes's children and feeding them to him in a banquet. Arcas has unintentionally reminded the king that the family has infanticide in its blood. (Later, Clytemnestre does so intentionally, to great and pointed effect.[7]) The personal is complicated by the political because it is Agamemnon's position as king that colors his dealings with his kin. The first word of verse 17 ("King") can be seen to influence all the others, syntactically and politically. Yet, if, in Arcas's eyes, the roles and relationships listed in verse 17 are the signs of Agamemnon's good fortune, the king undoubtedly considers the entire verse a brief but ironic litany of the ties that bind him to acceptance—another form of immobility.

But, at a time in French philosophical history when Stoicism had definitely lost the luster it possessed until the mid-seventeenth century, Agamemnon is typical; no Stoic he, he chafes at the thought of resignation, especially to death. Racine has established a balanced perspective toward the idea of accepting death. He divides his exceptionally large cast of major characters (six in all) along generational lines when the subject of death is broached. Once the members of the younger generation (Iphigénie, Achille, Eriphile) know that they are condemned to a premature death, they admit its inevitability and even justify it.[8] But the older generation (Agamemnon, Clytemnestre, Ulysse) discuss the central issue of Iphigénie's death to the point where these exchanges form the core of the play's text. Confrontations desired or feared, debates, and open and public quarrels give this tragedy its tensest moments; if Racine thought to increase the number of characters beyond his norm, he must have relished the idea of the spectacle of strong wills in conflict in *Iphigénie*. This "Cornelian" side is incontestably prominent, but let us not forget the intimate display of human frailty that distinguishes Racine's art, as when a father in distress seeks the ear of a sympathetic servant.

In his conversation with Arcas, Agamemnon explains the reasons for his conflicted state, including "These names of king of kings and of leader of Greece" (81) that he possesses. When, soon thereafter, Arcas wonders how Achille will react on learning that Agamemnon used his "name" (100) to lure Iphigénie to Aulide for a supposed marriage, we have a second indication, within a short span, of the importance of one's "image."[9] In a remarkable intrusion of the future in the present that distinguishes this play, the characters are preoccupied with how history or myth will depict them. Achille is totally taken with the pursuit of fame, which he will acquire, as is the case with heroes, through accumulated acts of valor and, more specifically, through that one defining moment, death. While caught up in the anticipation of glorious acts, Agamemnon is also concerned about losing his humanity (as father, husband) ultimately for the sake of nothing more than a bureaucratic function (as king, leader). As an older and mature figure, he worries somewhat more about shedding blood than spilling ink. There are two identities, then, for Agamemnon and the other characters of *Iphigénie*: a private life and a public image. Like Alexandre, Néron, and Titus, Agamemnon sees that he runs the risk of sacrificing the former to the latter.

The "virtuous and lovable" Iphigénie is not exempt from this pattern. If at first she expresses doubts about Achille's commitment to her (597–617), she ends on a note that has become familiar to us: "If he rushes off to Ilion [Troy], it is for my sake; / And, satisfied with a prize he seems to hold dear, / He wishes to do all while bearing the name of my spouse" (622–24). Here, as in several other places, Iphigénie speaks of herself with what a democratic audience might well consider to be arrogance. Like Achille, she is not averse to recalling the indispensable role that she will play in unleashing the Greek army for its conquest of Troy. But we must recall that Racine, who frequented royal society, was painting Iphigénie with all the self-awareness typical of the daughter of a king. In fact, Clytemnestre stresses this value when she counsels Iphigénie, upon learning of Achille's supposed change of heart about the marriage: "My daughter, it is up to us to show everyone who we are" (645).

In Claude Abraham's words, "*Iphigénie* is a drama of identity."[10] This search involves one's past, present, and, most critical for everyone except Eriphile, the future. Like the play itself, the characters' self-appreciation evolves from darkness to light, from mystery to knowledge. Racine allows us to glimpse the operations of this development in his characters in several ways, one of the most effective being the recourse to moments of phantasm; that is, the junctures when the characters are inspired to imagine events that will never take place, but which betray the heightened state of their emotions. Clytemnestre (1297–1300) and Achille (1602–08) have different visions of the events that will transpire on the altar, and Iphigénie dreams out loud (1537–52) of Achille's conquest of Troy, made possible, as she insists, by her willing self-sacrifice. Agamemnon's soul seems constantly traversed by imagined scenes involving all the other characters. Phantasm in *Iphigénie,* as in *Britannicus, Phèdre,* or *Athalie,* very effectively reveals cracks in the defenses of Racine's characters, for their dreams bear eloquent testimony to their real fears and desires.

In this play full of concealed sentiments, Eriphile is the most mysterious figure because she lacks a known identity. Agamemnon describes her early on as "This young beauty / [who] vainly tries to keep a secret that her pride betrays" (239–40), and she defines herself to Iphigénie as "a woman without a name" (708). She does not even have a home to anchor her self-consciousness because she is an exile. She misses what she believes to be her land, the isle of Lesbos devastated by Achille, since act 2 closes on her cry for "revenge."

Without realizing it, Eriphile's confidant Doris sums up the denouement when she attempts to convince the fatalistic captive that "At the moment when you will lose a false name, you will regain your real one" (434).[11] Moreover, Eriphile, who gives voice to one of the most flagrant understatements in all of Racine ("It is not a great burden to be a foreigner, unknown, and a slave," 470), is attracted to the illustrious warrior Achille because he represents everything she lacks: roots, fame, and status; that is, the components of an identity. The final revelation of that identity permits all the other characters to sail forward to their destiny.[12]

Clytemnestre's forceful statement to her husband at the beginning of act 3—"You control everything in this place" (803)—resumes the drama of reality and image for Agamemnon, for his domination is illusory: the gods, the Greeks, his wife, his daughter, and above all his own emotions are waging war over "control."[13] To defend himself, and to reaffirm control, Agamemnon engages in rhetorical tactics designed to deflect Clytemnestre's pursuit of the truth and, more to the point, to allow him to arrange the sacrifice of Iphigénie. Since Clytemnestre does not yet know his true designs, he can first be devious, and then, when his oratory does not have the desired effect, he simply ends the scene with a command: "Obey" (819). Michael Hawcroft has demonstrated that, if the second confrontation between husband and wife (act 4, scene 4) is a replay of act 3, scene 1, Racine has risen to the challenge of renewing interest in a previously discussed topic by having Agamemnon's motive clear from the start this time.[14] Since Clytemnestre is now fully aware of his intentions, his defense is weakened, and she rends it with a wounding personal attack that ends on a note of insubordination. Possessing all the facts, she can now rightly refuse to obey him and, replacing him as "dictator"—the one whose word is law—she orders Iphigénie to "Obey my dictates once more, for the last time" (1311–12).

Act 4, scene 4 is also remarkable for its complex portrayal of the psychology of the various family members. While there is evidence, here as elsewhere, of genuine affection, other, less positive qualities become apparent. Odette de Mourgues notes pertinently that "The very strong awareness the three characters in the play—Agamemnon, Iphigénie, and Clytemnestre—have of their relationships as parents and child, husband and wife, put them in a unique position to be hurt and to hurt."[15] In act 4, scene 4, Agamemnon and Clytemnestre use their daughter as the basis for assessing the effect of the gods' cruel demand on themselves, as if Iphigénie were, literally speaking, the "object" of debate. Agamemnon speaks of "my blood" (1244) that will be spilled in the sacrifice, and Clytemnestre describes Iphigénie as the purest element of "my blood" (1272). Racine insists on self-love as dominating behavior, even in circumstances in which it might come into conflict with the fate of a beloved child.

He elaborates on the self-centered nature of his characters in the long-awaited confrontation between Agamemnon and Achille (act 4, scene 6) in which they accuse each other, precisely, of selfishness. If Achille speaks of Iphigénie as being the object of "my vow, my love, my honor" (1341), Agamemnon counters with the notion that he alone has the right to "dispose" (1346) of his daughter and that, in any case, Achille's thirst for glory in Troy is the cause of the peril in which Iphigénie finds herself. While the well-known clash of Agamemnon and Achilles in Book I of the *Iliad* (148–57) is the source for this scene, which has no equivalent in Euripides, Racine stamps it as his own by narrowing and personalizing the import of the quarrel. It is not about

the future of Greek civilization, or the political ramifications of an inva-
sion of a foreign country, or even the spoils of war. It is an *ad hominem*
exchange between two egotists. Racine suggests in play after play that
this is representative of the true motivations for the great events of
human history.

The crisis for Agamemnon, leader of the most legendary military
campaign in Western history, occurs when Arcas, who was initially seen
in the dark of the predawn, sheds the first light on the king's plans to
use the altar for a sacrifice rather than a wedding. His statement, in a
verse that occupies the exact midpoint of the play (898), turns the plot
around. The significance of this moment is underlined by Racine, who
has everyone, except Agamemnon and Ulysse, on stage for this wrenching peripeteia that marks the passage from a dramatic to a tragic order.
The reaction to the revelation is swift, if not universal (we learn Eriphile's sentiments only in act 4). It is also intriguing in its form.

Unlike any other scene in the play, act 3, scene 5 is built for speed; it
contains rapid-fire exclamations from all the major characters, with one
line (913) being shared by four different speakers. This rhetorical device
of quick exchange, called stichomythia, was very useful to dramatists
who needed to open an occasional—and emotional—break in the deliberate pace of the long speeches that composed most of classical tragedy.
In this case, the short bursts momentarily, but very dramatically, sever
the pattern of relatively long passages of which the play is fundamentally constructed. One could attribute this format to the existence of an
unusually large number of principal characters, each of whom (so the
actors would demand) would have his or her own opportunity to
declaim at length.

But is Racine attracting attention to the pattern for another, comple-
mentary reason? If Racine had seen his old rival Corneille retire to the
sidelines in 1674, he now faced a new, multimedia threat in the exceedingly popular genre, the opera. Was he attempting to compete with the
"lyrical tragedy," as it was known, by creating an operatic spirit in this
play (and in *Phèdre*) through the use of a mythological framework and
long, lyrical stanzas, during which the characters often weep? When
Ulysse exclaims at the end, in an extended narration of the denouement
filled with references to mythological and allegorical figures, "You see
me in this happy moment / Filled with horror, joy, and rapture"
(1731–32), is he not alluding to the emotions that the new tragedy in
music was supposed to provoke? Jean Collinet perceives this element in

Iphigénie and concludes, "Rarely has anyone, with such subtlety, translated music by words."[16]

Iphigénie is, then, the ceremony of words and music through which the initial, irrational demand of the sacrifice of innocence is transformed in such a way as to permit Agamemnon to affirm his kingship, Greece to become a nation unified against a foreign power, and Eriphile to commit the existential act that frees both herself and the other characters.[17]

Chapter Twelve
Phèdre

Voltaire is credited with defining history as the tricks that we play upon the dead. One need not be as cynical as the Ferney patriarch to recognize that the most irresistible of temptations for those who profess to reconstruct the past is to deform it. This temptation may consist in applying a veneer of continuity to unconnected events or in unduly stressing a particular moment in time because it suits the historian's (if not history's) purposes. We would be guilty of the latter practice were we to claim that 1677, a very special year for Racine, blazons like a beacon in its decade, attracting the eye of even the most casual observer. Compared to the pregnant year of 1674, 1677 appears rather unexceptional. Nonetheless, as we have seen (see chapter 1) it was a pivotal year for Racine and closed on the image of a Racine securely anchored to a position at court. Despite its uncertain beginning, it turned out to be a year of crowning achievement for Racine. Yet, after all the conflicts and cabals have long been forgotten, there will always remain Racine's ultimate accomplishment of the year—*Phèdre.*

Ever since the 1687 edition of Racine's collected works, the title of the play has been *Phèdre,* not the original *Phèdre et Hippolyte.* While it is undeniable that the audience is interested in the fate of the couple Phèdre-Hippolyte, the title change defines the true focus of Racine's tragedy. He states in the first line of his Preface, "Here is yet another tragedy whose subject is to be found in Euripides." If the subject is Euripidean, the emphasis is surely Senecan, for Racine follows the Latin author in concentrating his play on the inner life of the queen Phèdre, rather than on her husband, Theseus, and his son, Hippolytus, as had been the case in the Euripidean version.

Racine thus presents his radically modified version of the Phaedra story, which had attracted a score of authors from Euripides (*Hippolytus*) to Mathieu Bidar (*Hippolyte,* 1675). It is the tale of a queen who, believing her husband dead, declares her love for her stepson, Hippolyte, who, unbeknownst to Phèdre, loves Aricie. King Thésée returns and, on the evidence of false statements by Oenone, Phèdre's confidant, condemns his son. Learning of Hippolyte's death, for which she is ultimately responsible, Phèdre takes poison and dies.

The Racinian play bears a close resemblance to Seneca's *Hippolytus*, except for one major aspect: the relationship between Hippolyte and Aricie, which does not exist in any of the ancient renderings of the Phaedra story. Structurally, *Phèdre* reflects the cyclical mentality characteristic of Racine's age. (For another example, see the concentric circles that form the structural basis of *La Princesse de Clèves*.) Inspired by biblical concepts of the identity of the patterns that govern human existence, and supported by the notion, dear to classical historians, of the cyclical rise and fall of empires, the seventeenth century believed that one day resembled the next from a philosophical, theological, and even sociological point of view. The moralist writer Jean de La Bruyère expresses the conception in these terms:

> In one hundred years the world will still exist entirely as it is now: it will be the same theater and the same decor, the actors will not be the same. . . . Other men will come upon the stage who will act out the same roles in the same play; they will fade away in their turn; and those who do not yet exist, will one day no longer exist themselves.[1]

Beyond their philosophical import, however, the circular patterns that Racine weaves into the text of *Phèdre* serve as a vehicle for certain basic themes. *Phèdre* is Racine's masterpiece, and the play's workings call for careful consideration.

The play opens as Hippolyte sounds the note of separation, of flight, even of exile, "I have made up my mind, Théramène. / I will leave the tranquil shores of Trozen." The multiple protestations of farewell by the characters, especially Hippolyte's and Phèdre's, are pierced by irony, and all of them will be immobilized in the unique setting of the play, Trozen, a city on the peninsula of southern Greece. Trozen, which Théramène describes as a "peaceful place" (30), will be the last place on earth for Oenone, Hippolyte, and Phèdre—appropriately and inevitably, for this play, like most of Racine's tragedies, represents what is, in fact, the last day of a life, the end of a journey.

The range of movement of the characters is wider and deeper than the physical universe, and it includes, for example, comings and goings into hell. Characters also project themselves and others into imagined places: Phèdre imagines Hippolyte in Crete, in act 2, scene 5; and Phèdre sees herself in hell with her father Minos in act 4, scene 6.

But Hippolyte insists on fleeing "this place," not, as Théramène suspects, because he has been persecuted by his step-mother Phèdre, but rather because, as he finally confesses, he loves Aricie, who is a kind of "forbidden fruit." Being the last of a family, the Pallantides, that opposed the claim laid to the throne of Athens by Hippolyte's father, Thésée, she must not bear children capable of renewing the Pallantides' pretension to royal power. Desperately, Hippolyte has tried to retain self-control and pursue his favorite activities, like the hunt, as a means of diversion, but to no avail. His solution is reiterated as the circle closes on scene 1, "Théramène, I leave today, and go to find my father" (138).

Seconds later, Phèdre herself expresses a desire to flee, during her first appearance on stage (act 1, scene 3), in a scene that is the counterpart to the one between Hippolyte and Théramène (act 1, scene 1). In fact, Théramène, who acts as a narrator within the play, had already linked the two characters in his descriptions of them: "Phèdre, struck by an illness she insists on hiding" (45), and "You [Hippolyte] are perishing from an illness that you hide" (136). In scene 3 it is Phèdre who is hesitant and reluctant and who complains to Oenone that, although she is attracted to the light of day, she cannot tolerate its glare and must withdraw before it. Phèdre's ascent from darkness toward the light betrays, in a classically symbolical fashion, her longing to escape her own personal hell for a world where she might recapture what she has lost. Feeling complicitous in the abandonment of her sister Ariane because Thésée left her to pursue Phèdre, the queen is instinctively drawn to the purity of Hippolyte. The whole play will thus be bathed in nebulous shades of responsibility where considerations of guilt, innocence, and obligation constantly reappear.

Convinced that she is guilty of what Catholic theology would call a sin of desire, Phèdre proceeds to accuse herself of crimes against nature. Words of self-accusation tumble from her lips as she speaks of her "shameful" pains, of her face "hot" with embarrassment, of impulses that have "deviated" from the path of righteousness. As a partial excuse she may offer the hereditary curse Venus cast on her family that was responsible for the unnatural desires that ruled her relatives. But she is her own most ruthless judge and shuns all contact with a humanity she has defiled. This perceptive self-evaluation sets Phèdre apart from the characters who have appeared to this point in Racine's oeuvre. The latter took themselves for Cornelian heroes who had wandered into the Racinian tragic space. On the contrary, from her first appearance on stage, Phèdre sees herself as powerless to commit those heroic—Cornelian—acts that might change the direction of her emotional life, but would also be unworthy of her as a tragic character. Phèdre knows, but her knowledge is useless.

Ignorant of the source of Phèdre's torment, Oenone reacts as Théramène had to Hippolyte's reticence, pursuing the matter with questions and hypotheses. But when Oenone pronounces the name of Hippolyte, she brings him alive in Phèdre's conscience to such a degree that Phèdre will stay and speak. There follows a series of verbal explosions in which Phèdre articulates her secret passions. Explaining how she valiantly attempted to avoid Hippolyte—to the point of having him exiled from Athens to Trozen—Phèdre only succeeds in giving voice to the desperate nature of her situation, while revealing that nothing has worked:

> Hardly had I been committed
> In marriage to the son of Aegeus [Theseus],
> And apparently secure in happy repose,
> When Athens showed me my proud enemy.
> I saw, I blushed, I paled.
> A deep stirring arose in my soul;
> I could not see nor could I speak.
> I felt my whole body chill then burn.[2]
> I knew the source was Venus and her terrible fires. . . .
> In vain on altars my hand lit incense,
> I prayed Hippolyte, and seeing him incessantly,
> Even at the foot of the smoking altars,
> I offered all to this god I dared not name.
>
> (269–88)

Phèdre's confession bears eloquent witness to her problem. Her physical attraction to Hippolyte ("I blushed . . . I could not see . . ."), the ease with which passion dominated reason, the hereditary curse of Venus on Phèdre's family that drives the individuals to an illicit, unnatural love (Phèdre's mother, Pasiphaé, gave birth to the minotaur, half-bull, half-man)—these autobiographical revelations appear in this passage.[3] Moreover, despite her efforts to separate herself from Hippolyte—emotionally and geographically—fate has reunited them in Trozen, and time has intensified her need for him.

Phèdre's avowal causes her as much suffering as it gives relief, for now the secret that had been festering within her has been unlocked.

Her shame has become more acute because of what she considers to be an incestuous desire for her stepson (Hippolyte is the son of Thésée and the Amazon queen Antiope). At the scene's end, in keeping with her original resolve, she vows to avoid light and life:

> I have told you all, and I do not regret it,
> Provided that, respecting the imminence of my death,
> You no longer afflict me with unjust reproach,
> And that you cease useless attempts to breathe
> Warm life into an almost cold body.
>
> (312–16)

As numerous observers have noted, the entire play can be said to take place between "Phèdre dying" and "Phèdre dead."

Immediately upon Phèdre's last word of verse 316, however, one of her attendants, Panope, rushes on stage to report the news of King Thésée's death. This development—one of the many occasions in classical tragedy when false news liberates characters—halts the circular movements in which both Hippolyte and Phèdre were entrapped. The king's death means the possibility of freedom, of new direction; Hippolyte may be able to pursue his love for Aricie, legitimately, and Phèdre, who ignores the existence of a rival for Hippolyte's heart, need not remain, guilt-ridden, in the shadows. Dazed by the news (and displaying no remorse for the loss of her husband), Phèdre yields to Oenone's insistence and permits her nurse to approach Hippolyte on her behalf for ostensibly "political" reasons: to achieve a coalition of forces to prevent Aricie's usurpation of the throne. On this note of hope, act 1 ends.

In act 2 we meet the object of Hippolyte's love, Aricie. The peripeteia of Thésée's apparent death has altered her situation as well. She is intrigued by a second piece of news disclosed by her confidant, Ismène: Hippolyte is attracted to her. Since both Aricie and Hippolyte descend, ultimately, from Jupiter, they share certain common traits, most notably a certain aggressivity. It is, in fact, the idea of having "conquered" the heretofore unconquerable young man that flatters a sadomasochistic tendency in Aricie:

> No, but to twist an inflexible will,
> To pain a soul supposedly invulnerable,
> To bind a slave dazzled by his chains,

And softly complaining of the pleasing fetters,
That is what I want, that is what excites me.
Hercules was more easily disarmed than Hippolyte.
(449–54)

The reference to Hercules is one of several throughout the text, because Thésée's exploits were performed in imitation of Hercules's. Every time that Hippolyte compares himself to his father, he is also implicitly measuring up to Hercules, in both of the peasant god's favorite pastimes: he was a mighty conqueror, protecting civilization against monsters, and he made many a conquest in the lists of love, for example, deflowering 49 virgins in a single night and siring 50 children as a consequence.

Hippolyte, the would-be Hercules, arrives (act 2, scene 2), with the intention of informing Aricie of her freedom, sputtering farewells, and finally, despite himself, declaring his love. His confession is punctuated with expressions of separation, of which the most revealing are those voicing an inner discontinuity:

Subject at last to the common fate,
By what disquiet am I estranged from myself ? . . .
And I for all my pointless pains,
I seek myself and find me not.   estrangement
My bow, my spears, my chariot,   confusion
All are now bothersome.
I have forgotten my training from Neptune.[4]
Only my laments echo in the woods,
And my idle steeds have forgotten my voice.
(535–52)

This moment reveals a new aspect of the theme of displacement visible throughout Racine's works: a strong emphasis on alienation. Hippolyte (and Phèdre) become increasingly conscious of the distance that separates them from what should be, or used to be, the center of their existence. In the last act of the play, Théramène describes Hippolyte in a state of total alienation. His horses no longer recognizing their master's voice, he is dragged to a ghastly death that renders him physically unrecognizable. Racine conjures up a final plastic image to reinforce the vision of Hippolyte's psychological shattering. The playwright's complex portrayal of physical, psychological, and emotional fragmentation was evidently so compelling that Charles Le Brun, the illustrator for the frontispiece of the first edition of the play, chose to depict the dying Hippolyte as the pictorial representation of the tragedy.

Scene 5 of act 2 represents a high point in the drama and is one of the legendary scenes in French theater. Phèdre has come to seek out Hippolyte, who has little patience for small talk with the queen. His aloofness only encourages Phèdre to be less circumspect. At first she is paralyzed by the sight of the prince (581): "He is here. My blood retreats toward my heart," a reflection of the Cartesian theory that when the blood withdraws from the extremities to the heart the individual becomes introverted (and vice versa). She then becomes suggestive, proposing that Hippolyte is so much the image of Thésée that the son's presence is a troublesome, yet idealized reminder of the lost father, to the point where, in a telling reversal, it is the son who lends physical features to the father:

> Yes, Prince, I languish, I am on fire for Thésée,
> I love him—. . .
> Your manner, your eyes, your speech were his,
> This noble virtue colored his cheeks,
> When he crossed the waves from our dear Crete,
> Worthy object of the dreams of Minos's daughters.
>   (634–44)

Phèdre gradually loses control, passing from the role of mother and wife of Thésée, to that of wife of the "new" Thésée, to that of lover:

> Love would have inspired the idea in me.
> It is I, Prince, I whose useful counsel
> Would have taught you the paths of the Labyrinth.
> How I would have toiled for this seductive face!
> Spooling out a thread would not have been enough for me,
> Loving companion in the danger you had to pursue,
> No, I would have gone on before you,
> And Phèdre with you in the Labyrinth
> Would have been found, or gladly lost.
>   (654–62)

In a passage that constitutes a labyrinth of words, Phèdre seeks out Hippolyte to teach the road to passion as an older, experienced woman to a younger man. When she clarifies her intentions, his horrified reaction deepens her sense of shame and reveals her conflicting heredity—as the daughter of Pasiphaé, she is seized by an immoral passion, but since her father, Minos, judges all creatures in hell, she also judges herself, harshly. Yet, one of the truths dramatized in *Phèdre*, as in much seventeenth-century classical literature, is that neither lucidity nor sincerity is necessarily helpful in resolving an emotional problem. *Phèdre* is the dramatization of how consciousness of failure is a noble human trait.

What the queen does not know, of course, is Hippolyte's assessment of himself. Consequently, she is in no position to calculate the real effect of her words on Hippolyte. The comparison to his hero father can only intensify that sense of inferiority he has expressed from the beginning. Instead of flattering him, she triggers an unwelcome fit of introspection. When he reacts to her open declaration (which, like all such statements, is an attempt at seduction), she instinctively tries to combine satisfaction and solution by imploring Hippolyte to slay her, or, if he cannot bring himself to do so, to lend her his blade. On her knees before the instrument of penetration, Phèdre pleads, "Give me it" (711). The temptation to view this scene through the prism of depth psychology is irresistible; clearly, Phèdre would be thrilled to die in a symbolic act of consummation with Hippolyte. That Racine's works often lend themselves to interpretations of this nature can be explained by the fact that, of all the tragic dramatists from the early Renaissance to the 1670s who took their cues from Seneca, Racine alone understood the dramatic effectiveness of portraying, as the Roman had done, the pathology of the sexual drive. The skillful (and daring) transposition of this element to the French stage constitutes one of Racine's signal achievements.

After Phèdre's frank declaration of love, Hippolyte still displays revulsion toward Phèdre's attempt at seduction; thus, Oenone can easily persuade her to exit before Théramène arrives. Hippolyte, confused and even ashamed of the role that he unwittingly played in Phèdre's personal drama, repeats his ironic formula, "Come, let us go, Théramène" (717), and decides to investigate both the current political crisis (Phèdre's son has been crowned king) and the rumor that Thésée may be alive. Thus ends the "Act of Declarations," as Jean-Louis Barrault has called it,[5] in which, precisely because the characters have verbalized their passions to the objects of their desire, "les jeux sont faits"—there can be no withdrawal from the game.

At the beginning of act 3, Phèdre, acutely aware of her shame, but nonetheless willing to pursue an Hippolyte who is now fully cognizant of her feelings, announces her decision to Oenone:

> At least I will not be left for a rival.
> All your advice is, finally, off the mark,
> Serve my passion, Oenone, and not my reason. . . .
> Go and find this ambitious boy, Oenone. . . .
> To bend him try every means. . . .
> Do not be ashamed to adopt a plaintive tone.
> I sanction all.
>
>   (790–811)

Then Phèdre goes one step further and implores her nemesis Venus to aid her in inspiring passion in the prince. The 12 lines of this short scene (act 3, scene 2) momentarily cast Phèdre in a new light, for she is ready to throw off the mantle of sorrow and guilt, having already opted to follow instinct, not reason.

The edifice of her hope collapses when Oenone rushes in (act 3, scene 3) to correct the inaccurate report of Thésée's death. This major peripeteia is reported, as in *Iphigénie,* in a verse that is the exact midpoint of the tragedy (827). Not only is he alive, but he has just arrived in Trozen. This second reversal of the action (the first was the report of Thésée's death) forces a return to the initial situation of the drama: a wife possesses an adulterous love for her stepson. If, however, Racine begins to trace a circle once again, its outlines are blacker than ever, for Phèdre has given expression to what was a secret desire. Phèdre argues that because suicide would leave her sons without protection, she must continue her accursed existence. Yet, we suspect that she is clinging to life, for life is hope, and she still longs for some miraculous union with the pure and purifying version of Thésée that she sees in Hippolyte. It becomes clear that the fact influencing Phèdre's conduct is not the return of Thésée, but her continued ignorance of the existence of a rival.

Dazed by the news of Thésée's reappearance—resurrection, practically, as he had been wandering in Hades—Phèdre passively accepts Oenone's proposal that Hippolyte be accused of trying to force his intentions on his stepmother. Oenone suggests that this reversal of the truth would be supported by the "evidence" of Hippolyte's sword, which he dropped in disgust at Phèdre's declaration of love in act 2 (a detail whose usefulness Racine learned from Seneca) and that the expected punishment would be limited to exile.

In act 3, scene 4 we meet Thésée. The return of the hero is not, as might be expected, a source of familial, perhaps even religious unification. Since its founding by Thésée's maternal grandfather, Pitthée, Trozen had been a refuge for those who seek peace and purification. Rather, Thésée is amazed to see his wife excuse herself and his son request permission to leave and "Disappear from any place traversed by your spouse" (925–26). The unsuspecting father—the only one of the three principal characters who has no clandestine passion troubling him—arrives home to preside over the dissolution of his family!

The two speeches that make up scene 5 deserve special attention, because they illuminate the relationship between the "new" and the "old" Thésée, as Phèdre would see it. The confrontation between father and son, alone on stage except for faithful Théramène, is a study in potential versus realization. Hippolyte once again dreams the heroic dream:

> But what duties now delay me?
> My idle youth has spent sufficient time
> In the forests pursuing small prey.
> May I not, shunning a shameful indolence,
> Redden my spear with more glorious blood? . . .
> Your feats allowed Hercules to rest,
> And to rely on you to pursue his tasks.
> And I, unknown son of such a famed father,
> I am far from rivaling even my mother's deeds.
>   (932–46)

Hippolyte ends his plea by speaking of monsters. If Hippolyte is another Thésée, he is a Thésée now tamed, immobilized, disarmed—literally, in the scene of Phèdre's confession of love. Phèdre and Aricie are attracted to him in their way, because of his virginity, his innocence, which is to say that he is not his father's son. He has not become the international seducer, the Don Juan, that is Thésée:[6]

> Permit, if any monster has escaped you,
> That I be the one to bring you its honorable remains,
> Or that, the testimony of an heroic death

Immortalizing the end of a noble career,
Prove to all posterity that I was your son.

(948–52)

It is precisely to this heroic image that Thésée responds, recounting how
he dwelled in the nether regions among beasts and monsters that he
succeeded in escaping. In Hippolyte's eyes Thésée's whole career has
been illustrated by positive, heroic accomplishments that excuse all of
his father's other conquests. Thésée has made war, therefore he can
make love. Hippolyte is sensitive to the need to prove himself as an
authentic hero, the better to condone his forbidden love for Aricie. Yet,
when offered the opportunity to slay a "monster"—a being whose existence is an affront to nature—in act 2, scene 5, Hippolyte dropped his
sword and fled in disgust.

Racine pursues the image of the monster (the word occurs 14 times
in *Phèdre* out of a total of 30 appearances in Racine's entire poetic corpus) so often that it assumes thematic and ironic proportions. In act 3,
scene 3 Phèdre had referred to Hippolyte as a "monster" (884). Not
only is he incapable of purging the earth of monsters,[7] but he has
become one himself. Racine underlines the negative character of Hippolyte by placing him among the objects of heroic endeavors. By this
transposition, Racine subtly previews, as it were, the demise of Hippolyte.

The prince is, however, very much alive at the end of act 3 as he
sounds a note of determination:

A future black with danger seizes my soul.
But innocence has surely nothing to fear.
Let us see by what happy tactic
I can recall my father's feeling for me,
And speak of a love he may wish to suppress,
But which all his power could never shake.

(995–1000)

Just as Phèdre made a decision to follow the dictates of her passion in
scene 1, so Hippolyte completes the cycle by proclaiming his own irrevocable love.

Irony seems to be implicit in the tragic vision, and Racine is nowhere
more ironic than in act 3: the mother finding solace in the lack of a rival,

the son exclaiming that innocence has nothing to fear, and the father-hero, seeking the security of the hearth—symbol of stability, of rooted-ness—discovering instead a family in disorder, almost in full flight.

We have noted in earlier chapters that the fourth act always contains the moment of greatest intensity in Racine's five-act plays. The tradition of French tragedy usually focused on act 4 considered in its largest temporal sense, that is, all that happens immediately preceding, during, and shortly after the fourth act. In *Phèdre,* Oenone has made her false accusation against Hippolyte in the few seconds that precede the reprise following the intermission. We may assign at least two reasons to explain Racine's conscious decision not to present Oenone slandering Hippolyte. (Given the seventeenth-century prejudice that noble birth is manifested in noble conduct, it would be unthinkable for Racine to have given this ignoble task to anyone but a social inferior.) First, the scene of Oenone's slander is unnecessary, dramatically, because the significant spectacle is not Oenone's performance but Thésée's reaction—which is, in fact, what Racine portrays as act 4 opens. The desire for concision is complemented, in this instance, by a sensitivity to public standards of decency. To depict Oenone outrageously offending justice by maligning the innocent prince might have shocked the audience. Racine, who may dare to be suggestive (Phèdre's open effort at seduction, a vocabulary of transgressive terms like *incest* and *adultery*), saw the advantage of practicing restraint in this case.

Thésée, whose willful temperament makes him ill-suited for adhering to stoic virtues, displays no patience or forbearance, "Ah! What have you said? The traitor, / Conceived this bold outrage to his father's honor?" (1001–02). His anger reaches a peak when the object of his wrath appears. Despite Hippolyte's discreet endeavor to defend himself without directly accusing Phèdre and by pointing to the only kind of reputation he has been able to acquire in the land—"I have made incivility a virtue. / . . . The light of day is no purer than the dark of my soul" (1110–11)—Thésée remains implacable. Indeed, the truth—that Hippolyte loves Aricie—only doubles the crime in Thésée's eyes: to lust is added perjury. He forthwith dismisses his son—"For the last time, leave my sight" (1154)—thereby giving Hippolyte the decisive impetus to undertake the escape he has been meditating for so long. Upon Hippolyte's departure, Thésée invokes Neptune's aid in exacting vengeance, in a scene (act 4, scene 3) short in time, but long in consequence.

One of the ironies of *Phèdre* is that Thésée, whose moral reputation is hardly impeccable, is called upon to play the role of judge—and jury.

The arrival of the king reestablishes law and order, at least apparently, and he proceeds to dispense justice in the manner of a magistrate. He listens to the accuser (Oenone), interrogates the accused (Hippolyte), and pronounces his judgment—condemnation, despite an evident conflict of interest as being both judge and plaintiff. In act 5, however, his growing doubts cause him to try to suspend the execution of his sentence, reopen the investigation, and seek the truth, which he finally discovers in the "Récit de Théramène" (Théramène's speech). The guarantor of order in the kingdom becomes guilty of irresponsibility through his curse on his innocent son, whom he thought guilty, and who believed his innocent love for Aricie was of a forbidden nature.

When Phèdre appears in act 4, scene 4, urged on by mixed feelings of remorse, love, and apprehension, Thésée is still reacting to Hippolyte's "lie," which he then repeats to Phèdre. This is a decisive moment in the play. Until this point Phèdre was willing to pursue Hippolyte whether or not her husband was alive, because of her belief that the only obstacle to union with the prince was the latter's inexperience, therefore reticence, in love. Now Phèdre has reached the moment of tragic illumination: there is a rival, Hippolyte is capable of love, all her plans were in vain.

After a brief surge of jealousy, Phèdre recites two of the most celebrated passages in Racine's theater, the second (1252–94) being particularly striking because it contains a heightened statement of Phèdre's situation:

> What am I doing? Where will my wandering reason go?
> I, jealous? And Thésée is the one I implore?
> My husband lives, and my passion still burns hot?
> For whom? Whose heart is the object of my desire?
> Every word makes my hair stand in horror.
> My crimes have exceeded human capacity.
>
> (1264–69)

This self-questioning leads Phèdre to a series of terrible visions. Her guilt becomes all the more insufferable because, she imagines, it is exposed to the view of all her relatives, starting with the Sun and then Jupiter. An immediate and very human solution presents itself: flight. But to what place?

> My ancestor is the father and master of the gods. . . .
> My forebears fill heaven and earth

> Where to hide? Let us flee into the night of Hell.
> What am I saying? My father there holds the fatal urn.
> (1275–87)

She may flee neither horizontally nor vertically. Here the impossibility of physical displacement joins the theme of alienation, for Phèdre realizes that she has become, as she herself has said, "Disowned by all of nature" (1241), the universal exile.

At the end of act 4, Phèdre curses Oenone (as Thésée had already done to Hippolyte) for having led her away from the original path she had chosen (death) and onto the road to a life worse than death in its moral implications. After calling Oenone a monster, she casts her out. It is at just such times that the significant question of Phèdre's motives and responsibility seems to cry out for elucidation. This noble, yet lamentable creature has insisted on her own liability from the start. Yet, we are also witness to her claims of persecution by Venus, who "inspired" an illicit love in Phèdre, as well as to her accusations against Oenone, who urged a course of action on her. Basically, the problem is one that has preoccupied human beings since at least the formulation of ethical systems: the nature of morality. To require Racine to furnish us with a coherent answer in his plays is to deform the tragedies into philosophical treatises. They are, first and foremost, dramas, and as such they expose the human condition in its complexity rather than through the logical filter of the discursive essay. Indeed, *Phèdre* does for tragedy what Molière's *Misanthrope* had done for comedy 10 years earlier: it crowns the evolution of its genre as a vehicle for the refined portrayal of character. The vision of both playwrights is unquestionably influenced by the strong tradition of philosophical and ethical observation and description that starts with Montaigne in the sixteenth century.[8]

But what of Phèdre herself? What seems to be operative in her case is a simple and human mechanism: a tendency to share a responsibility that has proven to be an overwhelming burden. Looking at the world through Phèdre's eyes, we can see that she is excruciatingly honest in accepting the consequences of her desires. Occasionally, she externalizes her feelings and they assume the shape of Venus (when it is a matter of the original source of the passion) or of Oenone (when it concerns the maneuvers designed to satisfy that passion). Phèdre makes a conscious decision within the play (act 3, scene 1), and she must acknowledge the consequences of it. Without the freedom to make such a choice, she would not be accountable for her acts; without such liability, the notion of guilt has no meaning. Revealingly, Racine never uses the word *fatality* in his plays. But because Phèdre's experience of guilt is constant, a fair conclusion would seem to be that, at the level of the characters in Racine's tragedies, freedom of will is not illusory.

The effects of the two maledictions of act 4 are observed in the fifth act. Hippolyte is first seen preparing to leave in the hope of rejoining Aricie in a temple at the gates of the city, where they will swear eternal faithfulness to one another in a ceremony reminiscent of the contracts known in the seventeenth century as a *mariage par paroles de présents* (a marriage effected simply through the vows of the two partners). Recognized by both civil and canon law, this form of agreement had the specific advantage of not requiring the consent of parents or authorities.[9] Obviously, such a formula suits the purposes of Hippolyte and Aricie to the letter.

When Hippolyte departs, Aricie has a brief opportunity to inspire the first of a series of doubts in Thésée concerning the accuracy of the testimony against the prince. Thésée's uncertainty is deepened when he learns from Panope of the suicide of Oenone, his primary "witness." By having Phèdre's nurse drown in Neptune's domain—an exceptional means of dying in Racinian theater[10]—Racine offers a first, potentially reconciliatory denouement by joining the houses of Phèdre and Thésée, since Thésée is supposedly protected by the god of the sea. Racine separates the two in the real denouement, when Phèdre admits to causing the death of Thésée's son.

After hearing of Oenone's death, Thésée is desperately imploring Neptune not to act precipitously when Théramène enters (act 5, scene 6) to describe the death of Hippolyte in the famous passage known as the "Récit de Théramène." This funeral oration on the death of the prince constitutes a fascinating achievement, for in it Racine bound up the salient features of Hippolyte's situation as they had been outlined from the curtain's rise.

Hippolyte's first move to leave Trozen turns out to be his last, thus terminating the theme of displacement on an ironic note. But, as in Phèdre's case, flight is associated with estrangement: this horseman is slain by his own steeds because they no longer recognize his voice, a voice whose last utterance is interrupted by death. Not even Aricie can distinguish his physical remains:

> Then Aricie in fear arrived.
> She came, Lord, fleeing your ire,
> In the presence of the gods to accept him as husband.

> She moves forward, and spies the red and steaming grass.
>
> She sees—what a sight for the eyes of a lover!—
>
> Hippolyte stretched out, without shape or color.
>
> Unsure, she hesitates to believe her misfortune,
>
> And not recognizing this hero she adores,
>
> She sees him and still asks for him.
>
> (1574–82)

He whose fundamental desire was to pursue monsters and who had become one, in a symbolic sense, dies after his unique attempt at slaying one. When, as Théramène depicts it, a horrible creature, part bull, part dragon, is said to have surged out of the water to frighten Hippolyte's horses, nature itself recoils in horror:

> Heaven in terror regards the savage beast,
>
> The earth recoils, the air is befouled,
>
> The wave which carried it withdraws in horror.
>
> (1522–24)

The beast's description (especially its bull-like qualities) recalls the minotaur; here again Racine suggests that one of the causes of Hippolyte's execution is his submission to a forbidden passion, one that made him lose mastery of himself—an element of unreason.

Thésée's tragic illumination is incomplete until he learns from Phèdre, to his great torment, that " 'Twas I who on your virgin and dutiful son / Dared to cast a corrupting, incestuous eye" (1623–24). Thésée now knows of the injustice he has perpetrated by preferring the testimony of his wife (and her intermediary, Oenone) to that of his son.[11] But Phèdre will not even give him the satisfaction of punishing the guilty party, for she has already seen to it. Described as dying in the very first act, Phèdre whispers, in the play's last scene, that she is near death:

> I poured into my burning veins,
>
> The poison that Medea brought to Athens.
>
> The venom having already reached my heart,
>
> It spreads cold where never it had been. . . .
>
> And death, clouding my eyes,
>
> Restores purity to the light of the world.
>
> (1635–44)

There is no point to continued existence for Phèdre. Hippolyte is dead, and with him any chance of satisfying that profound need she has so often described. Now, in a faint, but calm, almost reassuring voice, she reviews her unfortunate story for her husband: incestuous desire, guilt, remorse, and self-punishment. She recounts the past, whose cruelty, as Jacques Scherer reminds us, come from its being in Racine an "infinite accumulation of atrocious moments."[12] The light is extinguished in her eyes as it is restored in the world. Phèdre, sensitive to the evil that she has inflicted, considers herself a kind of second Eve, who deserves to be cast out into the darkness. Upon her disappearance, there will reappear that purity she has so long both sought and offended.

In the last verses of the tragedy, when a sober Thésée first indicates a desire to "flee this shore" (1605 – 06), he is only echoing his son's wish at the rising of the curtain. The circle of separation—at least, of a longing to depart—is completed. Nonetheless, legendary wanderer and agent of much familial discord the world over, Thésée then evidences a willingness to create order out of disorder, by accepting Aricie as his daughter and reconstituting his shattered family to a degree. Hippolyte will be buried with all the ritual of a hero, thus achieving in death at least a ceremonial and verbal heroism.[13]

But the ending is not entirely conclusive. The question of succession, for one thing, is never resolved. Even if Thésée treats Aricie as a daughter, she is not so by blood. Her eventual ascent to the throne would nullify Thésée's action of slaying her family, the Pallantides, and would certainly be contested by Phèdre's sons. Moreover, the fracturing of Hippolyte is the visible sign of a pervasive recourse to modalities of fragmentation we have noticed throughout the play: physical movement (recounted or desired), separation, alienation, and dismemberment. The couples of the play are all permanently estranged at the end: Phèdre and Thésée, Hippolyte and Aricie, and the two whose cycles supported the drama's edifice, Phèdre and Hippolyte. At the end all are victims, principally of having misused language: Phèdre should not have spoken, Hippolyte should have fully explained himself to Thésée, Aricie should also have been more direct and less suggestive with Thésée, and Thésée should not have spoken so quickly.

In his greatest tragedy, Racine boldly rejects the classical principle of order and proposes fragmentation, not unity, as an elementary human structure. He thereby intensifies the portrait of his title character as "disowned by all nature," and he announces the discontinuity of the modern world.

Chapter Thirteen
Esther

The creation of *Esther* was an inaugural occasion in the history of French religious theater because it was the first play ever presented at Saint-Cyr that was composed for the convent by an author exterior to the institution. Previously, Mme de Brinon, the Superior of the house, had had her own tragedies performed, as well as the *Marianne* of Tristan L'Hermite (probably in 1685) and Pierre Corneille's *Polyeucte*. *Esther* also opened the way for a small number of Christian tragedies with musical interludes performed between 1689 and 1700. It did not serve as a model, however, for the other plays, since its goal was at least as social as it was pedagogical. The superior artistic conditions of its performances, the select nature of the courtiers invited by Mme de Maintenon, and, in general, the ambitious financial support it enjoyed distinguish it from its successors that clearly privileged the didactic function.[1]

Despite its unique place in literary history, *Esther* has commanded little respect from critics until very recently, as if its brevity, compared to the other tragedies of Racine, translated its lack of quality. It was often dismissed as a divine bagatelle, a celebration of God's victory over temporal force that Racine was obligated to undertake in deference to Mme de Maintenon. Nonetheless, the close analyses of the play undertaken since the 1980s have been refreshingly positive about *Esther*'s merits, even if they are not as impressive as *Phèdre*'s or *Athalie*'s.[2]

It is striking that, of all the biblical material, Racine should have chosen the biblical Book of Esther, which has always occupied a marginal place in Scripture and whose content is secular; indeed, the name of God is never mentioned. Condensing the events according to his principle of selecting only the minimum necessary, he presents a situation in which a common biblical theme—attempted genocide—is treated in such a way as to demonstrate the triumph of the Judaeo-Christian tradition over its enemies. Moreover, perceiving the need for increasing the spiritual dimension of his play, he introduces a subtext involving an event of major importance to the development of the religious tradition of the West, namely, the Babylonian exile. In other words, Racine is again establishing the basis for exploring one of his favorite themes, alienation. This is accomplished early on through Esther's request to the chorus (act 1, scene 2) to sing of Sion and its misfortunes, principal among which is the exile from the homeland and its consequences. In Barbara Woshinsky's words, "In *Esther*, exile, idolatry and adultery are symbolically linked because they all represent humanity's wandering from the truth."[3]

In Racine's plot, Assuérus, King of Persia, is a powerful monarch who cannot initially distinguish truth from falsehood. He is, therefore, the prey of his minister Aman, who so hates the Jews for their lack of subservience to him that he has obtained a royal decree calling for their extermination. Esther, recently married to the king, is urged by her uncle Mardochée to protect her people; she does so effectively by entrapping Aman in what appears to be an act of disrespect toward the king. Assuérus learns that Esther is a Jew and that her uncle once saved his life by exposing an assassination plot against him. He has Aman executed, offers Aman's place and goods to Mardochée, and allows the Jews to practice their religion in a temple they will be free to reconstruct.

Woshinsky sums up the success of Racine's response to Mme de Maintenon's solicitation: "*Esther* . . . represents Racine's utopic attempt to make God and truth manifest on stage."[4] Having spent his entire public career, culminating in *Phèdre,* demonstrating humanity's powerlessness to bring order and reason to its affairs, Racine acquiesced to Mme de Maintenon's request for obvious political reasons, but perhaps also because it gave him the opportunity to show that there exists an "ordering principle," a supreme being capable of assuring ultimate coherence and justice. Racine calls on God in *Esther* to set things straight as Molière had solicited Louis XIV's intervention in *Tartuffe*. Odette de Mourgues concludes in this respect that "*Esther* represents a case where the pattern of order supersedes the tragic pattern completely."[5]

In his reading of the Book of Esther Racine had to have noticed the many allusions to feasting and fasting. The Bible is famous for such references, but the Book of Esther—that "secular" text—abounds in them: *mishteh*, the term for eating and drinking on special occasions, occurs fully 20 times versus 24 times in the rest of the Hebrew Bible. In point of fact, there are a half-dozen banquets in the Book of Esther reflecting a variety of the typical functions of the feast:

1.   Ahasuerus offers his high officers and chiefs of the army a banquet of 180 days' duration to demonstrate his superiority as a leader. This kind of "one-upmanship" is what anthropologists call "potlatch."

2. Ahasuerus next orders a feast for the people of Susa (the feast is described in the Greek text as a *potos,* a "drinking bout"), in order to display his liberality; that is, really to use a gift to obligate others toward him.

3. Queen Vashti, who does not appear in Racine's play, organizes a feast for her women in the royal palace as a sign of solidarity.

4. Once he chooses Esther as his new queen to replace Vashti, the king gives a banquet to all his officers and servants, announces a day of rest for all provinces, and distributes gifts. Here food as celebration come to the fore.

5. and 6. There are banquets to which Esther invites the king and Haman, his counselor, and which, although Haman initially assumes them to be validations of his rank as honored guest, prove to be examples of exchange of favors between Esther and the king. A festive meal is the moment for exchanges of all kinds.

All of the preceding incidents lead to the establishment of the feast of Purim at the end of the book, when the fourteenth and fifteenth of the month of Adar are designated as annual periods of joy and feasting, banquets and holy days. Certain commentators have even gone so far as to see in the Book of Esther an intention to supply a historical basis for this major feast whose character is more popular than religious, and symbolizes, appropriately enough given the frequency of food and drink in the narrative, the survival and regeneration of the Jews. Precisely owing to this characteristic, children traditionally play an important role in the celebration—a feature that made the subject a natural for the "young ladies" (Preface) of Saint-Cyr.

What struck Racine about the story of Esther is the very orality that the biblical text features and to which he then accords a central place in a play that is replete with references to "mouth," "voice," "tongue," and which derives a great deal of its impact from being sung. Statistical analyses by Charles Bernet bear out the impression that the vocabulary of *Esther* is surprisingly concrete and is especially rich in the areas of clothing and food.[6] Since the climactic moments of the play take place *after* the three-day period of fasting recorded in the Bible, Racine decided to put the emphasis on the diverse functions of the mouth—and not the deprivation of it—in a plot whose turning point occurs during a banquet. Since it is Esther herself who organizes this feast, we should begin with her. Given that her role is to speak the praise of God, she utters the word *mouth* more than anyone in a play where that term occurs more frequently than in any other Racinian tragedy.

As if for the sake of contrast, the first usage of *mouth* is in the phrase "impure mouth" (173) referring to Aman, whose actions cause consternation among the Jews, who fear being "devoured" by their enemies. The next occurrences are found in Racine's version of Esther's prayer (act 1, scene 4, verses 248–92), one of the Greek additions to the Hebrew Bible. Racine easily succeeds in reproducing the key moments that structure the biblical text. The initial allusion to *mouth* in the prayer is to the word of God:

> You were pleased, in your love, to choose our ancestors.
> You even promised them, from your sacred mouth,
> A posterity that would last forever.
>
> (252–54)

Then comes the supplication for protection of the Jews' ability to celebrate God's goodness:

> No, no, do not allow this savage people,
> Drunk on our blood, to close the only mouths
> That, in all the universe, make known your kindnesses;
> And reduce to silence all the gods that never were.
>
> (269–72)

Thereafter, Esther changes the focus from a description of the discursive function of the mouth to its gustatory uses:

> For me, whom you keep among these unbelievers,
> You know how much I hate their criminal feasts,
> And that I consider as desecrations
> Their table, their banquets, and their libations.[7]
>
> (273–76)

Finally, Esther ends her prayer by requesting that God

> Accompany my steps
> In front of this proud lion [Assuérus] who knows you not,
> Order that, upon seeing me, his anger subside,
> And make my speech so charming it will please him.
>
> (287–90)

Racine has cleverly reversed the order that the last two elements ("table" and "speech") had in the Bible to emphasize, in the ultimate position in the prayer, the power of speech and rhetoric.

The rest of the play is a veritable lesson on the uses and particularly the abuses of the organs of communication. Despite Assuérus's assertion to Aman, "Lying was never part of your discourse" (583), Aman's mouth misinforms, is guilty of calumny (which is described as a sin where one has "pity in the mouth," but "a tongue capable of murder"), and is even responsible for inspiring the king's recurring nightmares. If Aman's is a treasonous mouth, then Esther's is just the opposite: by transmitting the news to Assuérus of the eunuchs' plot to overthrow him (see verses 99–100), she renders an enormous political service to the state.

Or again, when Esther faints in the king's presence (act 2, scene 7)—perhaps from nervousness, perhaps from not having eaten for three days—the king revives her with his "salutary voice" (641), while it is feared that Aman may force the "timid mouth" of the Jews to commit the ultimate linguistic and theological perversion, blasphemy. Elise says to Esther:

> And suppose the impious Aman, in his murderous hand,
> Making a threatening blade shine before your eyes,
> Wished to force your timid mouth
> To blaspheme the name of the Almighty?
>
> (754–57)

This struggle over the opposing values of the mouth and its organs attains its natural climax in the banquet scene, the only festive occasion that Racine retained from the biblical ones previously enumerated. At the outset of the feast (act 3, scene 3), Esther's companions raise their voices in song, in the traditional linking of commensality and concert. According to them, "the blood of the orphan" and "the tears of the wretched" (952) will be Aman's "preferred dishes" (953) and his "sweetest drink" (954). When Esther reveals Aman's plot against the Jews and the traitor attempts to explain, the king immediately signifies his preference for Esther's word by cutting off Aman: "Silence. / Do you dare to speak without the king's permission?" (1091). The next time Aman opens his mouth, it is in an act of perfect hypocrisy, to convince Esther that "The interests of the Jews are already sacred to me" (1150) and to implore her to speak on his behalf to the king. Assuming the position of a supplicant at the feet of Esther—the position, ironically, that he had always wanted the disrespectful Mardochée to adopt in his presence—he is surprised by Assuérus and accused of having designs on the queen. The king's consequent fury and his quick decision to have Aman executed arise not only from a perceived attempt to steal his most prized possession but also from the specific setting of the alleged act. Even before Aman had left for the feast, one of his allies, Hydaspe, had noticed his inappropriate humor and had asked him pointedly, "Are you going to Esther's feast in such bad humor?" (911); that is, he was not bringing the correct attitude to a ritual of communion. Finally, with Esther lying on her side as Persians would at dinner, Aman's approaching her could well be construed as sacrilegious, as seeking to undermine the cosmic symbolism of conviviality by introducing an element of erotic violence.

We realize that Esther has won when one of the young Israelite women who are part of Esther's retinue proclaims, "[Esther] has spoken. Heaven did the rest" (1227). Since the perverting element disappears with Aman's death, the play can then end on the full chorus's call for the name of God "to be sung" (1283). If we usually categorize the mouth as possessing three basic functions—the nutritive, the discursive, and the erotic—we can see that Racine has chosen to combine the first two in Esther's banquet in order to create, in effect, an indispensable fourth in this play: the celebratory. God's truth will be praised in song, as, for example, by the girls at Saint-Cyr singing Moreau's music. Racine confirms this view when he writes in the Preface:

> [At Saint-Cyr] they also take pains to teach those who have a voice how to sing properly, and in so doing they do not allow the girls to lose a talent which can serve to amuse them innocently and that they can put to good use one day to sing the praises of God.

The reign of divine justice could not have occurred without the defeat of God's enemies, in this case Aman and his accomplice Hydaspe who exercises the functions of chief security agent for the palace of Assuérus in Suse. Aman is thus one of the many traitors in Racine's theater, but a special one because his treachery is judged against a suprahuman scale of values.

Who is Aman? In order to make the villain conform to seventeenth-century views about class and crime, Racine adds a detail absent from the Bible: Aman's origins are very modest, and he strives to "correct the injustice of his destiny." He notes the irony of his current position: "Delivered unto Persian hands as a young child, / I now govern the empire where I was bought" (451–52). Since Aman's birth is low, his soul is abject; he is therefore capable, as a former slave, of imposing on others the tyrannical treatment of which he himself had previously been the object. Working with Hydaspe, who knows all the secrets of the palace—even the details of the king's insomnia—Aman would normally win the day. He is nothing less than a Narcisse in a religious context.

But Aman has a human side lacking in Narcisse, and the audience can feel some pity for him. In a sense, he is a man without a country. Moved only by personal ambition, he is the exact counterpoise to the individual he despises, Mardochée, who lives only for his people, his God, and as a surrogate father for Esther. Mardochée assures the continuity of the Jewish religious tradition in a pagan world. Aman's hatred for him is transformed into a desire to eradicate all that Mardochée represents, which explains the initial crisis of the play, the Jews being mortally threatened by the royal decree for their extermination.

Ultimately, the question one has about Aman is this: if he is a traitor, what or whom does he betray? As with Narcisse, his crime is that he has misled and lied to the king in his own personal interest. The play is full of denunciations of the minister more concerned with self-aggrandizement than with the public good, which caused *Esther* to be seen by the contemporary public as having a particular reference to Louis XIV's aggressive minister, the Marquis de Louvois.

If the minister is interested only in himself, what of the king? One of the important themes in the play concerns blindness and light, especially the light of truth. Until Esther unveils both Aman's genocidal plans and her own status as a Jew, Assuérus was fully taken in by Aman and had even told him that "my own interest is the only goal you pursue" (584). Saint Augustine had referred to the Book of Esther in his argument for the efficacy of God's grace: once He gives it, it cannot be denied or refused. Assuérus—the specific example chosen by Augustine—is portrayed as undergoing something of a miraculous change in Racine, as if God has chosen to convert him, to elevate his vision in a manner reminiscent of what transpires at the end of Corneille's religious tragedy, *Polyeucte,* where Félix and Sévère are "enlightened." If Corneille's characters were influenced by the Christlike example of Polyeucte and his willful martyrdom, Racine elects to embody the "light" in Esther, who represents the truth to be unveiled only at the most propitious moment to defeat error. Racine gives this moment (act 3, scene 4) its own "space," as it were, by noting at the outset of act 3 that "The stage represents Esther's gardens and one of the sides of the dining room in which the banquet takes place." In other words, the world has now come to Esther and her values will henceforth dominate. She will uncover the truth, Aman will be unmasked, and Assuérus will see the light.

Esther is Racine's first religious play and his shortest tragedy, just barely longer than the only other three-act work in his oeuvre, *Les Plaideurs,* and it is the only time he gives each act of a play its own decor. In act 1, for instance, the setting is in Esther's apartment, which fulfills the familiar role of the "private space" found in other Racinian tragedies and also recalls the notion of sanctuary dear to the Jewish tradition. According to Perry Gethner, Esther turns the privacy of these rooms into a "sacred space in which she can reassume her true identity as a Jewess and pray."[8] But the striking formal departure from what preceded lies in Racine's composition of a "sort of poem where song was intermingled with the narrative" (Preface). The singing was performed by the chorus (of "young Israelite girls"), an idea that was inspired by Racine's intimate knowledge of Greek tragedy and its frequent staging of a chorus. He also admits that he borrowed two or three notions about Assuérus from the Greek historian Herodotus. Evidently, *Esther* reflects both new and tried aspects of Racinian dramaturgy.

When compared to his mastery of poetry in *Phèdre,* Racine's versification suffers somewhat in *Esther.* Yet, the first of his religious plays does deal with an epistemological problem—the nature of truth—that is one of the constant preoccupations of his characters from play to play. Moreover, Racine's reflections on the nature of religious tragedy in the instance of *Esther* served him extremely well in his next—and last—play: *Athalie.*

Chapter Fourteen

Athalie

Over the centuries, *Athalie* has been Racine's most controversial tragedy. Voltaire's opinion—that the play was the masterpiece at once of French poetry and of fanaticism—set the tone for the debate opposing those who object to the representation of "totalitarian spiritual power"[1] and those who, in the light of Racine's Preface, see *Athalie* as the spectacle of the accomplishment of the messianic promise through divine providence.[2] But this difference of views is but the second phase of the contentious history of *Athalie.* The first began almost immediately after the presentation of *Esther,* which Louis XIV enjoyed so much that he commissioned another religious play by Racine. Racine did not greet the task enthusiastically and resisted as best he could, pretexting his time-consuming and important duties as royal historiographer. Nonetheless, the monarch insisted.

If *Athalie* did not make its first appearance until 5 January 1691, almost two years after *Esther*'s premiere, the delay was due not so much to the necessity for two authors, a dramatist and a composer (Moreau), to harmonize their respective parts and to train amateurs (the young women of Saint-Cyr) in both theatrical and musical representation. Rather, the delay occurred principally owing to the snipings of Racine's jealous rivals and the opposition of ecclesiastics who were outraged by the idea of convent students yielding to the profane pleasures of theater. Abbé Testu, who was both a priest and a dramatist, wished to take advantage of the delay in mounting *Athalie* and even asked Mme de Maintenon to replace it with one of his own creations. Wisely, she declined. But the cabal against the play took its toll, for, to deflect criticism from the religious conservatives, *Athalie* was performed with a minimum of theatrical luster: no costumes, sets, or orchestra (only a harpsichord). The reduction of the play's "multimedia" aspect certainly impoverished the impact of this epic spectacle. It was, nonetheless, very well received—by the king and his entourage, at least.

Since there were no public performances of *Athalie* in Racine's lifetime, those outside the king's circle had to be content with reading the play. The result was—and is—that some readers cannot sufficiently appreciate the drama's spectacular historic vision or the titanic clash that Racine sparks between the title character and the God of the Old Testament without the supportive elements that the dramatist integrated into his production. The criticism has merit, and is born out by the fact that when *Athalie* was finally presented at the Comédie Française on and after 3 March 1716, even in a somewhat abridged form, it earned an enthusiastic reception from the spectators. The play competes very favorably with *Iphigénie* for the prize of the most spectacular of Racine's efforts, with crowds of armed, robed figures, a chorus, not one but two speaking roles for children, a setting in the vestibule of the famed Temple of Jerusalem that opens up, in act 5, to display the interior of the temple, and a breathtaking *coup de théâtre* when Athalie is trapped and Joas exposed.[3] It must be seen to be fully appreciated.

Unfortunately, the vast majority of us will always be limited to being readers rather than spectators of *Athalie*. Nonetheless, the text is sufficiently rich to be rewarding of itself. Racine drew his basic plot material for the tragedy of *Athalie* from the Old Testament (II Kings, II Chronicles) and the Jewish historian Josephus. If *Esther* depicted the rescue of the Jews, *Athalie,* which has a much broader sweep, deals with a critical episode in the entire history of the Judaeo-Christian tradition. Athalie, daughter of Achab and Jézabel, marries Joram, King of Juda, and has a son by him, Ahaziah (Ochosias in the play). On Joram's death, Ochosias ascends to the throne and is slain by Jéhu, who has been chosen by the prophets to kill all the idolatrous followers of Baal. Athalie is the embodiment of Racine's two favorite themes: she is passionate in her drive for revenge against Jéhu for slaying the descendants of her father Achab; and she has a developed political sense that counsels her to attempt the extermination of all of David's line—her grandchildren—to prevent challenges to her authority. Her plan is, however, frustrated by Josabet, wife of the high priest Joad, who saves one child, Joas. The play proper begins when Joad learns that Athalie plans to destroy the temple, where Joas has been hidden for years. Joad lures Athalie to the temple, where she meets Joas. Despite her material power and the counsel of the treacherous Mathan, high priest of Baal, she eventually falls into Joad's snare, is encircled in the temple, and is executed by the Levites. The coronation of Joas assures the continuation of David's line, which will culminate in the coming of Christ. The drama operates, then, on two levels: divine and human. The interaction between the two is the major source of the ambiguity that pervades this play.

A sense of conflict is impregnated in the drama from the beginning, as Racine opposes Jehovah and Baal, temple and palace, spiritual and material, patriarchy and matriarchy, parent and child.[4] Just as in *Andromaque* and *Iphigénie,* the first word of the tragedy is *oui*, as Abner responds to a comment made before the curtain's rise by Joad. The private conversation that we interrupt is full of details about biblical history: the struggle between Juda and Israel, Athalie's rule and revenge, the origins of the Chosen People, and the imminent threat posed by the crafty Mathan, who has convinced Athalie that Joad has hidden "David's treasures" in the temple. The main topic of the second half of scene 1, the longest expository scene in Racine's theater (164 lines), is the promise of a savior who will overthrow the enemies of David. Given Abner's concern about the lack of evidence for God's willingness to intervene on their behalf, it seems natural for him to ask questions, but Joad asks his share, too, often deploying them to avoid answering Abner. Racine is evidently creating all the elements for a plot based on unforeseen events and surprise, within a story whose ending all readers of the Bible know: Joas will be crowned, Athalie will be killed. Yet, he succeeds in inspiring two different emotions from the outset, embodied in two different spokespersons. Like Abner, we fear that evil will triumph, and like Joad we admire the workings of providence.

If one of the goals of the exposition is to capture the correct historic and cultural tone, its allusions must be the principal vehicle, and Racine does not fail in this respect. Yahweh is redoubtable (Joad, "I fear God," 64); the temple represents for Mathan a refuge for the Jews, while also personifying their God; Athalie has reigned for eight bloody years in defiance of God; and the divine promise is the motivating force for Joad and his people. Equally as important in setting the tone is Racine's deft recourse to proverbial phraseology recalling the Old Testament's, in such lines as:

> He who can calm the fury of the waves,
> Also knows how to foil the plots of the wicked.
> (61–62)

> What fruit (profit) do I gain from all your sacrifices?
> Do I need to spill the blood of goats and heifers?
> The blood of your kings cries out, and is not heard.[5]
> (87–89)

The references to bloodshed just noted are everywhere in *Athalie,* which is, appropriately, as violent as the Bible itself.[6]

Each of the two men involved in scene 1 has a role to play in the "grand design" as well as in the design of Racine's plot. Abner is not a complex figure. He has the warrior's sense of duty and loyalty, and, like a Burrhus in biblical garb, is far from being a revolutionary. For that reason, Joad refrains from informing him of the truth about Joas until relatively late in his plans. Thereafter, Abner can serve his new monarch with the same clear conscience as he did his former one, Athalie. His interlocutor, Joad, is a remarkable figure: part prophet, part tutor, and all politician. His faith seems to absolve him from the normal dictates of morality, like honesty and sensitivity to human life. He has plotted and planned for years for the day represented in *Athalie,* and his belief is far from passive: "Is passive faith an honest faith?" (71), as he asks Abner. He has both an unswerving conviction that his God will win and supreme confidence in the efficacy of his own actions, as they are authorized by the God of the Old Testament. (Typical of those who are convinced that they have been entrusted with a mission, Athalie also believes she has transcendental support: "Heaven itself has taken care to justify me," 470.) It is Joad's wily but aggressive leadership in bringing about the denouement that gives *Athalie* the necessary dimension—human—for it to be of interest to us.

For the drama is not a paean to the omnipotence of God, despite the opinion expressed by numerous critics who find one of the last lines spoken by Athalie to be definitive: "Pitiless God, you have plotted out everything" (1774). It is, in fact, Racine who plotted out everything so that the human element keeps our attention. Were *Athalie* a theological disquisition, we might conclude that it was exploring the two eternal but contradictory truths of mainline Christianity: God is all-powerful and the human being has free will. This was the crux of the quarrel between Augustinians and Jesuits in the seventeenth century, at least in its religious dimensions. But *Athalie* is, fortunately, not a theological meditation, and Racine is right to accord Joad the role of primary mover within the fulfillment of divine providence.[7]

If act 1 belongs to Joad, act 2 displays his adversary. Before her actual arrival—delayed until act 2 as is often Racine's preference for major figures—Athalie is painted in the darkest colors, especially by Joad (who seems to have little patience for women, including his wife Josabet[8]). Athalie is depicted as "the archetypal destructive mother of patriarchal mythology."[9] When she appears, we are surprised not to encounter a monster. What becomes clear is that there are two Athalies: the biblical murderess and the maternal figure whom Racine has chosen to draw in much more nuanced tones than one finds in the Old Testament. In order to elicit immediate sympathy for her, Racine presents her as having been chased from the temple and, therefore, almost as exhausted as Phèdre in her first appearance. Instead of a self-assured imperial presence, we discover a weary monarch; Athalie is changing, becoming more self-aware and sympathetic. Jean-Marie Apostolidès goes so far, in political terms, as to propose that she is the character in Racine's work "closest to an absolute monarch of the Ancien Régime. She endeavors to govern wisely, has put an end to hostilities with neighboring countries, is open to religious plurality."[10] The dream she relates in act 2, scene 5 is both the catalyst and the representation of her psychological shiftings. In the first part of the dream, Athalie experiences the loss of her mother, Jézabel, and in the second, she, the mother, is slain by a male child. The vision makes her acutely sensitive to her guilt and responsibility for the murders of her grandchildren, and explains her conversion from filicide to mother figure in the scene with Eliacin-Joas (act 2, scene 7):

> What new miracle troubles and confuses me?
> The softness of his voice, his childish appearance, his grace,
> Make my enmity, little by little,
> Turn to . . . Could I be touched by pity?
>
> (651–54)

Athalie's dream, which recalls similar passages in classical Greek literature, is not a sign of divine manipulation, but a time-honored theatrical technique that does two things: it reveals Athalie's inner workings and preoccupations, and it moves the plot along smartly. Since Mathan has practiced deception in telling Athalie that the Jews wish to crown Joas, she has a reason to enter the temple—her desire to placate the God of the Jews—and it is there that Racine has her come face to face with Joas. In a reminiscence of the episode of Christ teaching in the temple, Joas teaches Athalie in a dramatic reversal of roles, as the child becomes the counselor of the adult in the ways of God. As is the case with teaching at its best, more than information is transmitted, and Athalie is touched by the boy. Once she returns to herself, she plays the devil, tempting Joas with repeated offers of "pleasures" and implicitly opposing her "promises" (696) of a temporal kingdom to the messianic promise. When he resists, she recounts the litany of her vengeful deeds and, consequently, of her dehumanization. She then dismisses him, and the first confrontation between material power and spiritual innocence ends as a stand-off.

But the dream festers in Athalie's soul, and if it centers around Joas, it also prominently includes another member of the generational line, Jézabel. After noticing the glittering image of her mother, Athalie reaches out and finds

> a horrible mass
> Of bones and flesh torn and dragged in the mud,
> Bloodied shreds and frightful limbs
> That voracious dogs fought over among themselves.
>   (503–06)

The close proximity of exterior signs of wealth to a description of the decadent reality behind the illusion poses a central question for this play, asked later by Joad, "How has pure gold changed into base metal?" (1142). Since the vocabulary of corruption in this decidedly religious drama is matched by the lexicon of wealth and money, one might conclude that *Athalie*'s subtext contains a lesson on the vanity of materiality. But the quote from Joad has to do with Joas: how will this "treasure of David" commit fratricide against Zacharie?[11] The lesson really is that there will be a reverse Midas effect, in which everything will be turned from gold to dross. This ambiguity in Joas is equaled, in its way, by a certain sexual ambivalence in Athalie. She is first described as daring to enter one of the spaces "reserved for men" (397). Mathan later accords her both female and male traits:

> She is no longer that clear-headed, intrepid queen,
> Who rose above her timid sex,
> And overwhelmed her surprised enemies,
> And who knew the very cost of a wasted moment.
> The fear of wretched remorse troubles that great soul,
> She wavers, she hesitates; in a word, she is a woman.
>   (871–76)

Her indecision, born of her dream, reveals a human side to the queen, which is complemented by her courage in challenging the vengeful God of the Old Testament.

Act 3 is dominated by another confrontation, between Mathan and Joad. Mathan offered Racine an opportunity to create a traitor out of whole cloth because the references to him in the Bible are scant. Racine rose to the occasion and drew the portrait of "the total traitor"[12] who, once he lost the contest for leadership among his own people, the Jews, joined Athalie seeking revenge and power; he has renounced both his blood and his religion and is, consequently, the object of the most damning epithets in Racine's theater. He has become the high priest of Baal, though he has no faith in his new religion. He has a cunning and a diplomacy that have served him well and that distinguish him from Joad and his "inflexible bluntness" (939). Because Mathan is a sufficiently important figure, we need to know both him and his plottings well. Racine has, accordingly, given this counselor his own confidant, the self-seeking and unscrupulous Nathan, and it is to him that Mathan explains the choices that he made to flatter his ambitions. As Descotes notes, the operative word here is *choices*.[13] Unlike Narcisse, who felt the need to compensate for his low birth with high designs, Mathan pursues power freely and unconscionably through association with the mighty.

It is in act 3, scene 6 that Mathan, whose name rhymes with Satan in French, is the object of a lesson that Racine offers on the use of metrics for psychological effect. Just after Mathan has left the stage, never again to reappear, his name recurs at the midpoint—the caesura—of the alexandrine line; the repetition is reinforced by the interior rhyme of "Mathan" from one verse to the next:

> Peu s'en faut que *Mathan* ne m'ait nommé son père.
> Au perfide *Mathan* qui l'aurait révélé?
> Votre trouble à *Mathan* n'a-t-il point trop parlé?
> [Mathan did everything but name Joas's father.
> To the treacherous Mathan who would have revealed it?
> Did your confusion give you away to Mathan?]
> (1048–50)

Since interior rhymes are deployed sparingly by Racine, lest sound detract from sense, the triple rhyme here is noteworthy. Josabet and Joad fear that Mathan may have discovered the "hidden treasure." His name remains, after his departure, to haunt them, indeed, to taunt them—and the spectators—with the possibility of betrayal. Racine's tactic constitutes yet another form of the "absent presence," this time due to the reverberations of interior rhymes. This novel usage complements the kind we have come to expect, and in *Athalie* there is, in this vein, literally a *Deus absconditus,* a Hidden God, who is present in every scene. The Jewish people, who are deeply concerned about the fate of their kingdom and the survival of David's descendants, are also heard and felt, if not seen. God and the people extend the boundaries of the play vertically (metaphysically), then horizontally.

At the end of act 3, scene 6, Josabet's fears about Mathan's suspicions notwithstanding, Joad decides to take action and to crown the child before Mathan can formulate a contrary plan. The reversals operated in acts 2 and 3 are symptomatic of the twists in this play of and on reversal. The normally aggressive and confident Athalie is indecisive, and Mathan is confused. Joad, who has been prudent to this point, throws caution to the wind and in act 4 makes a firm decision to expose Joas. If Athalie and her followers were quick in decision and action, it is now Joad who wants to set the coronation in motion "before the appointed hour" (1096). Time, once the ally of she "who knew the very cost of a wasted moment," (874) seems to have switched camps. And it is not only a sense of time that has deserted Athalie and Mathan but a general appreciation of the true nature of their circumstances. Both have yielded to the temptation of becoming a law unto themselves and are thus insensitive to the beliefs of others, such as Joas and his preachings about the equity of a "law" (662) that distinguishes between the powerful and the lowly. Mathan is morally beyond rescue, and the description of his demise reveals his significance in the Divine Plan: he is given all of a half-line: "Mathan has been strangled" (1708). Athalie, however, is worthy of attention. She needs illumination.

But illumination comes first to Abner, as if Joad, who acts like a stage manager, were trying out his recognition scene first on a secondary figure, the better to prepare for the major uncovering when the scene changes—*"the backcloth opens, the interior of the temple is revealed"* (act 5, scene 6). The recognition is double: Athalie sees the truth, and the child is literally unveiled, since he was veiled earlier (1700). According to Cave, "It is striking that Racine chose a biblical subject for his only unequivocal recognition play."[14] Yet, he did not eschew elements from Greek tragedy to bolster his Old Testament material, such as the use of a chorus to comment on the emergence of knowledge. (We will recall that Racine had noted his intention, in his Preface to *Esther,* to "link, as in the ancient Greek tragedies, the chorus and its chant with the action," and he does so in *Athalie* by having the chorus on stage for all five acts.) The recognition of Joas as Athalie's grandson is unequivocal thanks to a physical, incontrovertible sign: Joas's scar from the original assassination attempt, which undoubtedly reminds anyone familiar with the New Testament of Christ's wound and its irrefutable proof of his resurrection. Joas's escape, if not quite a resurrection, is a prefiguration of Christ's triumph over death.

Despite her claim of perspicacity ("Yes, you [Mathan] open my eyes, / I begin to see clearly the meaning of this sign from heaven," 609–10), Athalie allows herself to be lured into the temple because she, like many tragic characters, is blind. It is as if she, not Joas, were the one wearing the *bandeau*, for the French word means both "diadem" and "blindfold." Although we have noticed a change in her, she still seems oblivious to the fact that her past actions have consequences that are weighed against a scale of moral values. These values, like those of tragedy, exact a penalty for ignorance and arrogance, and Joad makes this clear in a succinct statement pronounced to a Levite just before Athalie enters the temple:

> You, as soon as this queen, drunk with mad pride,
> Has passed the threshold of the Temple door,
> And can no longer turn back,
> Make sure that our martial trumpets
> Raise a sudden fear in the enemy camp.
>
> (1681–85)

Racine must have weighed the effect that presenting the queen in an ultimate confrontation with her opponents—Joad, Joas, and God—would have had against his normal practice of having a messenger recount the final events. Just as he had in one other instance (*Bérénice*), he decided that the determining actions had to be played out in full view. Therefore, he has Athalie move into territory foreign to her views. In fact, the early description of her as a "foreigner" ("étrangère," 448) has to do with place as an integral part of culture: she no longer shares essential values with the inhabitants of the temple. Once she enters hostile territory she steps beyond the point of no return, morally, physically—and politically, since her army will be terrified. Her cry of "Where am I?" (1731) only confirms her status as an outsider to that sacred space described by Joas as "my country" (640).

The failed filicide of Joas will be succeeded, according to Athalie, by a matricide when she is executed. This prophecy is the culmination of a series of references to the dream that is the most memorable set piece in the tragedy. Zacharie reports the queen's stunned reaction at the sight of Joas (act 2, scene 2), as does Athalie herself (act 2, scene 5). She is in disarray in the interrogation scene (act 2, scene 7) when the circumstances remind her once again of the slaying of her mother. An allusion to Jézabel turns up in Joad's curse of Mathan (1038), and Athalie refers to Joas in the recognition scene as a figure from a dream, a "repulsive ghost" (1729).[15] The dream serves as a point of reference throughout, scanning the major moments.

Corneille called *Polyeucte* a "Christian tragedy," while Racine named *Esther* a "tragedy" and *Athalie* a "tragedy drawn from sacred scripture." Should one read in Racine's choice of terms a desire to avoid titles like "Christian tragedy," or "sacred/holy tragedy" that indissolubly link religion and tragedy? If so, what is the problem, if one can judge from *Athalie*? Was Racine uncomfortable with the concept of a "religious tragedy" whose terms appear contradictory, for surely religion furnishes an explanation for and a comfort against the tragedies of human existence? There are several possible ways of approaching an answer. In the manner of Corneille, whose *Polyeucte* remains the most renowned religious tragedy of the seventeenth century, Racine may have chosen to interpret "tragedy" as casting his heroes into the closest proximity to failure (i.e., losing salvation)—even if they do not ultimately fail—so that the audience experiences trepidation over the fate of the Jews in the course of the play. Putting aside its knowledge of the Bible,[16] the public is deeply concerned about the realization of the promise of a redemptor and suffers both pity and terror. From another angle, if this is truly the tragedy of Athalie, whose ambition to compete with the God of the Jews could elicit admiration, and whose doubts and hesitations we find sympathetic, the tragedy might consist in her being the scapegoat, sacrificed to the patriarchal law. Having crossed the threshold of the "place reserved for men," the daughter of Jézabel was condemned by the Son of David. Finally, the apparent material and spiritual victory of Joas at the end has an ironic twist because, as a Racinian figure who will be true to his heritage, he will eventually turn on Zacharie and fulfill the prophetic curse that, in her last moments, Athalie addresses to God:

> I flatter myself, I hope,
> That in unbridled revolt and tired of your law,
> Faithful to Achab's blood that he received from me,

> Following his father, and his father's father,
> David's hated heir will be seen
> Abolishing your honors, profaning your altar,
> And avenging Athalie, Achab, and Jézabel.[17]
>
> (1784–90)

Athalie had already made the concession, "God of the Jews, you win!" (1768). Her curse, however, shows an awareness that the struggle is not over. When Joas utters his prayer (1797–99) that God protect him from the malediction, it is a moving moment, for the child's plea is compelling. Yet, we know his words will not be heard. Joas will be faithful to his murderous heritage. For whom is this a tragedy, then, if Athalie obtains a posthumous revenge? The text offers no unequivocal answer, but it may be that the postplay reversal is itself part of the mystery of the Master Plan that leads to the appearance of Christ. The chorus makes the point twice at the end of act 3: "O promise! O threat! O dark mystery! / How much evil, how much good are predicted one after the other?" (1212–13) and "Let us cease worrying: our God, some day, / Will unveil this great mystery" (1226–27). In all of this, Racine's role is to serve as the Master Plotter of the drama that celebrates the interaction between the human and the divine inscribed in that plan.

In his last theatrical effort, Racine gives every indication of taking as much pride in his work as he did in all the previous tragedies. Instead of being satisfied to respond to an official request with an inspirational drama dashed off for convent students, he attempted to create a new genre, integrating the music and the spectacular effects of the opera into the rigorous plotting of classical tragedy. In dramatic musicals, there was little expectation that the unities would be strictly observed. Yet, they are and in remarkably suggestive ways in *Athalie*. It goes without saying that action is unified.[18] The unity of place, which is rarely maintained in lyrical works of the seventeenth century with their spectacular effects, is unified in *Athalie,* but with significant nuances.[19] The stage is set "In the Temple of Jerusalem, in a vestibule of the apartment of the high priest," which means that we will not be permitted to see the Holy of Holies, the Inner Sanctum of the temple. That representation by Racine would be a form of profanation, but the actual setting does invite intrusion and, in the case of Mathan and Athalie, constitutes a sacrilege, punishable by death. Their entrances (hers in act 2, scene 7, his in act 2, scene 5) are the first of three invasions of the sacred place and each one is immediately characterized as unprecedented. In act 2, scene 2, Zacharie cries out that "The Temple is profaned" (381), a sentiment echoed by one of Athalie's women, Agar in 430–34, and by Mathan, "Great Queen, is this your place?" (459).

Mathan makes the next unlawful entrance in act 3, scene 1, which is again denounced by Zacharie, "Where are you going, in your rashness?" (848), and later by Joad (1025–26). The final intrusion is, of course, by Athalie in act 5, scenes 5–6. It is the most important of the three instances, the shortest in time, and the longest in consequence. The time Athalie spends on stage in her last appearance is not extensive, in part because she cannot be slain in full view of the public since both decorum (*"bienséances"*) and the rules of the Temple of Jahweh forbid it; French classicism and the Bible find common taboos in Racine's last play. Such interdictions are possible because, in conceiving *Athalie* as theater, Racine chose to unify his play in the most sacred place of all his tragedies.

In *Athalie,* Racine puts the unity of time to work in an exceptional way by having ideal time and real time coincide: the performance lasts only as long as the actions on stage should reasonably take. Moreover, there is no time lost between the acts because the chorus is on stage throughout to assure the liaison between not only scenes but acts. Racine establishes an especially tight connection between the end of act 4 and the beginning of act 5 by having the first verse of act 4 rhyme with a prominent verse of the last stanza of act 5: "Cher Zacharie, eh bien, que nous apprenez-vous" (1510) and "Courons, fuyons, retirons-nous" (1507). Racine's choice of day for the play also contributes substantially to its import. Since the Bible did not specify the day on which Athalie lost her throne and her life, Racine was free to turn that lapse to his own advantage. He chose the Jewish equivalent of the Christian feast of Pentecost and thereby underscored the message of the continuity of tradition between the Old Testament and the New. This one day witnesses the close of a long past and the opening of a future that culminates in the advent of Christ.

Since French tragedy fell into a gradual decline after *Athalie,* we cannot say that Racine's religious tragedy gave new and vital direction to the tragic genre in France.[20] *Athalie*'s success was rather international and cross-disciplinary in scope, for musicologists designate *Athalie* as a step toward the oratorios of Händel, who borrowed the subject of *Athalie* for one of his pieces.

Chapter Fifteen
Conclusion

Racine's theater is indelibly inscribed in the canon of western literature. Its lofty standing is secure because it is classic in several senses of the term. The principal meaning of *classic* is "of the first order," and conveys a distinction between the high art form of a Racine and popular culture. It is generally acknowledged that Racine was the leading literary figure of the French Classical Age, a privileged epoch that consciously sought to equal previous high moments of civilization, such as the periods of Alexander, Augustus, and the Medici. Moreover, the playwright, who as a student read the classics of Greek and Roman antiquity, himself became the exemplar "in class." Finally, the reason why he stands secure as a "classic" object of analysis and representation as we face the twenty-first century, is that his cosmic and disturbing vision of humanity broods over uneasy questions about the nature of good and evil, freedom and constraint, self and society, immanence and transcendence, our origins and our perspectives. Racine's views were unquestionably shaped by Jansenist doctrine and its insistence on the Fall as the explanation of the human condition. This austere religious orientation was surely aggravated by Racine's personal experience as an orphan; no surprise, then, that Racine's tragic characters all suffer a sense of loss, of incompleteness, and are tortured by a need to reunite with some sort of otherness.

But to see in Racine only the representative of our modernity is to repeat an error often committed in much criticism until the 1990s, that of reducing him to the status of a dramatist whose plays are "unplayable," even if they have in fact been staged and performed for over three centuries. While we should not underestimate the problems that any early modern text poses for a contemporary audience, an author's "unplayability" is, of course, based on perspectives that vary from period to period. Shakespeare was also considered strictly as a "literary" (non-representable) dramatist for 200 years, from the mid-seventeenth century on. As recent scholarship has demonstrated, we can now dismiss the notion that Racine is all poetry and no drama: in fact, he carefully considered every aspect of his works from the setting to the costumes and props to stage movements and even diction. The diction of Racine's actors, thanks to the coaching they received from the playwright, was so harmonious that Lully, Louis XIV's opera master, sent his singers to learn from their rehearsals. Racine required the members of the Hôtel de Bourgogne troupe to vary pitch and volume in their delivery; he even used full stops in his punctuation to delay the traditional rushing declamation of the actors.[1]

Racine's collaboration with his actors allows us a glimpse of his temperament: Racine was, in all respects, a perfectionist. If he defended every aspect of his art in his prefaces, it was in his utilization of language that he took the most pride because it was the vehicle that gave voice to the soul, all in furthering the drama. In Henry Phillips's words, "Speech in Racine possesses an essentially theatrical dimension in exploiting the excitement and sense of expectation involved in the utterance. However unlikely it may seem at first sight, Racine's tragedies are the paradigm of theatre itself."[2]

Thierry Maulnier, the author of an influential book on Racine (*Jean Racine* [Paris: Gallimard, 1936]), once wrote that Racine's poetry is to daily language what dance is to walking.[3] That same poetry allows Racine to express depths of feeling unprecedented in French theater. Contrary to the mannerisms of the poets and prose writers who constituted the socioliterary movement known as "Préciosité," which thrived in the first half of the century and which dealt exclusively in the hyperbolic expression of sentiment, Racine collapses the space between expression and sentiment. If the "précieux" writers claimed that they "burned" with passion, one could safely conclude that they felt some small spark of interest. But when Phèdre reveals that she still "burns" with love for Hippolyte although she is uncertain about her husband's death, we can be confident that she is seeking to convey the physical pain she experiences in the throes of unsatisfied passion. It is in this spirit that Racine creates a passionate, corporeal reality in what might otherwise pass for a harmless cliché or a literary convention.

That Racine's plays succeeded in eliciting powerful reactions from his spectators, especially weeping, betrays the profound understanding that all great classical authors have of the deepest emotional needs of their audience. In the seventeenth century poets strove to develop an intimate rapport with the public, and Racine established a remarkable closeness between the states of mind of his characters and those of the audience. Ironically, the area of Racine scholarship that has attracted the least attention is the basic vehicle of Racinian dramatic poetry: the alexandrine line. Were it not for the insightful remarks on the alexandrine present in Jean Dubu's book, *Racine aux miroirs,* there would be little to enlighten us on a topic that is perhaps as compelling as that of Racine's rhetoric, on which Peter France, Michael Hawcroft, and Gilles Declercq, among others, have written incisively.[4]

Further research on Racine's poetry would have to bear on his extraordinary talent for creating the perfect combination of words to express the violence that permeates his tragedies.[5] For instance, in the cruel refinement of her language, which she uses like a scalpel, Racine's Iphigénie becomes more ferocious than any of the murderers and criminals of Corneille.[6] Yet, the ritual of bloodshed that marks Racine's tragedies is transmitted in finely calibrated and rhymed alexandrines. Just as La Rochefoucauld undermined the severity of the message of his maxims through paradoxical forms ("Virtue is but vice disguised") that surprised and pleased the reader, so too Racine devised the melodiousness of his alexandrines and the assuring regularity of his rhymes as an aesthetic counterpoise designed to compensate for the transgressive content of his works. Clive Scott, the master of studies of rhyme in French literature, proposes an even broader conclusion:

> It is precisely the function of rhyme in French neo-classical tragedy to imply that all has already been thought of, that the accidents and spontaneities of speech are an illusion, have already been foreseen as part of a preordained design. It is the imperturbable assuredness of the alexandrine couplet which conveys, to use Attridge's words (1979, p. 68), "the sense of a world where nothing happens by chance," which maintains "the impression of a human dignity which even the extremity of feeling cannot destroy."[7]

Drama is speech between two silences and speech is the medium between two spaces: the visible and the invisible, the action on stage and the events conjured up by the characters' desires and dreams. One of the most notorious lines in Racine speaks splendidly to the dramatist's ability to plumb the depths of a character's soul, as if in a reverie. Hippolyte offers this earnest self-appraisal, sober in its succession of monosyllables: "Le jour n'est pas plus pur que le fond de mon coeur" (The light of day is not as pure as the dark of my soul [*Phèdre,* 1112]). That the son of Thésée should be torn to shreds because a monster unexpectedly surges out of the sea is symptomatic of Racine's strategy of taking the heroic events of epic and transforming them into the constraining, powerless world of tragedy. Racine's representation of our human limitations is the lesson of his tragedies, and it has impacted heavily on the history of the tragic genre. Racine is the precursor for a host of major dramatists from Ibsen and O'Neill, to Beckett and Artaud. One can thus only concur with Heinrich Heine, who bestowed on Racine the title of first modern poet.[8]

Notes and References

Preface

1. "Oh! Mon doux Racine, c'est dans tes chefs-d'oeuvres [*sic*] que je reconnais le cœur des femmes! Je forme le mien à tes nobles poésies! Si la lyre de mon âme ne pleure pas toujours à tes accords divins, c'est que l'admiration laisse tout mon être dans l'extase.

> Rachel
> Turin 16 obre [*sic*] 1857 [1851?]"

This quote is found on the fly-leaf of a volume that belonged to the celebrated actress Rachel and that is now in the collection of the Princeton University Library: *Racine, Œuvres dramatiques . . . avec les notes de tous les commentateurs* (Paris: Lefèvre, 1844), vol. 1. Rachel was not alone in her passion, as an actress, for Racine. In France actresses have had entire careers based on Racine (e.g., Marie Bell in *Phèdre*), which has never been true of Racine's rival, Pierre Corneille. For the French actress, Phèdre is as exacting a role as Hamlet or Lear for the Anglo-Saxon actor.

2. Robert Lowell, *Phaedra: A Verse Translation of Racine's* Phèdre (London: Faber and Faber, 1961), 8.

3. Christopher Ricks, *Essays in Appreciation* (Oxford: Clarendon Press, 1996), 246.

4. Patrick Swinden, "Translating Racine," *Comparative Literature* 49, no. 3 (Summer 1997): 209.

Chapter One

1. Spanheim, the special envoy of the prince of Brandenburg to the court of Louis XIV, has written a fascinating portrait of Racine, from which the above quote is taken, and which is to be found most conveniently in Raymond Picard, *Nouveau Corpus Racinianum* (Paris: CNRS, 1976), 263.

2. I have drawn my material for this biography of Racine mainly from Raymond Picard, *La Carrière de Jean Racine* (Paris: Gallimard, 1956); Alain Viala, *Racine: La Stratégie du caméléon* (Paris: Seghers, 1990); Jean Dubu, *Les Lettres d'Uzès de Racine* (Nimes: Lacour, 1991); and the erudite Notices to the plays contained in Jean-Pierre Collinet's edition of Racine's *Théâtre complet,* 2 vols. (Paris: Gallimard, 1983).

3. In "Racine et Port-Royal: un épisode inconnu" (in *La Guirlande di Cecilia* [Fasano: Schena Editore, 1996], 557–65), Jean Mesnard examines a document he recently uncovered that suggests, at the same time, a later date— 1666—for Racine's break with Port-Royal and an earlier one—1676—for his return to the Jansenist fold than had previously been thought.

4. Voltaire, in his *Commentaires sur Corneille* (Commentaries on Corneille), spread a number of myths about Racine. The most improbable is the one that suggests that *Bérénice* describes the moment when Henrietta and Louis XIV decided to put an end to their mutual attraction.

5. See the various chronological possibilities offered by Collinet, *Théâtre complet*, 2:13.

6. Marc Fumaroli, "Melpomène au miroir: la tragédie comme héroïne dans *Médée* et *Phèdre*," *Saggi e Ricerche di Letteratura Francese* 19 (1980): 175–205.

7. The event of his acceptance speech at the Académie Française was less than memorable. Undoubtedly paralyzed with stage fright, Racine spoke in an inaudible monotone throughout, embarrassing his protector, Colbert, who made his first visit to the Académie for the occasion. The content of Racine's remarks was evidently no more impressive than his delivery, since, as his son Louis tells us, Racine destroyed all copies of the speech, including those kept in the archives of the Académie. On 2 January 1685 Racine gave a formal address before the Académie to hail the entrance of Pierre Corneille into its ranks; he was this time, from all reports, up to the task.

8. Madame de Sévigné, *Correspondance*, ed. Roger Duchêne (Paris: Gallimard, 1978), 3:487–88.

Chapter Two

1. See Armand Hoog, *Littérature en Silésie* (Paris: Grasset, 1944).

2. For a selection of Phaedra plays in French that have not been available in recent times, see Allen G. Wood, ed., *Le Mythe de Phèdre: les Hippolyte Français du dix-septième siècle* (Paris: Honoré Champion, 1996).

3. Jean Rohou, *Le Classicisme* (Paris: Hachette, 1996): 122–23.

4. Raymond Picard, *De Racine au Parthénon* (Paris: Gallimard, 1977), 71.

5. See Norbert Elias, *The Court Society*, trans. E. Jephcott (New York: Pantheon Books, 1983), esp. 141.

6. For those interested in the relationship between history and dramatic literature in the seventeenth century, especially as reflected in Corneille's theater, John Lyons's, *The Tragedy of Origins* (Stanford, Calif.: Stanford University Press, 1996) is indispensable.

7. Margaret McGowan, "Racine's 'lieu théâtral,' " in *Form and Meaning*, ed. William D. Howarth, Ian MacFarlane, and Margaret McGowan (Amersham: Avebury, 1982), 166–86, esp. 170.

8. The characters of French tragedy express themselves almost exclusively in the alexandrine meter after 1660. Between 1637 and 1639 two-thirds

of the French tragedies have moments where the meter of 12 feet per verse line is interrupted by a lyric monologue, called the "stances," composed of lines of varying length (6, 7, 8, 10, or 12 feet). The most famous example occurs when Rodrigue debates his dilemma at the end of act 1 of *Le Cid* in what are known as "Les Stances du Cid." However, by the late 1650s they were included in barely 20 percent of tragic productions. They disappeared shortly thereafter, the victim of verisimilitude.

9. "Qu'en un lieu, qu'en un jour, un seul fait accompli, / Tienne jusqu'à la fin le théâtre rempli," verses 45 – 46 of Chant 3.

10. Margaret McGowan makes an important point about dress also contributing to the concentration on the emotions: "The fact (to judge from the drawings and engravings which survive) that there was little to distinguish the dress of characters from that of spectators had significant consequences for the way in which seventeenth-century court audiences responded to plays and for the assumptions Racine and others could make about their public. Since the terrain was familiar, interest centered on the quality of performance and on the expression of feeling" (McGowan, "Racine's 'lieu théâtral,' " 171).

11. David Maskell demonstrates Racine's effectiveness in occasionally leaving the stage empty, to better create pregnant silences. See David Maskell, "Entrées et sorties dans la tragédie classique," *Papers on French Seventeenth-Century Literature* 24, no. 47 (1997): 421– 44.

12. See especially David Maskell, *Racine, A Theatrical Reading* (Oxford: Clarendon Press, 1991).

Chapter Three

1. My practice throughout will be to retain the French names for the characters of French plays (Phèdre, Oreste), but to use the English form for the classical forebears of those characters (Phaedra, Orestes) and for mythological and historical figures who do not appear in the plays. Also, for the rare quotes from the original text of Racine, I have used the edition of Racine's *Œuvres complètes,* ed. Raymond Picard for the Pléiade series, 2 vols. (Paris: Gallimard, 1950).

2. Christian Biet, *Œdipe en monarchie* (Paris: Klincksieck, 1994), 242; see also chap. 4.

3. Georges May, "L'Unité de sang chez Racine," *Revue d'Histoire Littéraire de la France* 72 (March–April 1972): 209–33.

4. On Racine as a precursor of modernity, see, for example, Marie-Florine Bruneau, "Racine's *Phèdre* or the Labor Pains of Modernity," *Renaissance Drama* 22 (1991): 123 – 45.

5. Terence Cave was the first to draw attention to the significance of this 1697 variant in *Recognitions: A Study in Poetics* (Oxford: Clarendon Press, 1988), 328 n.3.

6. For an analogous vision, see the ode "Un Corbeau" (A crow) by the seventeenth-century baroque poet Théophile de Viau.

7. It is equally not surprising that of the 326 occurrences of *sang* (blood) in Racine's dramatic corpus, almost a third appear in *La Thébaïde*. See the vehicle by which French studies entered the age of technology, Bryant C. Freeman and Alan Batson, *Concordance du théâtre et des poésies de Jean Racine*, 2 vols. (Ithaca, NY: Cornell University Press, 1968). This is the first computerized concordance of any French author.

8. For more on this matter, see my *Racine and Seneca* (Chapel Hill: University of North Carolina Press, 1971).

9. Valérie Worth-Stylianou, "La Querelle du confident et la structure dramatique des premières pièces de Racine," *Littératures Classiques* 16 (1992): 229–46.

10. Richard Parish, *Racine: The Limits of Tragedy* (Tuebingen: Papers on French Seventeenth-Century Literature, 1993), 109.

11. Marcel Gutwirth has explored the subtleties of the rapport between Racine's sense of tragedy and the concepts of purity and innocence in "La Problématique de l'innocence dans le théâtre de Racine," *Revue des Sciences Humaines* 106 (1962): 183–202.

12. Bernard Weinberg, *The Art of Jean Racine* (Chicago: University of Chicago Press, 1963), 37–38.

Chapter Four

1. See the "Notice" to *Alexandre* in *Théâtre complet de Racine*, ed. Jacques Morel and Alain Viala (Paris: Garnier, 1980), 66.

2. For a study of the reflections of Versailles in Racine's work, see Jean Dubu, *Racine aux miroirs* (Paris: SEDES, 1992): 299–309.

3. See Michael Hawcroft, *Word as Action: Racine, Rhetoric, and Theatrical Language* (Oxford: Clarendon Press, 1992).

4. Jacques Scherer, *Racine et/ou la cérémonie* (Paris: Presses Universitaires de France, 1982), 166–67.

5. See Michael Hawcroft and Valerie Worth's critical edition of *Alexandre le Grand* (Exeter: University of Exeter Press, 1990), xxxvii.

6. For an example from the visual arts of the identification of Louis XIV with Hercules, see the portrait of the king by Robert Nanteuil (1623–1678), dating from 1672, with the hide of the Nemean lion (the traditional attribute of Hercules) arranged above the monarch.

7. Timothy Reiss, "Banditry, Madness, and Sovereign Authority: *Alexandre le Grand*," in *Homage to Paul Bénichou* (Birmingham, AL: Summa Publications, 1994), 113–42.

Chapter Five

1. Paul Bénichou, *Man and Ethics: Studies in French Classicism* (Garden City, NY: Doubleday, 1971), 164.

2.   Racine must have rejected out of hand the option of using a name that would, of itself, occupy almost half of any alexandrine meter.

3.   Racine never presents the moment when his characters fall in love, the "innamoramento." Racine's vision of humanity and his dramatic sense combine in his theater to reduce the onstage elements to the absolute essentials by focusing not on cause but on effect, not on origin but on consequence.

4.   Noémi Hepp, "Sur le mensonge racinien," *Travaux de Langue et de Littérature* 25, no. 2 (1987): 65–78.

5.   This recalls Molière's *Tartuffe,* in which the apparent impregnability of the hypocrite, the falsifier par excellence, forces the family, to which Molière has confided the high moral ground, to resort to speaking ill of Tartuffe.

6.   See Robert Hartle, "Symmetry and Irony in Racine's *Andromaque,*" in *Paths to Freedom: Studies in Honor of E. B. O. Borgerhoff,* ed. Ronald W. Tobin, special issue of *L'Esprit Créateur* 11 (1971): 46–58.

7.   This substitute ending has the added advantage of confiding the throne eventually to Astyanax and, in so doing, illustrating the myth, dear to the French monarchy, that the Frankish line of kings descended from the heroes of Troy.

8.   Nonetheless, there exists some ambiguity about the point. In verse 1615, Oreste says that heaven is relentless in its attempts to punish him, which could mean that this is not Oreste's first crime. It could also refer to Oreste's "star-crossed" situation relative to Hermione.

Chapter Six

1.   In his edition of Racine's *Théâtre complet,* Collinet discusses the collaboration on *Les Plaideurs* in the light of Louis Racine's recollections (1:461–62).

2.   Louise Horowitz, "Justice for Dogs: The Triumph of Illusion in *Les Plaideurs,*" *French Review* 52, no. 2 (1978): 278.

3.   Claire Carlin, "Racine's Classicized Baroque," *Cahiers du Dix-Septième* 2, no. 2 (Fall 1988): 41.

4.   Maya Slater, "Racine's *Les Plaideurs*: A Tragedian's Farce," in *Farce* (New York: Cambridge University Press, 1988): 83–97. When Slater concludes that Racine is portraying "a collection of eccentrics" (92), she uses an image that is even better suited to a 1637 comedy by Jean Desmarests de Saint-Sorlin, *Les Visionnaires* (The lunatics) in which each of the nine characters has a particular "vision" or "delusion." Because the play influenced both Corneille (*Le Menteur* [The liar]) and Molière (*Misanthrope*), it could hardly have escaped Racine's notice when he was conceiving his obsessive figures.

5.   Slater, *Farce,* 87.

6.   Nina C. Ekstein, "The Comic Récit: *Les Plaideurs,*" *Papers on French Seventeenth-Century Literature* 12, no. 23 (1985): 525–40.

7. Ibid., 528.

8. This is Jacques Morel's conclusion in *"Les Plaideurs*, réécriture et provocation," *Littératures Classiques* 27 (1996): 339–41.

9. For Harpagon the reference is to a thing ("it"), for Valère to his beloved ("her").

10. Maskell, *Racine, A Theatrical Reading,* 84. The *Mémoire de Mahelot*, composed by a stage designer, is a valuable document for our knowledge of practical conditions and considerations, including box office receipts, of Paris theaters in the seventeenth century.

11. Children pitted against parents is probably the most common theme in Racine's tragedies, but nowhere does it attain greater effect than in *Britannicus*. Nathan Gross speculates that Racine was composing both *Les Plaideurs* and *Britannicus* at about the same time. See Nathan Gross, *"Les Plaideurs* and the Racinian Canon," *Modern Language Notes* 80 (1965): 318–35.

Chapter Seven

1. Another explanation, which has some credence given the seventeenth-century public's penchant for wanting to cheer heroes and hiss villains, is that the role of Néron was originally given to an audience favorite, Floridor. The popular affection for him was apparently such that the audience was reluctant to indicate disapproval of the unattractive character he was playing.

2. The first Preface dates from 1670. For the editions that appeared between 1676 and 1697 Racine rewrote the Preface. The quote is taken from the latter Preface.

3. Georges Forestier, ed., *Britannicus*, Collection Folio Théâtre 25 (Paris: Gallimard, 1995), 12.

4. Volker Schröder has gone into great detail on the political and dynastic importance of Junia Calvina in "Politique du couple: amour réciproque et légimité dynastique dans *Britannicus*," *Cahiers de l'Association Internationale des Etudes Françaises* 49 (1997): 455–91.

5. Actually, at his feet: he kicked her so violently, she died.

6. There exists another play on the theme of Arria and Poetus, a five-act tragedy written after *Britannicus* by one of the relatively small group of woman dramatists practicing between 1650 and 1750 in France: Marie-Anne Barbier's *Arrie et Pétus* of 1702. One can find a recent copy in *Femmes dramaturges en France, 1650–1750:* pièces choisies, textes établis, présentés et annotés par Perry Gethner (Tuebingen: Papers on French Seventeenth-Century Literature, 1993). Gethner has also selected this play for inclusion in an anthology of women's plays in English translation from the same period. See *The Lunatic Lover and Other Plays by French Women of the Seventeenth and Eighteenth Centuries* (Portsmouth, NH: Heinemann, 1994).

7. See Jules Brody, " 'Les Yeux de César': The Language of Vision in *Britannicus*," in *Studies in Honor of Morris Bishop*, ed. J.-J. Demorest (Ithaca, NY:

Cornell University Press, 1963): 185–201; and Louis Van Delft, "Language and Power: Eyes and Word in *Britannicus,*" *Yale French Studies* 45 (1970): 102–12.

8. The expression is taken from Ralph Albanese, "Patterns of Tragic Irony in *Britannicus,*" *Australian Journal of French Studies* 14 (1977): 242.

9. The point in history that this play addresses occurred after Nero had been emperor for five years. It is possible that Racine reduced it to three years so that Néron would not have spent so long in a state of at least official or political virtue for him credibly to become a "monster."

10. Scherer, *Racine et/ou la cérémonie,* 61–62

11. Claire Carlin "Racine, Mauron, and the Question of Genre," *Bulletin of the Rocky Mountain Modern Language Association* 36, no. 1 (1982): 25–33.

12. Racine's portrayal of a violent emperor having a taste for acting and dancing is said to be the reason why Louis XIV, who took dancing lessons for 20 years, decided to refrain from dancing in public after 1669.

13. Picard, *Œuvres complètes,* 1:391.

14. The human trait of attempting to impose one's obsession on others is effectively satirized in Molière's *Les Fâcheux* (The bores).

15. Charles Baudelaire, "Salon of 1846," in *Œuvres completes,* ed. Claude Pichois (Paris: Gallimard, 1976), 2:480.

16. In a significant document of French literary history, the Préface de *Cromwell,* Victor Hugo, who led the Romantic opposition to classicism, criticized Racine for deciding to present the narration of Britannicus's death over the other possibility. "If Racine had not been paralyzed, as he was, by the prejudices of his century, if his work had not been torpedoed by classicism, he would . . . not have relegated to the wings that admirable banquet scene in which Seneca's student poisons Britannicus with the cup of reconciliation" (Victor Hugo, Préface de *Cromwell,* ed. Roger Pons [Paris: Hatier, n.d.], 61). As Michael Hawcroft indicates, Hugo did not see the confession and the justification inherent in Burrhus's speech. See Michael Hawcroft, "Racine, Rhetoric, and the Death *Récit,*" *Modern Language Review* 84, no. 1 (January 1989): 26–36.

Chapter Eight

1. The word *passionately* does not appear in the original Latin text and is an early indication of how Racine wishes us to view the Titus-Bérénice relationship.

2. The standard reference to the language of vision in Racine is to Jean Starobinski, "Racine et la poétique du regard," *L'Œil vivant* (Paris: Gallimard, 1961): 68–89. But see also the exciting study that illuminates the self-centered nature of vision in Racine: Renée Morel, "Narcisse mortifié et mortifère: le regard chez Racine," *French Review* 64, no. 6 (1991): 921–33.

3. John Campbell, "*Bérénice*: The Plotting of a Tragedy," *Seventeenth-Century French Studies* 15 (1993): 145.

4.   Harriet Stone, *The Classical Model: Literature and Knowledge in Seventeenth-Century France* (Ithaca, NY: Cornell University Press, 1996), 79.

5.   Maskell, *Racine, A Theatrical Reading,* 27.

6.   The equivalent in comedy is undoubtedly Molière's *Tartuffe*, in which the underlying problem is one of censorship, of denying the right to speak. See my "Authority, Language, and Censorship," *Approaches to Teaching Molière's* Tartuffe (New York: Modern Language Association, 1995): 26–32.

7.   Richard Goodkin "The Performed Letter, or, How Words Do Things in Racine," *Papers on French Seventeenth-Century Literature* 17, no. 32 (1989): 89.

8.   See Hepp, "Sur le mensonge racinien," for a full treatment of lying to others and to oneself in Racine's theater.

9.   For a full development of the Titus-Britannicus-Néron triangle, see Jacques Scherer's edition of *Bérénice* (Paris: SEDES, 1974), 61–63.

10.   Richard Parish expatiates on Bérénice's critique of Roman traditions in *Racine: The Limits of Tragedy,* 18–22. See also the pages on "*Bérénice's* Oriental Law: The Emperor's New Clothes," in Stone, *The Classical Model,* 77–94.

11.   J. Dainard, "The Power of the Spoken Word in *Bérénice,*" *Romanic Review* 67 (1976): 159.

12.   David Maskell points this out in *Racine: A Theatrical Reading,* 212.

13.   Titus states it unequivocally: "My reign will be nothing less than a long banishment" (754).

14.   Picard, *Œuvres complètes,* 1:474.

15.   Harriet Stone offers this striking image of the end of the play: "Titus is framed in the mirror of representation that figures him at the feet of Bérénice like an infant in the arms of its mother" (*The Classical Model,* 85).

16.   Roland Barthes, *Sur Racine* (Paris: Seuil, 1963).

17.   For a thorough investigation of the pros and cons of Planchon's interpretation, see Noémi Hepp, "Le Personnage de Titus dans *Bérénice*: essai de mis au point," *Travaux de Linguistique et de Littérature* 18, no. 2 (1980): 85–96

18.   As Hepp points out ("Le Personnage de Titus," 91), the fact that Titus speaks these lines to his confidant Paulin argues heavily in favor of his sincerity.

19.   Odette de Mourgues, *Racine or the Triumph of Relevance* (Cambridge: Cambridge University Press, 1967), 12. Campbell sees suspense amidst the interminable instants: " 'Suspense' might seem an odd term to use in the same breath as *Bérénice*. Yet the whole play could be seen as organized according to the rhetorical figure of suspension: the heightening of interest by delay of the main subject" (Campbell, "*Bérénice*: The Plotting of a Tragedy," 148).

20.   Jacques Scherer has stimulating ideas on time in Racine in *Racine et/ou la cérémonie,* 215–23. In "Playing for Time in *Bérénice,*" (*Nottingham French Studies* 32, no. 2 [1993]: 23–28), John Campbell analyzes time in this particular tragedy and concludes, "In this never more melancholy tragedy, as charac-

ters strive to retain what is already a memory, time as a living experience predicates the inescapable in life, and takes on the character of a tragic fatality" (28).

21. Georges Forestier "Où finit *Bérénice* commence *Tite et Bérénice,*" *Onze études sur la vieillesse de Corneille* (Paris: Klinckiesck, 1994): 53–75. D. C. Potts offers an addition to the bibliography of the quarrel when he speculates that certain coincidences of phrasing in Racine's Preface and in a letter by Mme de Sévigné of 12 July 1671 may betray an attempt by one of Corneille's most devoted admirers to devalue the claims Racine had made in the Preface. See D. C. Potts, "Undercutting Racine?" *French Studies Bulletin* 59 (Summer 1996): 14. If this is so, then the letter in question takes its place in a thick dossier of polemics for and against *Bérénice* published in the late seventeenth and early eighteenth centuries.

22. H. C. Lancaster, *French Dramatic Literature in the Seventeenth Century* (Baltimore, Md.: Johns Hopkins University Press, 1940), part 4, 1:76.

Chapter Nine

1. Racine's contemporaries were far from convinced of the authenticity of Racine's portrayal of Turks. Several modern critics have tended to agree, but the majority are of a mind with Judd Hubert, who sees in the exotic atmosphere of *Bajazet* the secret of the play's success rather than the source of its supposed weakness (Judd Hubert, *Essai d'exégèse racinienne:* Bérénice, Bajazet, Athalie [Paris: Nizet, 1985], 52). For an exhaustive review of the linguistic elements that compose the play's local color, see Maria G. Pittaluga, *Aspects du vocabulaire de Jean Racine* (Fasano: Schena, 1991), 81–117.

2. Molière changed Mutaferraca into Mustapha Raca for his spoof of fancy-dress Turks, *Le Bourgeois gentilhomme* of 1670.

3. For more details, consult T. Sarah Peterson, *Acquired Taste: The French Origins of Modern Cooking* (Ithaca, NY: Cornell University Press, 1994).

4. For a review of seventeenth-century French attitudes toward the Ottoman Empire, see Michèle Longino Farrell, "Early Orientalisms," *L'Esprit Créateur* 32, no. 3 (1992): 5–12.

5. Pierre Voltz, "*Bérénice, Bajazet, Athalie*: réflexions dramaturgiques à partir de la notion d'espace dans la tragédie racinienne" in *La Romaine, la Turque et la Juive,* ed. P. Ronzeaud (Marseilles: Université de Provence, 1986), 51–75, offers a detailed analysis of space in the three plays cited in his title. He also points out (64–65) that the *Serrail* is only the visible part of an extensive imaginary setting. For example, Acomat speaks of the "dark path" (209) that leads to it; mention is made of a personal space (*appartement*) belonging to Roxane and another to Bajazet; and there exists a refuge where Atalide vents her emotions in private.

6. Jean Dubu addresses the questions of the anomalous capitalization and spelling of *Serrail* and its unstable meaning in *Racine aux miroirs*, 137–48.

7. I translate *cependant* as "nonetheless" in keeping with the interpretation of Catherine Spenser in her stimulating piece, "*Bajazet*: la personne interposée ou la dérobade," *Papers on French Seventeenth-Century Literature* 9, no. 16 (1982): 253–69.

8. Susan Tiefenbrun, *Signs of the Hidden* (Amsterdam: Rodopi, 1980), 209.

9. The one restraint that Amurat has observed until the day of the tragedy concerns the necessity of assuring a successor to the throne. Since his reign has yet to produce an heir, he has kept Bajazet alive in case the siege of Babylone were to prove fatal to him. This inviolable tradition of the Ottoman Empire creates an ironic situation in which the holder of absolute power is prevented from dispatching a potential rival.

10. See Mourgues, *Racine or the Triumph of Relevance*, 112–34.

11. For a subtle investigation of Roxane's passage from illusion to illumination, see Jules Brody, "*Bajazet* or the Tragedy of Roxane," *Romanic Review* 60, no. 4 (1969): 273–90.

12. Racine often integrates stage directions in the text because one could not count on the spectators being able to see certain reactions, such as Bajazet noticing Atalide's distress in this scene and saying, "What do I see? What is the matter? You are weeping" (955). Atalide's lack of verbal reaction is also only one instance of the many expressive silences built into the rhythm Racine conceived for the performance of his texts.

13. J. H. Phillips, "Racinian Letters," *Modern Language Studies* 27, no. 1 (1991): 39.

Chapter Ten

1. Racine concentrates events that stretched across many years in reality. He makes Monime and Xipharès contemporaries, whereas Xipharès was in fact the son of the woman who succeeded Monime in Mithridate's affections. Both Xipharès and Monime died before Mithridate.

2. Collinet, *Racine: Théâtre complet*, 2:499.

3. Louis Racine, *Remarques sur les tragédies de Jean Racine* (Amsterdam, 1752), 1:487–88.

4. Michael O'Reagan, *The Mannerist Aesthetic: A Study of Racine's Mithridate* (Bristol: Bristol University Press, 1980), 37.

5. Interestingly, *secret* reappears with heightened frequency in the cluster of plays beginning with *Britannicus* (21 times), *Bérénice* (15), *Bajazet* (19), *Mithridate* (21), and *Iphigénie* (16). In the tragedy most famous for the secret passion of its title character, *Phèdre*, the verb *cacher* ("to hide") replaces the adjective *secret* as the operative item.

6. "Maxime Supprimée 64," in La Rochefoucauld, *Maximes*, ed. J. Truchet (Paris: Garnier, 1967), 150.

7. Henry Phillips, *Racine*: Mithridate (London: Grant & Cutler, Ltd., 1990), 38.

8.   See Robert Mantran, *L'Empire ottoman du XVIe au XVIIe siècle* (London: Variorum Reprints, 1984), 383.

9.   *Cognitive mapping* is a term devised by postmodern geographer Kevin Lynch to define what occurs when people's perceptions of significant barriers, landmarks, and pathways that facilitate movement and placement help give them a sense of efficacy in space. See, for example, Edward Soja, *Postmodern Geographies* (London: Verso, 1989). In tragedy, of course, the characters are more conscious of restraints than of freedom of movement.

10.   Phillips, *Racine*: Mithridate, 63.

11.   See Jean Rohou, *L'Evolution du tragique racinien* (Paris: SEDES, 1991).

12.   William Cloonan, "Fathers and Sons in *Mithridate*," *French Review* 49 (1976): 515.

13.   Clive Scott, *The Riches of Rhyme* (Oxford: Clarendon Press, 1988), 155.

14.   Donna Kuizenga sums up the play enviably when she ends her article with "Mithridate's tragic greatness lies in the fact that he is the sole fully conscious witness of his own eclipse" ("Racine's *Mithridate*: A Reconsideration," *French Review* 52 [1978]: 285).

15.   See Charles Bernet, *Le Vocabulaire des tragédies de Jean Racine* (Geneva: Slatkine, 1983), 209.

Chapter Eleven

1.   E. B. O. Borgerhoff, *The Freedom of French Classicism* (Princeton: Princeton University Press, 1950), 168.

2.   Philippe Sellier, "Les Tragédies de Jean Racine et Port-Royal," *Carnets Giraudoux-Racine* 3 (1997): 59.

3.   Maurice Delcroix, *Le Sacré dans les tragédies de Racine* (Paris: Nizet, 1970), 392.

4.   In the most intense scene of the play, Clytemnestre has a vision of Calchas slaughtering Iphigénie as if she were a sacrificial animal:

> A priest, surrounded by a complicitous crowd,
> Will place his criminal hand on my daughter,
> Tear open her chest, and, to satisfy his curiosity,
> Will consult the divine omens in her beating heart.
> (1297–1300)

5.   Terence Cave underlines the point when he notes that "it is a consequence of Racine's rewriting of the plot that Agamemnon appears to be the victim of what looks uncommonly (uncannily) like a practical joke or pun devised by Calchas and doubtless, the gods" (Cave, *Recognitions*, 343).

6.   John Lapp, *Aspects of Racinian Tragedy* (Toronto: Toronto University Press, 1956), 4.

7. She says, "Yes, you are of the blood of Atreus and Thyestes: / Executioner of your own daughter all that remains / Is for you to serve her, as a horrible meal, to her mother" (1246–48).

8. For more on the differing perceptions of death by the characters, see Dubu, *Racine aux miroirs,* 149–58.

9. The French word for "name" (*nom*) appears 26 times in *Iphigénie,* by far its highest frequency in any Racinian tragedy.

10. Claude Abraham, *Jean Racine* (Boston: Twayne, 1977), 114.

11. Besides being Eriphile's confidant, Doris adds one other element to the plot: the only one who knew Eriphile's real identity was Doris's deceased father.

12. In Richard Parish's elegant formula, Eriphile reveals "all the characteristics of the Racinian psychology of the sexually passionate woman—complex, complicated, pitiable, yet embittered" (Parish, *Racine: The Limits of Tragedy,* 66).

13. This is one instance of irony in a play so replete with it that its tone sometimes flirts with the comic. There is an occasional flash of black humor, for example when Iphigénie, attempting to console Clytemnestre for the anticipated loss of a daughter, exclaims, "Your eyes will see another me in my brother Orestes" (1657). For a seventeenth-century public intimately familiar with Greek mythology the irony is that Orestes will avenge his father's death by slaying his mother (as an extension of the action of *Andromaque*).

14. Hawcroft, *Word as Action,* 118–28.

15. Mourgues, Racine or the Triumph of Relevance, 49.

16. Jean Collinet, "Racine et ses personnages invisibles: le cas d'*Iphigénie,*" in *The Equilibrium of Wit: Essays for Odette de Mourgues,* ed. Peter Bayley and Dorothy Gabe Coleman (Lexington, KY: French Forum, 1982): 176–92; esp. p. 190.

17. Jean-Marie Apostolidès shares this conclusion by noting, "The element of sacrifice reestablishes the vertical flow between men and gods, and permits the latter to start up the world's engine again." See "La Belle aux eaux dormantes," *Poétique* 15, no. 58 (1984): 153.

Chapter Twelve

1. La Bruyère, *Les Caractères* (The characters), ed. R. Garapon (Paris: Garnier, 1962), 252. This circular conception is not espoused by Descartes or others who propose a linear, progressive view.

2. For an explanation of these apparently contradictory physical symptoms, see Jean-Michel Pelous, "Métaphores et figures de l'amour dans la *Phèdre* de Racine," *Travaux de Linguistique et de Littérature* 19, no. 2 (1981): 71–81.

3. Some of Racine's contemporaries recognized the influence of Sappho's ode "To the Beloved" in the passage just quoted. For a feminist explanation of "Racine's appropriation of the voice of female passion in order to bring

about the downfall of the female desiring subject . . . as a response to the threat of a female literary origin," see Joan DeJean, "Fictions of Sappho," *Critical Inquiry* 13 (Summer 1987): 804.

4. Neptune is the god of horses and horse training for Hippolyte, but for Thésée, Neptune is the deity of the sea.

5. Jean Racine, *Phèdre,* ed. Jean-Louis Barrault, Collection "Mise en scène" (Paris: Seuil, 1946), 105.

6. We might recall that Thésée's father, Egée, threw himself into the sea, thereafter called Aegean, when he did not see the white sail on Thésée's ship, the sign of his son's safe return. Thésée neglected to raise the sail because he was too busy making love.

7. The verb *purger* exists only in *Phèdre,* among all of Racine's plays, thus suggesting that there is a link between monstrosity and a need for purging.

8. Bénichou's *Man and Ethics* treats all of the major authors of the seventeenth century in the context of ethical thought, and Pierre Force compares Molière with the French moralists in *Molière, ou le prix des choses: morale, comédie et économie* (Paris: Nathan, 1994).

9. See Georges Couton, "Le Mariage d'Hippolyte et d'Aricie ou Racine entre Pausanias et le droit canon," *Revue des Sciences Humaines* 111 (1963): 305–15.

10. Racine has Phèdre die in a fashion that is opposed to Hippolyte's death. If he is torn apart, she is allowed to retain her physical integrity, unlike the preceding Phèdres who die by the sword or by hanging, more typical of a woman in classical literature.

11. *Phèdre* and *Iphigénie* have in common a series of actions (or verbal actions) that lead a father to sacrifice his child. This scenario is authorized by the highest authority for French classical dramatists, Aristotle.

12. Scherer, *Racine et/ou la cérémonie,* 216.

13. Racine undercuts any attribution of true (i.e., monster-slaying) heroism to Hippolyte by never having Théramène say explicitly that Hippolyte "killed" the sea creature.

Chapter Thirteen

1. See Anne Piéjus, "*Esther,* un modèle paradoxal de théâtre musical pour Saint-Cyr," *Papers on French Seventeenth-Century Literature* 24, no. 47 (1997): 395–420. Piéjus also informs us of the fact that *Esther* is by far the most "musical" of these tragedies because 30 percent of its verses are sung, compared to, for example, not quite 7 percent in *Athalie.*

2. For a dissenting voice among the chorus of praises, see Parish, *Racine: The Limits of Tragedy,* 42–44.

3. Barbara Woshinsky, Signs of Certainty: *The Linguistic Imperative in French Classical Literature* (Stanford, Calif.: Anma Libri, 1991), 92.

4. Ibid., 86.
5. Mourgues, Racine, or the Triumph of Relevance, 131.
6. See Charles Bernet, *Le Vocabulaire de tragédies de Racine* (Paris: Slatkine, 1983), 216.
7. Racine makes a point of defending the use of *libations* in his Preface where he states: "But I did not consider it necessary to believe the word of this same Herodotus, when he says that the Persians constructed neither temples, nor altars, nor statues to their gods, and that they never served libations in the course of their sacrifices."
8. Perry Gethner, "The Staging of Prayer in French Theater of the Seventeenth Century," *Papers in French Seventeenth-Century Literature* 9, no. 16 (1982): 32.

Chapter Fourteen

1. J. Mambrino, "*Athalie* de Racine et *Dom Juan* de Molière," *Etudes* 353 (July 1980): 64.
2. John Campbell has noted the major participants in the debate in his indispensable article, "The God of *Athalie*," *French Studies* 43 (1989): 401, n.5.
3. The roles of the children in *Athalie*, which is the only play by Racine to present them on stage, is explored by Derek F. Connon, "The Child on the Tragic Stage in 17th- and 18th-Century France: Racine, La Motte, Saurin," *Romance Studies* (Swansea) 27 (1996): 15–29.
4. In the introductory remarks ("Présentation") to his edition of *Racine, théâtre complet*, 2 vols. (Paris: Imprimerie Nationale, 1995), Phillipe Sellier discusses the phantasm of the slaying of a child: "The fear of being beaten, put to death by a paternal figure constitutes a part of our archaeology, a forgotten hieroglyph . . . This phantasm appears to be one of the elements of the realm of Racine's imagination" (13).
5. By their very nature, the choral chants are filled with biblical reminiscences, notably of the fertility of the land of milk and honey. See, for example, act 1, scene 4.
6. Another set of images, concerning filth, decadence, and corruption, is also impressively rich in *Athalie* and has been investigated with illuminating results in Lillian Corti, "Excremental Vision and Sublimation in Racine's *Athalie*," *French Forum* 12, no. 1 (1987): 43–53.
7. John Campbell expresses the same point in this fashion: "It is an inescapable fact that what happens in *Athalie* happens because of decisions taken by characters and because of reactions to those decisions" (Campbell, "The God of *Athalie*," 389).
8. Ian MacLean has enlightening things to say about misogyny in the French seventeenth century in his *Woman Triumphant: Feminism in French Literature 1610–52* (Oxford: Oxford University Press, 1977).

9. Helen Bates, "Matricide and Filicide in Racine's *Athalie*," *Symposium* 38, no. 1 (1984): 57.

10. Jean-Marie Apostolidès, *Le Prince sacrifié* (Paris: Minuit, 1985), 128.

11. Using the quote about pure gold as the basis for her conclusion, Helen Bates proposes that *Athalie* is about the "inevitable transformations . . . of innocent children into murderous adults" (Bates, "Matricide and Filicide," 64).

12. Maurice Descotes, "Le Visage du traître dans les tragédies de Racine," *Revue d'Histoire Littéraire de la France* 78, no. 4 (1978), 560.

13. Ibid.

14. Cave, *Recognitions,* 360.

15. For *Athalie* as a "ghost story" see ibid., 367.

16. One wonders if the seventeenth-century audience was as familiar with the story of Athaliah as we might think. If not, then the play is all the more suspenseful.

17. Zacharie would pass for a flaw in Racine's normally rigorous dramaturgy because he is not necessary to the action, were it not for the fact that he puts a face on the future crime of Joas, thereby ensuring its permanent place in the consciences of the spectators.

18. In the Preface to his play *Cromwell,* Victor Hugo proposes that there are really only two unities, time and place, since a good author will always unify his plot.

19. See Jacques Truchet, "Remarques sur le lieu et le temps dans *Athalie*," *Information Littéraire* 37, no. 5 (1985): 195–97.

20. In a far-reaching article, Pierre Voltz theorizes that French tragedy owed its decline specifically to the inability of tragic authors after Racine to follow his lead in developing a "spatial realism" on stage that responded to public expectations. See Voltz, "*Bérénice, Bajazet, Athalie,*" 51–80.

Chapter Fifteen

1. See Maskell, *Racine: A Theatrical Reading*, 127.

2. Phillips, *Racine*: Mithridate, 55.

3. Sellier, *Théâtre complet,* 1:38.

4. Peter France, *Racine's Rhetoric* (Oxford: Clarendon Press, 1965); Hawcroft, *Word as Action*; Gilles Declercq, "A l'école de Quintilien: l'hypotypose dans les tragédies de Racine," *Op. cit.* 5 (1995): 73–88, to cite just one of his articles.

5. The late Raymond Picard once told me of his chance encounter with André Malraux in a train. Upon learning that Picard was a Racine specialist, Malraux quoted a passage and asked Picard to identify it. Although it sounded perfectly Racinian, Picard could not place it. Malraux, who had an abiding interest in minor seventeenth-century authors, explained that the pas-

sage came from a tragedy written by one of Racine's disciples, La Grange-Chancel. It would be interesting to learn more about the qualitative differences that separate Racine's poetic language from that of his imitators.

6.   Sellier, in his "Présentation" to the *Théâtre complet*, offers a similar view: "From *La Thébaïde* to *Athalie*, strangling, carnage, laceration are proposed 'as a deadly spectacle,' with a single-mindedness and an emphasis that goes beyond the *diasparagmos*—the ritual tearing—of the *Bacchantes* of Euripides" (1:15).

7.   Clive Scott, *The Riches of Rhyme: Studies in French Verse* (Oxford: Clarendon Press, 1988), 158. The internal reference is to Derek Attridge, "Dryden's Dilemma, or, Racine Refashioned: The Problem of the English Dramatic Couplet," *Yearbook of English Studies* 9 (1979): 68.

8.   Bénichou, *Ethics,* 166.

Selected Bibliography

PRIMARY SOURCES

French Editions

Racine, Jean. *Œuvres complètes.* Ed. Raymond Picard. Bibliothèque de la Pléiade, 2 vols. Paris: Gallimard, 1950. The standard critical edition of Racine's writings. A new edition of the theater in the same series, edited by Georges Forestier, is forthcoming in 1999.

———. *Théâtre complet.* Ed. Jacques Morel and Alain Viala. Paris: Garnier, 1980. Handy, one-volume edition with adequate notes.

———. *Théâtre complet.* Ed. Jean-Pierre Collinet. 2 vols. Paris: Gallimard, 1982 and 1983. Edition of great erudition with many references to Picard's *Nouveau Corpus Racinianum.*

———. *Lettres d'Uzès,* rev. ed. Ed. Jean Dubu. Nîmes: Librairie Lacour, 1991. Furnishes a wealth of information on Racine's stay in the south of France and its impact on his life and career.

Translations

The Complete Plays of Jean Racine. Trans. Samuel Solomon. 2 vols. New York: Modern Library, 1969. The only translation of Racine's complete theater. Useful for plays not covered by others.

Jean Racine: Britannicus, Phaedra, Athalia. Trans. C. H. Sisson. New York: Oxford University Press, 1987. Close to literal translation, renders Racine accessible to literate public.

Jean Racine: Four Greek Plays: Andromache, Iphigenia, Phaedra, Athaliah. Trans. R. C. Knight. New York: Cambridge University Press, 1982. Work of high literary merit, longer in English translation than in French original.

Racine, Jean. *Iphigenia, Phaedra, Athaliah.* Trans. John Cairncross. Baltimore: Penguin Books, 1964. The translation of *Phèdre* may be the best in English.

SECONDARY SOURCES

Background Materials

Cabeen, David C., and Jules Brody. *A Critical Bibliography of French Literature,* vol. 3: *The Seventeenth Century.* Syracuse, NY: Syracuse University Press,

1961. Racine chapter, compiled by Georges May, contains 299 annotated items. Complemented by the Racine chapter, compiled by Ronald W. Tobin, in the Supplement to the above volume, ed. H. Gaston Hall. Syracuse, NY: Syracuse University Press, 1983. Coverage ends in mid-1970s.

Gossip, Christopher J. *An Introduction to French Classical Tragedy*. Totowa, NJ: Barnes & Noble Books, 1981. Solid and comprehensive view avoiding superficial generalities.

Klapp, Otto. *Bibliographie der französischen Literaturwissenschaft*. Frankfurt: Klostermann, 1956 to date. Most reliable annual bibliography of French literature.

Picard, Raymond. *Nouveau Corpus Racinianum. Recueil-inventaire des Textes et Documents du XVIIe Siècle Concernant Racine*. Paris: Éditions du CNRS, 1976. Collection of almost all the references made to Racine in the seventeenth century. Major scholarly undertaking.

Truchet, Jacques. *La Tragédie classique en France*. Paris: Presses Universitaires de France, 1975. Updated bibliography as of 1997 printing. Excellent review of major trends and methods in the criticism of French classical tragedy since 1950. Judicious synthesis of the critical controversies surrounding Racine's tragedies.

Critical Materials

Backès, Jean-Louis. *Racine*. Paris: Seuil, 1981. Original essay on all of Racine's writings. Good analysis of rhetorical structures.

Barthes, Roland. *On Racine*. Trans. Richard Howard. New York: Hill and Wang, 1964 (original French version, 1963). Application of structuralist principles to Racine's tragedies. Some brilliant and dramatically formulated insights, but methodology is faulty. Source of longlasting polemic over the objectives of literary criticism, starting with Raymond Picard's *New Criticism or New Fraud* (Pullman: Washington State University Press, 1969) (original French version, 1965).

Bénichou, Paul. *Man and Ethics: Studies in French Classicism*. Trans. Elizabeth Hughes. New York: Doubleday, 1971 (original French version, 1948). Despite some dated perspectives, still towers over all socioliterary studies of seventeenth-century France.

Bernet, Charles. *Le Vocabulaire des tragédies de Racine: analyse statistique*. Geneva: Droz, 1983. A helpful tool for those interested in a quantitative, specialized analysis of Racine's vocabulary.

Biet, Christian. *Racine*. Paris: Hachette, 1996. Good introduction to Racine, with special emphasis on the expressive function of tears.

Dubu, Jean. *Racine aux miroirs*. Paris: SEDES, 1992. Essays on a wide variety of topics concerning Racine's work, always within the context of the history and culture of seventeenth-century France.

Edwards, Michael. *La Tragédie racienienne.* Paris: La Pensée Universelle, 1972. Controversial, often schematic attempt to counterbalance general critical view that Racine's tragedies are totally pessimistic. Stimulating analyses.

Ekstein, Nina C. *Dramatic Narrative: Racine's Récits.* New York: Peter Lang, 1986. Useful examination of the 195 narrations that extend the imaginary boundaries of Racinian tragedies.

Freeman, Bryant C., and Alan Batson. *Concordance du théâtre et des poésies de Jean Racine.* 2 vols. Ithaca, NY: Cornell University Press, 1968. First computerized concordance of a French writer. Indispensable tool.

Hawcroft, Michael. *Word as Action: Racine, Rhetoric, and Theatrical Language.* Oxford: Clarendon Press, 1992. Compelling analysis of the affinities between rhetoric and theatricality in the tragedies.

Knight, R. C., *Racine et la Grèce.* 1950; rpt. Paris: Nizet, 1974. Outstanding study of Racine's debt to classical Greek authors.

Lapp, John C. *Aspects of Racinian Tragedy.* Toronto: University of Toronto Press, 1956. Remains one of the most enlightening thematic approaches to Racine.

Maskell, David. *Racine, A Theatrical Reading.* Oxford: Clarendon Press, 1991. Indispensable contribution to an appreciation of Racine's remarkable theatricality refutes the perception of the dramatist as fundamentally verbal and abstract.

Morgues, Odette de. *Racine, or the Triumph of Relevance.* Cambridge: Cambridge University Press, 1967. Excellent introduction for the general public to the workings of Racine's plays and how they succeed in conveying the feeling of tragic conflict

Niderst, Alain. *Racine et la tragédie classique.* Paris: Nizet, 1978. Clear analysis of the role of the tragic heroes in revealing the psychology and the morality of the plays.

Parish, Richard. *Racine: The Limits of Tragedy.* Tuebingen: Papers on French Seventeenth Century Literature, 1993. Indicates how Racine turned to good advantage the limits of genre, of the stage, of order, and of language. Insightful on space in the plays.

Phillips, J. Henry. *Racine: Language and Theatre.* Durham, England: University of Durham Press, 1994. Subtle study of the degree to which characters' concerns about speaking contribute to the tragic effect.

Picard, Raymond. *La Carrière de Jean Racine.* Paris: Gallimard, 1956. Monumental, exhaustive work superseding all previous biographical studies. Elegant study of Racine's use of theater as a vehicle for social ascension.

Rohou, Jean. *L'Evolution du tragique racinien.* Paris: SEDES, 1991. Analysis of the plays as reflecting the psyche of Racine.

———. *Jean Racine: bilan critique.* Paris: Nathan, 1994. Clear treatment of the reception of Racine's plays, their vision, themes, style, and structure. Includes important "Guide bibliographique."

Scherer, Jacques. *Racine et/ou la cérémonie.* Paris: Presses Universitaires de France, 1982. Comprehensive, rich study of the complexity of Racine's theater. Perhaps the best general book on Racine in French.

Spencer, Catherine. *La Tragédie du prince.* Tuebingen: Papers on French Seventeenth-Century Literature, 1987. Examines the role of intermediaries, especially traitors and the unloved, in the political dimension of the tragedies.

Tobin, Ronald W. *Racine and Seneca.* Chapel Hill: University of North Carolina Press, 1971. Comprehensive study of the relationship between Racine and Seneca and of the influence of Seneca on French tragedy of the sixteenth and seventeenth centuries.

Viala, Alain. *Racine, la stratégie du caméléon.* Paris: Seghers, 1990. Breezy biography of Racine as an insecure *arriviste.* Based on intimate knowledge of Racine's work and the culture of seventeenth-century France.

Zimmermann, Eléonore M. *La Liberté et le destin dans le théâtre de Racine.* Saratoga, Calif.: Anma Libri, 1982. Explores the dialectic of freedom and fate in Racine's tragedies.

Index

The Author

Ronald W. Tobin, professor of French and associate vice chancellor at the University of California, Santa Barbara, holds a B.A. from Saint Peter's College and a Ph.D. from Princeton University. He is editor-in-chief of the *French Review* and vice president of the Société Racine. The French government named him Chevalier, then officer in the Order of the Academic Palms, Chevalier in the National Order of Merit, and Chevalier in the Order of Arts and Letters. His books and editions include *Racine and Seneca, Tarte à la crème: Comedy and Gastronomy in Molière's Theater, Le Corps au XVIIe siècle,* and *Paths to Freedom: Essays in Honor of E. B. O. Borgerhoff.*

The Editor

David O'Connell is professor of French at Georgia State University. He received his Ph.D. in 1966 from Princeton University, where he was a National Woodrow Wilson Fellow, the Bergen Fellow in Romance Languages, and a National Woodrow Wilson Dissertation Fellow. He is the author of *The Teachings of Saint Louis: A Critical Text* (1972), *Les Propos de Saint Louis* (1974), *Louis-Ferdinand Céline* (1976), *The Instructions of Saint Louis: A Critical Text* (1979), and *Michel de Saint Pierre: A Catholic Novelist at the Crossroads* (1990). He has edited more than 60 books in the Twayne World Authors Series.